DOWNFIELD!

DOWNFIELD!

Untold Stories of the
Green Bay Packers

Jerry Poling

Prairie Oak Press
a division of Trails Media Group, Inc.
Black Earth, Wisconsin

Prairie Oak Press
a division of Trails Media Group, Inc.
P.O. Box 317
Black Earth, WI 53515

Typeset by KC Graphics, Inc., Madison, Wisconsin
Printed in the United States of America by Sheridan Books, Inc.
06 05 04 03 02   6 5 4 3

Library of Congress Cataloging-in-Publication Data

Poling, Jerry, 1958-
    Downfield!: untold stories of the Green Bay Packers / Jerry
Poling.—1st ed.
        p.   cm.
    ISBN 1-879483-33-5
    1. Green Bay Packers (Football team)—History. 2. Football players—
United States—Conduct of life. 3. Football players—Wisconsin—
History. I. Title.
GV956.G7P65 1996
796.332'64'0977561—dc20   96-29365
                                                            CIP

To my wife, Lynn, whose encouragement gave me the inspiration to start the book and whose patience and understanding gave me the time to write it. To my sons, Jerad and Matthew, two fine young men and Packer fans. To my parents, Edna and John C. Poling, my coaches in life, and to all my family, my favorite team.

—Jerry Poling

CONTENTS

FOREWORD

When *Instant Replay,* my first book, was published, Gary Knafelc, one of our tight ends, said to me, "Hey, you should have called your book "Half of It." I said, "Half of It?" And he said, "Yea, that's all you told— half of it." He was right. I generally only told about the positive side of my pro football experience. I didn't mention the amphetamines, the partying, the ladies, or any of the really negative aspects of pro football. I couldn't at that time.

Jerry Poling gives us a look at all sides of the pro football experience. The successes and the failures, both on and off the field, both during and after the players' careers. Good and bad. Sweet and sour.

Pro football players have a platform at a very young age. Normally a person had to be a bit gray or have some sort of political or business success to gain the attention of the community. Not so with pro ball players. At the ripe old age of 22 people plead with them for a few words. They have a wonderful platform. Some of them are smart enough to realize it and use that platform in a positive manner.

Pro football players are like any other group. To generalize about them is to misinform. The group is made up of individuals, good and bad, mature and childish, smart and not so smart. In short, they are representative of the general population in almost every respect, except one. They played professional football and played it very well. The experience generally changed and defined their lives. Chester Marcol wandered through that wilderness they call the NFL and came out the other side scarred and bruised. He's now living a life very much like he might have had he never played a down in the NFL.

There is a glamour side to pro football, and there is a harsh reality that pro football is also a big business. After the applause, after the cheers have died, life goes on often in pain, often in poverty, but always with a difficult adjustment to real life.

After their careers, many players have to refocus their lives or, as Ezra Johnson put it, try to become a good husband and father, focusing on the more meaningful aspects of life—God, family, and profession.

I hope you enjoy reading *Downfield* as much as I did. Remember the next time a player makes a spectacular play, it's no more or less than we're all capable of. Remember the next time a player screws up—they are boys playing a game.

Jerry Kramer

INTRODUCTION

My first recollection of the Green Bay Packers was in 1966, when I was eight years old. I watched at my grandparents' house as the Packers won a championship. The room full of my aunts, uncles, and cousins, normally staid people, was wild with excitement. I figured that the Packers must be important. In 1972, by then a full-fledged Packer fan, I sat dejectedly in my basement as the Packers lost in the playoffs to Washington. Ditto a decade later, when their playoff hopes ended in Dallas.

My days of just watching the Packers came to an end in 1989 when an old friend, editor Al Pahl, asked me to track down a former player every week and write a story for the *Packer Report*. Suddenly, I was an interactive fan, talking to and writing about the men I had grown up watching. My avocation was a fan's dream, not necessarily a journalist's. Variously called "Where are they now?", "What ever happened to . . . ?", or "Flashback," these staples of the newspaper world satisfy our curiosity like a class or family reunion.

For five years I ferreted out about 120 former Packers of the more than 1,300 who have played since 1919. I found them all over the country doing all sorts of things: coaching, preaching, running businesses, working in factories, or working in law enforcement. The magic of Ma Bell resurrected men who had passed on to the football nether world.

In addition to satisfying my curiosity, I began to see the significance of the pro football experience still alive in the players. When I stopped writing for *Packer Report*, I kept hearing those voices on the phone, those voices of Packer history. So I started talking back.

I began *Downfield* in 1994 by hunting for more former Packers and relocating some I previously had talked to. I called them, went to their homes and businesses, or met them at restaurants and tried to peel away some layers of Packer history and personal experience to see what had been digested.

I wanted to know what scoring touchdowns and making tackles meant to them now. What did they gain or lose from all that exertion? Where did it take them? What Packer experiences were significant to them decades later, and why?

Most men talked at length to me, a person they had never heard of or only vaguely remembered from a phone conversation years earlier. I think I know why they talked. Playing pro football is such an intense, life-altering experience that these men seemed to enjoy analyzing and ruminating 10, 25, and even 50 years after the fact. Football still was part of their lives in many ways.

I talked to star players of the 1960s, wondering if their memories ever would dim. I also looked for average players from average Packer teams, players like Steve Odom, David Greenwood, Phillip Epps, and David Whitehurst, who couldn't live off their fame or their Packer salaries. Where did pro football leave these lesser gods? I wanted a realistic look at a broad spectrum of people who shared a unique American experience—playing in that most illogical of pro football cities, Green Bay, Wisconsin.

I focused on former players who provided a meaningful cross-section of experiences and memories. Some players I couldn't track down, many are dead, and a few chose not to be interviewed. One Packer from the early 1980s eluded my investigative grasp entirely. Not one ex-teammate, relative, or even his ex-wife had a clue where he was. Unfortunately, he sounded like he could use a friend.

I hope that *Downfield* widens our view of professional football players while bringing some new perspectives to Packer history. I'm confident you will get as much satisfaction and enjoyment reading the stories as I did writing them.

To all of the players I interviewed, I offer my sincere thanks for their time and their thoughts. This book is for all the men who once were Packers and for the great fans who cheered them on.

Along with the many players, my thanks go to editors Jerry Minnich and Kristin Visser of Prairie Oak Press for their dedication to the project; Jerry Kramer, whose insightful comments about the manuscript kept me focused; Lee Remmel, Packer public relations director; the late Shirley Leonard, Packer public relations secretary; Al Pahl, former editor of the

Packer Report; ex-Packer John Biolo, organizer of the Packer Alumni Reunion; librarian Diane Robb at the *Green Bay Press-Gazette*; the reference desks at the Eau Claire and Green Bay public libraries; historian Joe Horrigan at the Pro Football Hall of Fame; and to my employer, the Eau Claire Press Company and *Eau Claire Leader-Telegram*, for the use of file photos and computer time and for a lot of cheerful support.

Jerry Poling,
Eau Claire, Wis.
April 11, 1996

DOWNFIELD!

1

The Brockington Myths

John Brockington
Running back, 1971-1977

After rushing for more than 1,000 yards each of his first three seasons in pro football, John Brockington, barrel-chested and bull-necked, looked like the next Jim Taylor for the Green Bay Packers, the next Jim Brown of the National Football League. Brockington not only had Taylor's Packer rushing record in his sights, he wanted to break Brown's NFL all-time rushing record of 12,312 career yards.

Anything seemed possible for the powerful 6' 1", 225-pound fullback from Ohio State. The Packers were so excited in 1974 that they gave Brockington a $450,000 signing bonus and a no-cut contract worth about $150,000 a year, more than five times what he had been making.

But his dreams of glory were not to be. He rushed for 883 yards in 1974, dropped to 434 yards in 1975, and to 406 yards in 1976. He looked totally out of sync at times, like a race horse trying to trot. He developed a stutter step and seemed hesitant to hit the holes that he had galloped through so forcefully in the early years of his career.

Everyone from the Packer front office on down to the fans mumbled that Brockington simply had lost his amazing skills, or worse, had been ruined by his big contract. Coach Bart Starr said Brockington, at age 28 in 1977, should have been in his prime. Instead, Starr cut him one game into the 1977 season. "His fall from greatness was a complete mystery," Starr said later.

Now, nearly two decades later, Brockington said it was no mystery. "His fall" was part of the fallout and confusion when coach Dan Devine packed up and Bart Starr returned as coach to finish off the inglorious 1970s for the once-golden Packers. John Brockington was a victim of the great Packer meltdown.

Now age 47 and a financial services broker in San Diego, Brockington wants one thing about his reputation cleared up: He is adamant that his demise had nothing to do with a fat wallet and lack of desire. "I don't know of any ballplayer who thinks about money on the field," Brockington said. He was insulted when he found out that a former Packer executive committee member, the late John B. Torinus, in the book *The Packer Legend*, related Brockington's yardage drop to the salary increase. Brockington said, "I was thinking about winning football games and playing well. When they benched me in Green Bay I was in tears, sick. It was awful. I wanted to play 10 years and finish up. I wanted to beat Jim Brown's record in the same time or less." Several former teammates also attested that the affable, goal-oriented Brockington wasn't the type of person who would be changed by money. Blaming Brockington's fall on money apparently was no more than a convenient answer to a perplexing problem.

Brockington's personal explanation—the one he will take to his grave—is simple: The Packers for some unexplained reason took away his favorite play and tried to make him a different type of runner. For his first three seasons, Brockington got most of his yards on what he called a "36-37" play, which gave him a hole between the guard and tackle. It was the perfect ram-it-through play for a man with locomotive-like legs. "It was the same off-tackle play that Taylor and other successful runners used for most of their yards," Brockington said.

Starting in 1974, the "coaching staff changed. They came with a totally new offense. They took my best play away and said, 'make yards.'

They scrapped it. It was totally gone," Brockington said. "I felt naked out there." Suddenly, the Packers wanted Brockington to run more horizontal on what he called a "38-39" play, which called for him to start parallel to the line for a few steps before breaking sharply up field. His job was to spot whatever hole developed, unlike the old play in which he hit a specific, assigned hole. "I was not that kind of runner. It was a developing-type play, run to daylight, and I never felt comfortable with it. It was very tough, not something I was used to doing," Brockington explained. So Brockington would look for the hole and get stuck en route to daylight. "The complaint was that I was running too fast so I couldn't make the cut. I could not get the mechanics right. When I did it was too late."

Several of Brockington's teammates, including Jim Carter and Gale Gillingham, agreed that Brockington was forced into a type of running that didn't suit him. "All of a sudden it looked like he was running east and west instead of north and south," Carter said. Quarterback Scott Hunter remembers yelling at Brockington in the huddle once for not turning that "38-39" play up field when he should have, resulting in a one-yard loss. Later he realized that Brockington "couldn't square his shoulders that fast. He needed to be running where his shoulders were square to the line of scrimmage," Hunter said.

According to Brockington, the "38-39" play was the favorite of assistant offensive coach Paul Roach, who arrived in 1975 with Starr. "[Roach] was in love with that play." However, Brockington didn't confront Roach or Starr because players didn't do that then, unlike today when highly paid players often speak out.

Former defensive back Willie Buchanon believes there was a deliberate attempt by the Packer front office to ruin Brockington. Several of the assistant coaches on Starr's staff were leftovers from Devine's staff. "Once Mac [Lane] was gone they tried to break John. They completely demoralized him. I saw it. They belittled him so much that his confidence was not there. They messed him up," Buchanon said. "Dave Pureifory and I used to talk to one coach and tell him to leave John alone. Get off him and leave him run. They decided they didn't want John Brockington to run or do anything. It came from upstairs and filtered down to the coaches," Buchanon recalled.

Not the least of Brockington's problems was Starr's decision in 1975 to trade his key blocking back, MacArthur Lane. During a divisive 1974 players strike, when several Packers crossed the picket line, Lane took an active role representing the striking Packers. In 1975, Starr, in one of his first significant moves as the new coach, traded Lane when it was suggested that Lane was a trouble-maker. Starr later admitted that he made a mistake by listening to his staff. Lane agreed that Brockington needed him. "That's when things went downhill. John's game went down. He had no lead blocker," said Lane, who was traded to the Kansas City Chiefs. Lane and Brockington were so punishing that the Packer defense even dreaded practicing against the duo, linebacker Jim Carter remembered.

Brockington believes his output was also hurt by turnover in the offensive line. Gale Gillingham sat out in 1975, and Ken Bowman and Malcolm Snider had retired, among other changes. "Sometimes there were not any holes there. I needed a little crack. It got to the point where there were not any cracks. The offensive line was in a state of flux. I got most of the blame for it," Brockington recalled. Gillingham concurred, saying, "Everything changed after 1974," including "terrible" assistant coaches brought in by the inexperienced Starr.

During the 1976 season, Brockington lost his starting job to Barty Smith. Brockington was released after the first game in 1977. In that game he gained 25 yards in 11 carries and became the 24th NFL player to top 5,000 career yards. He wound up with 5,024 yards, more than 3,000 behind Packer career leader Taylor but still third on the Packer all-time rushing list.

For two years he tried and failed to catch on with another team. Finally, he gave up and went into the real estate business in Oceanside, California, near San Diego, in 1980. He began selling financial services with the Equitable in 1988 and went into business for himself in 1993. Now he works out of a home office up to 60 hours a week. He was divorced in 1979 and has two grown daughters.

While he called pro football a "wonderful life," he said that playing in Green Bay was odd at times. He remembers Devine and assistant coach Bob Schnelker engaged in a virtual tug of war one time as each tried to send in plays in 1971. "Schnelker grabbed a player and gave him a play. Devine grabbed him and changed the play, and Schnelker grabbed another

player. This is pro football!" Brockington said that players deliberately
would sabotage the defense "so we would lose and get Devine out of
town." During one game, defensive coordinator Dave Hanner called a
particular defense. The backs ignored the call and ran their own defense.
When Hanner questioned why they didn't run what was ordered, one of
the backs simply replied, "We called that [expletive] off," Brockington
recalled with a laugh. "That's how bad it was. It was really a trip playing in those days."

Although he finished with a fractured career, Brockington's NFL
memories remain a part of his identity because "it's who I was and I know
how tough it is to get to the NFL."

He didn't even intend to play football. Growing up in a Jewish section of Brooklyn, New York, he decided to go out for the Thomas Jefferson High School football team one day when he came home and saw
his big brother, Freeman, wearing a football uniform. "I decided I wanted
one of those too," Brockington said. So he went out for the team, only
to find out that the coach, Moe Finkelstein, was a disciplinarian. The players were forced to wear a jacket and tie on Wednesdays and Fridays. And
when Brockington showed up late for practice one day, he found out that
Finkelstein had no slack in his reins. Brockington was told that he had
one minute to decide whether or not he was serious about playing football. He was. He never again arrived late for practice.

Finkelstein provided the spark that was missing in Brockington's life.
His late father, a post office worker, and mother, a domestic worker, usually weren't home after school, leaving John, Freeman, and their sister
Linda unsupervised. "I was headed down that road so many kids head
down. I did what I wanted to do. Sometimes I didn't feel like going to
school. There was no discipline. [Finkelstein] straightened me out quick,"
Brockington said.

Brockington eventually made all the honor teams in the New York
city area and got a scholarship to attend Ohio State. He didn't get a chance
to play full time at OSU until his senior year, when he topped 1,000 yards
rushing for coach Woody Hayes. When he got to the Packers, Ray
Nitschke told him he should thank Ohio State for having played just one
year because he wasn't burned out. With fresh, young legs, Brockington
busted out with 1,105, 1,027, and 1,144 yards in his first three years. In

1971, he was NFL Rookie of the Year, All-Pro, made the Pro Bowl, and set a rookie rushing record.

Then his best playing days ended amidst the departures of Lane and Devine, and Starr's coaching changes. Brockington knows that he was one of the NFL's best, but only for a short time, too short a time in his mind. He is irritated when he sees NFL highlight films that feature great players; he keeps looking for himself and coming up empty. "I see guys who didn't do jack. I don't ever see myself. Did all that film [of me] get water damaged?" he asked rhetorically.

John Brockington didn't finish his career—at least not the way he had envisioned. "I wish I could go back, but I know I'm 47 now and I can't go back. I just watch the young kids now."

Green and Gold and Black

Bob Mann
Wide receiver, 1950-1954

George "Tiger" Greene
Safety, 1986-1990

When *Jackie Robinson broke the color barrier in baseball by playing for the Brooklyn Dodgers in 1947, America marked it down as a social milestone in the mercilessly slow advancement against racism.*

Because of the significance of that event—a change in America's most traditional game often is seen as a barometer of change in America itself—often forgotten is that the integration of blacks and whites in professional sports was already under way when Robinson walked to the plate at Ebbets Field on April 15, 1947.

The first major athletic color barrier was broken in football, not in baseball. It happened September 26, 1946, in Los Angeles, when running back Kenny Washington caught a 19-yard pass during the Rams' season opener against Philadelphia at the Coliseum. Another black, Woody Strode, also played for the Rams that season. Ironically, Washington

*and Strode had played on the same UCLA football team with the most
famous black athlete of all, Robinson, who actually signed with the
Dodgers in 1945 but didn't make his major league debut until 1947.*

*Integration in pro basketball occurred in 1950 when three players
signed with NBA teams.*

Bob Mann

In 1948 a small, fast wide receiver, Bob Mann, made All-Big Ten at
the University of Michigan. He was aware that a few courageous blacks
were gaining acceptance in professional sports, and he was encouraged
to give it a try. More than that, as a matter of principle, he knew in his
heart he could play in the NFL after going against many NFL-bound players from the Big Ten. "I felt I could play pro ball. No question about it,"
said Mann. Encouraged and determined, Bob Mann made history. Not
once but twice.

Mann's parents showed him by example that color was no barrier to
success. His father was a physician, his mother a school administrator in
his hometown of New Bern, North Carolina, a city of about 13,000 people
in the southeastern corner of the state. Mann attended Hampton Institute
(a black college in Hampton, Virginia) before transferring to the University of Michigan to major in zoology. He left school to serve in the
Navy in World War II and returned to a new country of sorts. Robinson
was on his way up with the Dodgers, and a rival new pro football league,
called the All-America Football Conference (AAFC), was pushing to sign
black players. One team did. The Cleveland Browns of the AAFC, under
Coach Paul Brown, signed Marion Motley and Bill Willis in 1946,
although the signing of Kenny Washington and Woody Strode by the LA
Rams in the older league that spring was perceived as the breakthrough.
Most teams signed two black players at a time so that they could room
together. The Rams, in their first year in LA after moving from Cleveland under owner Dan Reeves, are credited with the true breakthrough
because it was in the NFL where a color barrier existed from 1934 to
1945, a seldom-mentioned, shameful era in NFL history.

In 1948, Mann signed as a free agent along with Melvin Grooms to
become the first blacks to play for the Detroit Lions. In 1950, Mann went
a step further. He went to northeastern Wisconsin—where there were few

black people at all—and became the first black football player in the 31-year history of the Green Bay Packers.

The Packers actually had two black players on their roster during training camp in 1950, guard Jimmy Thomas and halfback Jim Clark, both from Ohio State. They were released before the regular season began, but their presence caused a stir. Several white Packers grumbled and one requested not to be photographed with his black teammates, according to Art Daley, a Green Bay newspaper reporter at the time.

Later that season, coach Gene Ronzani heard that Mann was available. In 1949 with the Lions, Mann had caught 66 passes for more than 1,000 yards to rank second in the league. After a salary dispute with the Lions, he was traded in 1950 to the New York Yankees for future Hall of Fame quarterback Bobby Layne. Despite his outstanding season with the Lions, when Mann got to New York he was released after the preseason. Mann said he was "railroaded" out of the league. The Yankees had three black players and Mann believed they had a black quota. He was the black man out. Mann went back to Detroit, disheartened, and looked for a job.

Then Ronzani called. It all seemed so simple. Mann went to Green Bay the Saturday after Thanksgiving, November 25, 1950, talked to Ronzani ("a nice man," Mann said), signed a contract, and made Packer history when he walked into the Packer locker room hours later to meet his new teammates, who were practicing for Sunday's game. Halfback Billy Boedeker was cut to make room for Mann.

Mann remembers the historic moment only as an "unusual situation, I guess," although walking into all-white work and social situations had become almost commonplace for him. He was used to it, but his new Packer teammates weren't. "I remember the first time he walked into the locker room. There was silence," said Clayton Tonnemaker, a rookie center on the 1950 team. "We knew he was coming, but in that locker room it was a big deal, like Jackie Robinson joining the Brooklyn Dodgers. We had a lot of southern guys on the team, a lot from Texas. They had never played with a black before." Tonnemaker, from Minnesota, and Mann, from Michigan, had played against each other in Big Ten games.

Tonnemaker decided to break the silence. "I went over and introduced myself."

The next day, Mann played in the Packers' 25-21 victory over the San Francisco 49ers at City Stadium. A crowd of just 13,196—the worst of the season—turned out on a snowy, cold day. Mann caught one pass for eight yards and was credited with delivering a key block in a 57-yard TD run by Billy Grimes. The loss broke a six-game losing streak for the Packers, and it was their third and last win in a 3-9 season. The 49ers, a former AAFC team in their first year in the NFL, were on their way to a 3-9 record also. Their star was their first black player, fullback Joe Perry, a future Hall of Famer.

Neither the *Green Bay Press-Gazette* nor The Associated Press, in their coverage of Mann's signing and first game mentioned that Mann was the Packers' first black player. When blacks were integrating sports, media often would single out black athletes in their reports, referring to them as Negro, colored or black. The integration of the Green Bay Packers didn't make headlines in 1950; it didn't even make the news.

Mann was just one of 17 blacks out of a population of 52,735 in Green Bay, according to the 1950 U.S. Census. Packer players say the only other Green Bay black they remember was a man who shined shoes in a local hotel. Despite the situation, it generally was an auspicious debut for the black athlete in Green Bay. Mann was accepted by his teammates, and while he may not have felt at home he was made to feel as comfortable as possible in a white city and on a white team. "It was very nice," said Mann, who has been an attorney since 1970 in Detroit. "The Green Bay people were nice and warm. They all talked football. It was a wonderful football town. I have no complaints." Mann never was denied service in a Green Bay restaurant or at a hotel because of his color, he said.

Considered a quiet man and a fine player—he averaged 15 yards a catch as a Packer—Mann "was a popular guy. He came out with us at night after the ballgames. We'd go someplace and dance. All the wives would dance with him. He was well-accepted by everyone," said Dick Wildung, a tackle and captain of the team.

Mann and several other players stayed at the Northland Hotel—a popular rooming site for Packer players—and at a motel in downtown Green Bay during the season. He lived in Detroit during the off-season.

He was accepted in Green Bay, but his life was far from easy. On the road, Mann faced segregation. When the Packers went to Baltimore to play in 1953, Mann wasn't allowed to stay with the team at the whites-only hotel; he was sent to a black hotel. In Dallas in 1952, he and the team's second black player, back Bill Robinson, suffered the same indignity. Mann handled the situations with dignity, accepting the humiliation without protest for the sake of the team. "It's a situation where you really can't do anything about it," he explained.

Still single, Mann often would get special passes from Ronzani to go to Milwaukee or Chicago to socialize. The 5'11", 175-pound Mann roomed with Dick "The Bruiser" Afflis, a broad-chested 250-pounder who doubled as a pro wrestler, and with guard Ray "Dippy" DiPierro. "It was a lonely life. He had no place to go socially. It was kind of a hermit's life," DiPierro said. "I can't say enough for the character of the person. He never complained. Bobby just did his job quietly. Bobby was accepted."

Mann was accepted, but at the same time up to a dozen players on the team "were fighting inside." They accepted Mann "for the sake of the team," according to DiPierro. "You've got good guys and bad guys. He was a good guy. There's so much more being said there than people realize. He has a theory that everything in life balances out." Things did balance out. After Mann had been on the team for a while, several teammates from Texas confided in Mann. They told him that playing with a black was "like anything else," Mann recalled.

Mann caught six passes for 89 yards and a touchdown in the last three games of the 1950 season. The next year, still the only black, he led the team with 50 catches. He was the first Packer since Don Hutson (who retired in 1945) to catch 50 passes in a season. Mann was good enough that once when playing the Bears he heard that coach George Halas offered $50 to anyone who would knock off Mann's mustache. "For $50 I would have cut it off myself," Mann laughed. On another occasion, Mann found himself alone in the end zone waving his arms for QB Tobin Rote to throw him the ball. As Rote scrambled, an upset Halas ran into the end zone alongside Mann and began yelling for a Bears defensive back to get back and cover Mann. "He was a dirty coach really," Mann remembered.

During the late 1940s and early 1950s, the black athletes from all sports formed a bond. Mann was friends with the few NFL blacks like Len Ford, Marion Motley, Bill Willis, Woody Strode and Kenny Washington. Motley and Willis chose not to play in a 1946 game in Miami because of a death threat. While with the Lions, Mann once sat out an exhibition game in New Orleans, where blacks were not allowed to play.

Mann also was friends with Jackie Robinson. Mann himself was a fine baseball player, having signed with the Kansas City Monarchs of the Negro Leagues in 1949; a separated shoulder ended his baseball career. Jackie Robinson also had played for the Monarchs before debuting with the Dodgers.

Mann's football career came to an end in the 1954 preseason when he tore knee ligaments and retired. Mann, who has been married to his second wife, Vera, for 40 years, went into the real estate business for several years after football. He returned to school and earned a law degree at age 40 in 1970. He specializes in trying criminal cases at the Federal Court Building in downtown Detroit.

Although he played just three full seasons and didn't set any receiving records, Mann was inducted into the Packer Hall of Fame in 1988, a tribute to a good receiver but also to a man who helped change an organization, one that has employed black athletes every year since.

As many as 13 blacks played for pro football teams in the sport's infancy from 1920 through 1933. The first black players in the formal NFL (blacks played in early pro leagues around the turn of the century) were Fritz Pollard and Bobby Marshall, who signed in 1919 with Rock Island-Independence, Illinois. Pollard then signed in 1920 with the Akron (Ohio) Indians of the American Professional Football Association, which became the NFL in 1921. In 1922, Pollard played for the Milwaukee Badgers, the only team to have three blacks during that period (the others were Paul Robeson and Fred "Duke" Slater). Pollard became the NFL's first black head coach when he led the Hammond (Indiana) Pros in 1923-1924. As many as six blacks were in the NFL in the early 1920s, but the number dwindled to one or two per season beginning in 1927.

In the 1920s and 1930s blacks were also banned in pro baseball, which gave rise to the Negro Leagues. According to the late Arthur Ashe, Jr., who wrote *Hard Road to Glory*, a three-volume history of black athletes in pro sports, white football players pressured owners to get rid of black players when jobs got scarce during the Depression. By 1934, no blacks were in the league. While blacks disappeared, NFL owners actually increased team rosters from 20 to 24 in 1935 and to 33 players by 1940. According to Joe Horrigan, historian at the Pro Football Hall of Fame, there is no written proof that a ban ever existed, but he is convinced after researching the subject that there was "at least a gentlemen's agreement" among the owners to keep blacks out of the league.

Ashe, the first black to win the U.S. Open (1968) and Wimbledon (1975) men's singles tennis titles, called the NFL color barrier "one of the blackest spots on the record of American professional sports. All NFL records should properly show asterisks besides any records made during this era." The color barrier meant that Hall of Fame receiver Don Hutson, for example, who played from 1935-1945 with the Packers, never competed with a black in his pro career. Hutson set numerous NFL records, including one for touchdown receptions that stood for almost 50 years.

Official NFL fact and history books, which trace the history of pro football, do not discuss the color barrier. The books simply acknowledge the re-emergence of blacks after World War II. The director of communications for the NFL, Greg Aiello, acknowledged there were no blacks from 1934-1945. "There was no written policy or formal official ban of black players from the league during those years." He reasoned that there were no blacks for 12 years because the NFL was "a product of society at that time."

In 1995, the NFL recognized the 50th season of modern integration in the league by making a $1 million donation to the United Negro College Fund. It was a fine gesture, but the league did not address its oversights during the 12 years when blacks did not play. The NFL was attempting to address a problem without ever admitting that one took place—the equivalent of pleading no contest in a court of law without actually acknowledging one's guilt.

One of the most powerful men in the NFL in 1934 was Earl "Curly" Lambeau, the coach and general manager of the Packers. The Packers won three straight championships from 1929-1931. With Lambeau at the helm, the Packers were influential in league decisions when blacks disappeared in 1934.

The NFL's other leading men at the time included owners George Halas of the Chicago Bears, Tim Mara of the New York Giants, Bert Bell of the Philadelphia Eagles, Art Rooney of the Pittsburgh Pirates [Steelers], and George Preston Marshall of the Boston [Washington] Redskins. Joe Carr was league president until he died in 1939, and Elmer Layden became the NFL's first commissioner in 1941, serving until 1946, when he was replaced by Bell. The Bears, Giants, and Packers were the oldest and strongest teams in the league; the Redskins, Eagles, and Pirates were virtual newcomers to the NFL.

With his league-wide influence and close association to the owners, Lambeau certainly had to be privvy to knowledge about the disappearance of blacks from the league. It is reasonable to assume, under the circumstances, that he played a role in the color barrier. Unfortunately, little about the NFL's or Lambeau's role has been documented, most likely because of its unseemly nature or perhaps because of the league's apathetic approach to the use of black athletes.

Lambeau was a dynamic, charismatic leader largely responsible for the unlikely survival of an NFL franchise in a small city. He was one of the founders of pro football and was at the forefront of all league changes on and off the field for more than three decades. He was with the Packers from 1919 until his resignation as coach early in 1950. Born in Green Bay in 1898, he died in 1965 in the Door County vacation area northeast of Green Bay.

George Halas, in a 1979 autobiography *Halas on Halas,* said the early NFL owners "were a tight little group" who helped each other build a financially successful league. Halas and Lambeau were good friends. Halas wrote in detail about the early years of the Bears and the NFL, but he did not discuss the disappearance of blacks or mention their return to the NFL after the war. His only mention of the black issue was an acknowledgment that the Bears drafted their first black in 1952.

At least Halas can say that he drafted and used black players. Lambeau cannot. The fact remains that no blacks ever played for Lambeau during his 31 years with the Packers, even during the two periods when they were accepted in the NFL (1920-1933 and 1946-1949).

Furthermore, Lambeau's denial of black players went well beyond Green Bay. Lambeau coached and was vice president of the Chicago

Cardinals in 1950 and 1951. He had no black players there, either. The Cardinals got their first modern-era black player (actually three of them) in 1952. As in Green Bay, blacks began playing with the Cardinals the year after Lambeau left.

Lambeau then coached the Washington Redskins under owner George Preston Marshall in 1952 and 1953. Again, he hired no blacks. Thus, when his storied coaching career ended in 1953—eight years after blacks had returned to the league—Lambeau still was fielding all-white teams.

Lambeau finished his career with a team infamous for its indifference to black rights. The Redskins were the NFL's lone team from the South and the league's embarrassing holdout when it came to signing black players. They were the last NFL team to integrate, not signing a black until 1962; Marshall still was the owner. According to Joe Horrigan, the NFL historian, Marshall rebelled against using blacks because "his was the team of the South. The South was segregated and he planned to keep his team that way." Marshall only gave in to signing black players in 1962 when he faced protests and boycotts. "He was coerced," Horrigan said.

The availability of good black players had to be apparent to Lambeau. Blacks played collegiately at northern schools and at black colleges until they were accepted at southern colleges after the 1960s civil rights movements. Lambeau was a tireless recruiter who did not isolate himself in Green Bay. Lambeau, for example, traveled to Los Angeles in 1935 for the Rose Bowl to get a look at Alabama star Don Hutson. In the late 1940s, Lambeau spent off-seasons on the West Coast, where blacks had been playing for years with the Rams, the Los Angeles Dons of the AAFC, and in the Pacific Coast League. Lambeau regularly scouted and signed players from across the country. Author Ocania Chalk wrote in *Pioneers of Black Sport* that as early as 1940 "there was a virtual plethora of outstanding black football players and All-Americans." In 1939, Kenny Washington was an All-American and led the nation in total offense while at UCLA.

Although he never employed blacks or apparently never attempted to employ them, Lambeau is remembered in Green Bay as fair-minded and unprejudiced. Lambeau's first wife, Marguerite Lambeau, whom he divorced in 1935, is 97 and still lives in the Green Bay house that Lambeau's father built. "I don't remember him ever not liking black players. I don't know how he really felt, but he was very broad-minded. He was interested in football players whether they were black, pink, or yellow," she recalled.

John Biolo played guard under Lambeau in 1939, when the Packers were NFL champions, one of three titles (also 1936 and 1944) they won when the NFL color barrier existed. "Nothing ever was said that he objected to [blacks]," said Biolo, who still lives in Green Bay. "Way up here in the north country there were no blacks living here. You would hear comments that blacks wouldn't attract any customers [to games]. That's the kind of stuff you heard. Take it for what it's worth."

However, as early as the 1920s other northern cities had black players. Bobby Marshall played with the Minnesota Marines in 1922 and with the Duluth Eskimoes in 1927, and the Milwaukee Badgers had an unprecedented three blacks in 1922. One of the early great black players, Paul Robeson of the Milwaukee Badgers, was a two-time All-American end at Rutgers in the early 1920s. Joe Horrigan said that Lambeau's decision not to use blacks "doesn't reflect on Curly Lambeau so much as it does on the [Green Bay] community at that time."

Art Daley, who started covering the Packers in 1942 for the *Green Bay Press-Gazette* and is a member of the Packer Hall of Fame, said he doesn't remember black players ever being the subject of a conversation with Lambeau. Daley saw Lambeau virtually every day during the season for eight years. Several former Packers from the 1940s said they were not aware of a color barrier and questioned that it existed.

Howard Levitas was equipment manager for Lambeau from 1928 through 1940. He said Lambeau was not openly against blacks but was a fair person. Once, Levitas recalled, a Jewish player was tackled in front of the Packer bench and a Packer yelled, "Kill that [expletive] kike. Lambeau said, 'If I ever hear that kind of talk on this bench again you won't be on the team.' I'm Jewish. I remember that very well. That's a good example of the kind of person [Lambeau] was," said Levitas, 81, who still lives near Green Bay.

The Packers were the fifth team to integrate out of the eleven teams that began play in the NFL in 1946. Amazingly, complete integration of the NFL took 17 years, a period in the NFL that Ashe refers to as "tokenism." Now more than 60 percent of NFL players are black, and they have overcome stereotyping to play every position, including quarterback and middle linebacker, which in the early years after reintegration they were not allowed to play; one historian called it the NFL's "caste system."

The slow acceptance of blacks in the NFL is reflected in the chronology of Packers who have made the Pro Football Hall of Fame. Thirteen white Packers were elected to the Hall (starting with charter member Lambeau in 1963) before a black Packer was chosen (Herb Adderly in 1980).

After the Packers signed Mann, it was two years before they signed another black player. Mann was the lone black on the Packers in 1950, 1951, and 1953. There were three blacks in 1952 (Mann, Bill Robinson, and Tom Johnson). When Mann retired in 1954, halfback Veryl Switzer, the top draft pick, became the lone black.

In 1955, the Packers drafted Charles Brackins of Prairie View, Texas, in the 16th round. Brackins, 6' 2", 210 pounds, was only the fifth black to play quarterback in the NFL. He played special teams and threw just two passes (both incomplete) for the Packers that season before being released on November 7. Brackins was released despite the poor play of starting quarterback Tobin Rote, who completed just 45.9 percent of his passes that season and had 19 interceptions to rank near the bottom of the league.

In 1958, Len Ford, from the University of Michigan, played for the Packers in the final season of his great 11-year career. The 6' 5", 260-pound tight end/defensive end, who died in 1972, was inducted into the Pro Football Hall of Fame in 1976. Ford was the first black to play for the Los Angeles Dons of the AAFC in 1948-1949, and he played for the Cleveland Browns from 1950-1957. With the Packers, he played mostly defense and didn't catch any passes.

In 1959, when Vince Lombardi left the New York Giants as an assistant to become head coach of the Packers, he brought along Emlen Tunnell. In 1948, Tunnell had become the first black to play for the Giants, where he became one of the great defensive backs in the NFL. He set an NFL record with 79 interceptions, was the first black coach in the modern

NFL (assistant with the Giants in 1963), and in 1967 was the first black inducted into the Pro Football Hall of Fame.

Tunnell played for the Packers from 1959 through 1961, a time when Lombardi's demands went beyond excellence on the football field. "In the first meeting we had on the field he called us all together—about 60 guys—and [Lombardi] said, 'If I ever hear nigger or dago or kike or anything like that around here, regardless of who you are, you're through with me. You can't play for me if you have any kind of prejudice,' " Tunnell remembered.

When Tunnell arrived, defensive end Nate Borden was the only other black with the Packers. Borden had been drafted by the Packers in 1955 in the 25th round out of Indiana. He faced some of the same obstacles that Mann had faced five years earlier—not everyone on the Packer roster was comfortable playing with blacks. Bart Starr recalled that many Packers from the South refused to live in the same hotel as Borden, forcing Borden to move into a "shanty" type of building. Starr also was from the South but had been "exposed at an early age to integration" because his father was a career military man; Starr befriended Borden.

"It was bad for blacks [in Green Bay]. Real bad," Tunnell said. "Nate was staying in a place where I wouldn't have kept my dog. Vinnie changed all that. He gave the people who were renting the room to Nate hell and then he moved him into a decent place. There were never any second-class citizens on the Packers, black or white. In the three years I was in Green Bay he picked up my hotel bill at the Northland [Hotel]. He didn't have to do that." Tunnell died of a heart attack July 23, 1975, on the practice field while an assistant coach. He was 50.

In his autobiography, Ray Nitschke said that under Lombardi the Packers "never had any serious racial problems, the way some other clubs had. . . . The black players had some problems in their off hours, living in a small city like Green Bay where there weren't too many places they liked to go to relax. But they learned to accept this. . . . Lombardi made everybody on his team feel like part of one family."

By 1968, the Packers had 16 black players out of a squad of 47.

One black player, tackle Francis Peay (1968-1972), believed that playing in Green Bay was one of the best things that happened to him. "It was a great place for me. The quiet community gave me a lot of thought time to decompress a bit and see who I was and who I was going to be. I really started to read quite a bit when I was in Green Bay, and it's something I still avidly do. I learned more about myself and people in Green Bay than I could hope to discover in New York City. My political consciousness developed. Community became important. My level of social consciousness heightened," said Peay, who went on to coach Northwestern University and devote time to charitable causes.

George "Tiger" Greene

In April 1995, George "Tiger" Greene was going about his work at Indian Hills Country Club in Atlanta. A few hours' drive away in Augusta, Georgia, preparations were under way for the annual Masters Tournament. One of the members of the mostly white, private Indian Hills club approached Greene and congratulated him on qualifying for the prestigious Masters. Greene, the first assistant pro, was a little embarrassed. Yes, people call him Tiger. Yes, he is a black golfer. But they had him confused with Tiger Woods, the famous young amateur player who was making his debut at the Masters.

In a line of work where few people are black and even fewer are named Tiger, Greene knows there are bound to be cases of mistaken identity as he pursues a career as a golf professional. Worse, he has seen stereotyping and racism in golf and expects to see a lot more as he moves up the PGA ladder and attempts to get his Class A card. He hopes to become a head pro.

Greene's golf career is somewhat of a miracle. He has a scratch or zero handicap but only began playing in the mid-1980s.

He's prepared for the long, cold, stares of incredulous white golfers when they see him behind the pro shop counter or on the practice tee giving lessons. Greene is ready to endure because he has a lot of experience. Growing up in Flat Rock, North Carolina, he attended a predominately white high school. Except for two seasons in Atlanta, he spent most of his pro football career in mostly white Green Bay, where he admits that being black wasn't easy and the stresses contributed to the breakup of his marriage.

The first week of September 1993, Greene tried to qualify for the Greater Milwaukee Open. He failed, shooting a five-over-par 77, but his friend, pro Tim Simpson, introduced him to some other tour pros. Tour star Chip Beck gave Greene some advice. "He said if I ever could qualify for one of the tournaments the sky would be the limit for me because I'm left-handed, black, and an ex-NFL player. First and foremost, I'm black. He said there just aren't any blacks out there [on tour] at all. He said don't ever give up and don't let people deter you."

Many times Greene has felt like walking away. He got the job at Indian Hills in the spring of 1994, but only after a three-year search. Several times he lost assistant pro jobs to whites who had inferior credentials. Other times he was told that jobs were filled when they really weren't. "I've been through more than you can imagine," he said from his apartment in Smyrna, Georgia. "It's still kind of weird going to sectional tournaments where there are 250 to 300 pros and only two or three are black. It's still the good ol' boys network. Country clubs are still places that people can call their own, I guess."

As a football player, Greene, 6 feet, 190 pounds and a tough, sure tackler, was undrafted coming out of Western Carolina College in 1985. After he signed as a free agent with the Falcons and was released in 1986, he found a home in Green Bay with Forrest Gregg, who was dropping Bart Starr's holdover players. On October 19, 1986, Greene, defensive back Ken Stills, and linebacker Tim Harris all got their first starts in a 17-14 win over Cleveland. It was the Packers' first win after starting the season 0-6.

Greene liked playing in Green Bay, but he wasn't comfortable. "Green Bay taught me a lot. I learned how to bite my tongue at times and how to speak up at times." Although black players "ended up fitting in pretty good" in Green Bay and although they were treated very well by fans "80 percent of the time," living there wasn't easy. Greene often cut the hair of black teammates, who couldn't find a suitable barbershop except in Milwaukee. Black players couldn't find their favorite foods, including cornbread, chitlins, and collared greens, in Green Bay grocery stores. "We just assumed the food would be there, but it wasn't. When we got to Milwaukee, 60 percent of the players would go to this one soul-food place."

Alphonso Carreker, Greene's teammate for three seasons, concurred that such basic things as haircuts, food and entertainment were hard for black players to get. "When I first got there it was culture shock. I couldn't even find a *Jet* magazine. I couldn't find hair-care products," Carreker said. "I lived in [the suburb of] Howard and bought a house. The neighbors and everything were great, but if you didn't grow up playing hockey it was hard to get into it. There wasn't much for a 22-year-old millionaire to do."

John Brockington felt the awkwardness of being black in Green Bay. "I was treated different because of who I was. People in that town didn't have much use for you if you were not playing football," Brockington said. He recalled when he and his wife were in search of a place to live in Green Bay. In one neighborhood they visited, a rumor went around that "black people were trying to move on the street. When they found out it was me, everything was fine. That's the way it was in those days," he said with a chuckle.

Carreker mentioned the legal problems of James Lofton and Eddie Lee Ivery, who were involved in an alleged sexual assault, and Mossy Cade, who was convicted of a sexual assault, while playing for the Packers in the mid-1980s. Other black Packers became leery of venturing out into bars. "There was absolutely nowhere to go. It was so small guys would get together and have card parties and try to stay out of the clubs. We'd get together and chug beer. Basically you were stuck at home with the snow and couple cases of beer," Carreker recalled.

Greene found much to like about Green Bay, but he remembers how little there was for players to do and how little privacy they had. When players did go out to have a drink, fans sometimes would call the front office to report them. "That was one of the toughest things. We had no privacy," Greene said. The players in Green Bay who got in trouble with the law were weeded out because the team "was more concerned about what people thought about players than what players did for the team." Greene cited Tim Harris, who "had a lot of problems and did a lot of things he shouldn't have but when Sunday came he was ready."

Greene contrasted the Green Bay situation with Atlanta, where players knew their off-field activities would have no bearing on their standing with the team. In Green Bay, "it was hard to be a player. You had to walk a thin line. It was different I tell you. I enjoyed playing ball in Green Bay, but I wish basically that the team was moved to Milwaukee. I think both parties would benefit. I think [Green Bay] is too small of a city," Greene stated.

Greene still is hurt when he remembers one of Gregg's assistant coaches saying during a team meeting that certain color players were made to play certain positions, a racist sentiment that was thought to have disappeared from sports years before. "They were Jimmy the Greek-type comments. We were sitting there and we couldn't believe what we were hearing. I had a lot of respect for that man. After that I lost a lot of respect for him. It was amazing."

The good days came in 1989 when the Packers went 10-6. Greene was making a solid six-figure salary and Lindy Infante was on his way up as coach. But in 1990 and 1991 the Packers lost too many games and Infante was fired by new general manager Ron Wolf. "Lindy was great until we went 10-6. Then I guess it went to his head. He changed. When he was first there he was a player's coach. When we went 10-6 people praised him as the new guru. He didn't care about the players anymore. He got rid of the 10-6 guys because they were holding out. There's a lot of stuff that went on there that people have no idea." Packer fans, Greene suggested, should take less interest in players' personal lives and more interest in how the team is managed.

Greene was one of the players Infante cut in 1990. He also was one of the 18 veteran players—including Don Majkowski, Ron Hallstrom, and Ken Ruettgers—who held out in a contract dispute. "They let a lot of good players go. That was their downfall. I think Lindy regretted it. Personalities got in the way. A guy's personality off the field shouldn't dictate what he does on the field," Greene said. In his book *The Packer Tapes,* retired trainer Domenic Gentile suggested the mass of holdouts were unwarranted after the Packers had just one good season. "Lindy wanted to teach these guys a lesson. He wanted to prove to them that they couldn't hold a gun to the Packers. Lines in the sand were drawn, and they dissected the team. There was a great deal of animosity and bitterness between players and management," Gentile said.

Greene never was a star with the Packers, playing in 56 games from 1986-1989 but starting only 15. He had four sacks and four interceptions in that period and was a special teams standout. After Greene was cut by the Packers he played for a year with Miami before being released, and retiring. Worst of all, his marriage broke up in 1991. His ex-wife and young son, Anthony, also live in the Atlanta area. Greene said Green Bay didn't help his marriage. "She hated Green Bay. She absolutely hated it. There never was anything for her to do. If I had to do it over I would have found something for her to do in Green Bay, taken her with me to games. It was not just Green Bay but football had a lot to do with it, a lot." The divorce rate is high among ex-NFL players, Greene said, because players and their wives get used to "walking in the store and buying things. Once football is over, the money's not there. You get spoiled. The adjustment has not been a major problem with me. I understand you don't have to have a big house and a fancy car to be happy. I wish I would have learned that six years ago."

As he moves away from his "dream come true" of playing in the NFL, Greene finds himself missing the camaraderie of football, but "I don't miss the crap you have to go through with coaches and the politics. I try to steer my boy away from football. I don't want him to go through what I went through."

CHAPTER

The Polish Fisherman

Czeslaw "Chester" Marcol
Place-kicker, 1972-1980

In 1972 Chester Marcol made 33 of 48 field-goal attempts, led the NFL in scoring and was All-Pro. It was quite a six months for a 22-year-old baby-faced man who just seven years earlier was suffering through the loss of his father, didn't know what a football was, and was unable to speak English.

Helping lead the Packers to the NFC Central Division title, he was seen as a sign of the second coming of glory. Packer fans called him the "Polish Prince" and the "Polish Messiah." One of the earliest soccer-style kickers in the NFL, he seemed to descend magically on Green Bay bearing god-like powers.

Nearly a quarter-century later in the twin cities of Hancock and Houghton, Michigan, where he has lived since 1990, Chester didn't mind talking about his glory days but was glad to have them far behind. As he drove through town on a spring day when the rivers were full of snowmelt, he suggested a new nickname: "I just want to be known as Chester the Fisherman. I'm a good fisherman."

He wasn't kidding. He was smiling one of those content, self-confident smiles. The Prince was at peace.

The cleft chin was still there, but the cherub face, frizzy hairdo, and innocent look of the young kicker had been eroded by a decade of pain. He wore a baseball cap with an "M" on it for Marlboro, his favorite brand of cigarettes. His hair, dark and wavy with streaks of gray, framed his mature, handsome face. He was thick through the shoulders and a small pot belly pushed out his Madison Muskies T-shirt at the waist.

Living on the Keweenaw Peninsula, which juts into Lake Superior, he seemingly had gone back to where he had come from—nowhere. It's a place where 300 inches of snow can fall in a winter, where Marcol can ice fish until May, where snow can fall in July, where even the coldest place in the NFL, Green Bay, is 212 miles to the south.

But at age 47, Chester Marcol was proud to say he liked it just fine up north, a place that to him is as beautiful as a 60-yard field goal. He truly has been to a place called Nowhere and never wants to go back. The Upper Peninsula of Michigan looks like heaven to him.

In his last few years as a Packer, Marcol began to drink heavily. He started using cocaine in his last season with the Packers, and it ultimately led to his being cut by Bart Starr, although Starr and most players were unaware of his drug problem, Marcol said.

His drug use set in motion a downward spiral that took him to a hellish suicide attempt in 1986. On the day he decided to die, he drank battery acid.

Since moving to the UP his life has stopped spinning. He found a doctor who diagnosed a chemical imbalance as the root of his drug and alcohol problems. He takes medication to control the roller coaster he rode for 10 years. Minus cocaine and alcohol for about five years, Marcol is happier than he's ever been, content to fish, hunt, help at his father-in-law's Union 76 gas station/bait shop, and watch as much hockey as possible. He remarried after moving to the UP. He and his wife, Carole, 30, have a young daughter, Mariah, with hopes of another child. They also have a 10-year-old daughter, Ashley, from Carole's first marriage. Life in their second-story apartment is unpretentious—just the way Chester wants it. It's a very normal life now for the football Messiah.

"I feel good when I come back here to the apartment. It was a turning point in my life when I met Carole. Prior to that I was almost irresponsible. I was living for myself. Since I met Carole my life has been really, really positive," Chester said. He talked about the other good friends he has made in the UP and how the simple life there has been the social tonic he needs. He has a support group at his church that reaffirms the value of his life. "I don't have a fancy home or the finest car, but that's so minimal."

The apartment kitchen and living room blend together. Game balls from Chester's career are scattered about. His Pro Bowl helmet sits atop the antlers of a deer mount in the living room. The centerpiece of the home is a large framed Packer 75th Anniversary print, and Chester proudly points out his signature along with those of other Packer greats. He was inducted into the Packer Hall of Fame in 1987. On the refrigerator is the quarter-century-old clipping of Chester as a collegian after he kicked a national record 62-yard field goal. The headline said "70 yards next for Hillsdale kicker?"

A lot of great things happened to him in football but none were greater than his comeback from the doorstep of death, a doorstep that he desperately wanted to cross. He was so depressed in the winter of 1986 while living in Lansing, Michigan, he "became comfortable" with suicide. "Peace came over me because I knew by taking my life I wouldn't have to suffer anymore. For a few months I was planning how. Three of every four seconds I was thinking how I could do it."

He had seen his life go "totally, totally insane and downhill. There's no doubt in my mind that the suicide attempt was led to by my cocaine use. It got to the point where my life or mission or whatever was completed." He might get up in the morning and feel fine, then "out of the blue, it was like turning on a switch and off to the races I'd go" into depression. "Then I'd use [drugs] or find something for relief." He was too proud to see a therapist about his problems, and he didn't think he was an alcoholic because he thought alcoholics were street bums, not ordinary people like him.

Ironically, he was working at the time as a counselor at a home for troubled youths. He could help them, but he could not help himself. Yet the day he drank the battery acid in February 1986, he saved his life by reaching for help. After quickly becoming extremely ill, he called a friend, who got him to a hospital. His condition was critical and he was given last rites during his 12 days in intensive care.

He spent one year in a group home while regaining his strength. Recovery came slowly. For the next five years, he continued to struggle. Because the acid damaged his esophagus, he needed to have the tube stretched twice a week so that food could pass through it. He had three surgeries to repair damage to his stomach caused by the acid. "My ability to lift is gone," he said; he proved it when he hesitated and then only gingerly picked up his young daughter. He still has the esophagus stretched occasionally now, a procedure that "takes me a few days to recover from." When he feels food becoming stuck in his throat, he makes an appointment with his doctor. In a positive groove now, Chester can see daily how far he has come, not how far he was down; his glass is half-full again.

For several years after the suicide attempt, he continued to battle with alcohol and cocaine use. "I was up and down for a long time. I would use, not use. Drink, not drink. It depended when the money was available." He has no money left from the $120,000, three-year contract he signed as a rookie and his six additional years of Packer earnings. He depends on disability income.

Life suddenly began to clear when he got to the UP, and he now finds that living each day without vices—save cigarettes—gives him great satisfaction. He is satisfied with keeping life as simple as possible. He knows he could return to work as a counselor but doesn't want to look beyond fishing, hunting, and watching his favorite TV programs. "I get up early, work my crossword puzzle, and have coffee. And it's OK to do that. I feel comfortable with myself." He fishes for walleye, salmon, and any other kind of fish he can eat fried or smoked. Carole says, somewhat incredulously, "All I have to do is let him hunt and fish and he's happy."

"I thank God I've been able to turn it around," Chester said. "It was a long, long road. . . ."

It was a road that began in postwar Poland in the southeastern city of Opole Lubelskie, between Warsaw and Krakow, about 60 miles from the Soviet Union. Czeslaw Boleslaw Marcol was born in 1949. He soon became one of the best young soccer players in Opole, population 50,000. When Chester was 14, his father, an engineer, died of an apparent heart attack, and in 1965 his mother moved her four children to Imlay City, Michigan, 40 miles north of Detroit, to be with family. Chester not only was without a father but was in a new country where he couldn't speak the language and couldn't find anyone to play soccer. "The only thing that kept my sanity was my mom's relatives and family gatherings," he remembered.

Marcol's extended family knew that he had athletic talent, but they steered him toward helping out on the family farms and assumed he eventually would work in a Pontiac, Michigan, auto factory. All that changed one day in sophomore gym class when one of the teachers brought out some footballs and told Chester to kick them across the gym. His missile kicks began soaring across the gym and off the walls, grabbing everyone's attention. "I knew something was happening because people were stopping to watch. They took me outside and I was kicking field goals from 60 yards."

A week later he was playing football, a sport he never even had heard of in Poland. At 5' 7", 155 pounds, he was a fine punter and wide receiver. He went to Hillsdale College, a small National Association of Intercollegiate Athletics school in south-central Michigan. There Coach Frank "Muddy" Waters saw an NFL leg in the making and got Marcol to plan for the future and give up on his idea of playing wide receiver. Marcol was NAIA All-American four years in a row and the top kicker in the nation in 1971. His record-setting 62-yard field goal got him national attention. He often booted 70-yarders in practice and once had a 77-yard attempt fall inches short.

The Packers made him their second-round draft pick in 1972. Going from Hillsdale to a star in the NFL almost overnight may have been too much for Marcol. "It all happened in one year. Sometimes it's bad to get a start like that."

Marcol had All-Pro seasons again in 1973 and 1974 (when he led NFL in scoring again), but then missed virtually all the 1975 season with an injury. He had solid seasons in 1976, 1977, and 1978 but missed the last part of 1979 because of knee surgery.

During those years, Marcol began to drink heavily after games and during nights out with his teammates, occasionally putting himself in embarrassing situations. Once he was scheduled to speak at a banquet in La Crosse, Wisconsin, and showed up drunk. He thought little about the dangers of drinking because he began at age 10 in Poland. Beer was sold there on corner stands, and young Chester would "have my beer with the adults and think nothing of it."

But as his Packer career continued, people around him saw signs of his problem. One of the team secretaries, the late Shirley Leonard, who acted as a sort of den mother to the players, asked him once, "What happened to the down-to-earth, humble Polish guy?" Team trainer Dominic Gentile, still one of Marcol's close friends, told Marcol that his drinking was making him look bad. "As much as I didn't like it, I knew at that point they were right," Marcol said. After retiring, his drinking got so bad that he would keep a quart of beer by his bed to satisfy cravings he got during the night.

Everyone assumed that the bottle was to blame when Marcol's performance began to fall short in 1980. Reality hit Marcol when during kicking drills the coaches began using machines instead of him to get the ball down field. His kicks had become wobbly and short.

Earlier that summer Marcol had gone drinking with friends. One of them went to get a gram of cocaine. Surprised, Chester said he never heard of it. But he gave it a try. "Shortly thereafter I was using regularly. I used [cocaine] that season. There's no doubt it affected my performance. It really slipped." Few people, even his teammates, knew he was using cocaine. He adds that cocaine use wasn't a widespread problem among Packer players.

The end came abruptly. About a month into the season, Marcol was called into Starr's office and cut. Starr didn't mention alcohol or drugs or inquire about Marcol's deteriorating skills, Marcol remembered. "It was just a normal, down-to-earth talk. I knew deep down inside why [I was being cut], but nobody else knew. Everybody was puzzled."

Marcol had beaten out Tom Birney for the kicking job in the 1980 training camp, but with Marcol gone Birney took over. By November, the Packers had cut Birney and signed Jan Stenerud, who was coaxed out of retirement by Starr.

Marcol was signed by Houston and finished the 1980 season there. But the Oilers didn't re-sign him for 1981 after he was arrested for disorderly conduct in Green Bay during the off season.

"There's no doubt in my mind that if I didn't use [drugs and alcohol], I would be playing well into my 40s. Three years ago with jeans and street shoes I was kicking 50-yard field goals. My career came to an end in Green Bay in a totally different way than I wanted it to happen. I cheated myself, my teammates and the Packer organization out of some really good years," Marcol said.

Ironically, Marcol's last season provided his greatest memory. In the 1980 opener against the Chicago Bears at Lambeau Field, the score was tied 6-6 in overtime. Marcol came in to attempt a potential game-winning 25-yard field goal. The kick was blocked, but Marcol caught the ball in the air. Few delirious Packer fans would have guessed that Chester Marcol was on cocaine and on his last legs in the NFL when he sprinted around 11 Bears into the end zone for a touchdown to give the Packers a 12-6 win at Lambeau Field.

By 1981, at age 32, his NFL career was over. "I thought my life had kind of ended. My identity was sports. My self-esteem was sports." He got a divorce that year and continued using cocaine and drinking heavily. He and his first wife, Barbara, had a daughter and adopted a son. He returned to college and got his bachelor's degree, but he had lost all that was important to him. He still is trying to repair relations with Barbara and their daughter.

The pains of the 1980s are as far away as Opole Lubelskie, Poland, to him now. He's clinging to all of the new important parts of his life, starting with his new family and his rebuilt self-esteem. He's Somewhere and plans to stay there.

"The biggest difference in my life now is that I don't have to do stupid things. I can influence people in a positive way. Anything that happened in my life I wouldn't trade for what I have now. It was a lot of good times, but the majority of it was floundering. It was hard. Now there's more caring, more love, more concern and friendships.

"I don't want to be mentioned as just a great football player. It's a small part of my life. I just want to live to be a good example. When I die I want people to say what a great person he was . . . and he played football."

CHAPTER

Love Lost

Jim Carter
Linebacker, 1970-1978

I*f you ask former Packers whether or not they enjoyed playing in Green Bay, most say it was the highlight of their football careers. In Green Bay, they'll tell you with emotion in their voices, they felt not only appreciated but heroic. It's something they never forget.*

The players probably never knew that five times—as early as 1922— fans came to the financial rescue of the team with stock drives and fundraisers. They only could sense something special each time they stepped on Lambeau Field, winning or winless, to waves of welcoming cheers, or were asked for autographs while at the grocery store. They only could sense that the Packers were America's team, not a multimillionaire's.

What is America's team? It's millions of Packer fans, long-suffering Wisconsinites, former Wisconsinites and converts who simply love the underdog or love the fact that the Packers are the only publicly owned, and hence American-owned, NFL team (with 1,800 to 1,900 shareholders). These fans supply the circulation for two Packer fan newspapers, make up America's Pack fan club, belly up to Packer bars on Sundays across the country and surf the Internet for information about the team.

Without America's team, Green Bay would be just another Great Lakes port city and blend unnoticed into the Midwestern landscape. It wouldn't get national headlines or be on national newscasts with Los Angeles, Chicago, or New York. So the fans eagerly pay their homage to their Hollywood, their Sears Towers, their Empire State Building—the Packers. It's love requited. Former players often return for reunions or guest appearances and repeat the mantra: Once a Packer always a Packer. The fans and players are warmed by the mutual admiration and family-like bond.

That intangible bond between players and fans is the magic behind the Green Bay Packers. It's how Packer players mounted one last frozen-finger drive against Dallas in 1967. It's how Packer fans revel at the chance to sit for hours in numbing cold. It's how southern natives like Brett Favre somehow excel in subzero Green Bay weather. It's why people from Wisconsin donated as much money as people from Tennessee toward the rebuilding of Reggie White's church in Knoxville in 1996. It's how Packer merchandise (the city has only 97,000 people) was the fifth best seller in the NFL after the 1995 season. It's how the small-town Packers sell out every game outside in December when a metropolitan team like the Minnesota Vikings struggled in 1995 to give away indoor tickets. It's how the Packers have a season-ticket waiting list of 23,000. It's how Green Bay inexplicably has had a team for more than three-quarters of a century while pro football has been remapped dozens of times in all the major cities in the land.

In Green Bay, football is a matter of love.

The love relationship between the Green Bay Packers and their fans was plain for Jim Carter to see when he arrived in 1970, just two years after the Packers' third straight title. He had grown up a six-hour drive west of Green Bay in St. Paul, Minnesota, hearing about players like Starr, Nitschke, and Hornung. "I was pretty excited to be a Packer. It sounded glamorous," he recalled.

It was. Until he tried to replace the ultimate football soldier, Ray Nitschke, at middle linebacker. The ugly experience—being booed by his own fans—left a scar on Carter's psyche, one that irritates him still, even though he is a successful businessman who has put almost 20 years of tracks between himself, football, and Green Bay. He has three new and four used car dealerships with $70 million annually in sales and has given up drinking in favor of community involvement. Carter has built a new life separate from football, one he's proud of. Yet he is discomforted at the thought of returning to what is considered the greatest football city in the country.

Since retiring in 1978, he hasn't been to a Packer game in Green Bay, although he would like to return for a pending reunion of the 1972 Central Division champion team. "If I ever went to Green Bay for an alumni game I fear I'd get booed. I never want to go through that again. It had a profound effect on me. It was degrading. Maybe that's why I made a new life of not being interested in football," he said from his office at Jim Carter Ford in Eau Claire, Wisconsin, as he sat behind a desk the length of an offensive line. He pointed to a wall where three helmets—University of Minnesota, Pro Bowl, and Packer—were displayed in a case, the only visible evidence that he once was at the top of a different profession. Unlike many Packers of the 1960s, he doesn't use his Packer past as a business builder, doesn't throw footballs around in his commercials, doesn't schmooze with the Packer elite to sell cars. He played in an era when the Packers were losers; losing doesn't sell.

Jim Carter acknowledges that Packer fans and the franchise are one-of-a-kind, but he remains detached from Green Bay for good reason. The good life—or a life of doing good, in Carter's case—didn't really begin until he left Green Bay.

He retired from football with $50,000 and opened his first dealership in Eau Claire. After struggling through two years of high consumer interest rates and low sales, he slowly built a regional auto empire, with businesses in St. Paul and the Wisconsin cities of Eau Claire, Chippewa Falls, La Crosse, and Wausau. In his mind, he's finally had some successes. He has done well enough so that he could build a new, trendy-looking Jim Carter Ford in 1994 in Eau Claire, well enough so that he can downhill ski 10 days a month in the winter at his second home in Winter Park, Colorado. He employs about 150 people, and he is regarded as a fair but forceful boss.

In Eau Claire, he has been head of the Chamber of Commerce, a small business person of the year, and a state auto dealer of the year, impressive stuff for a man who believes he wasted his first decade of adulthood. "I like what I've done the last 15 years a lot more. But we still have lots of work to do. I've made opportunity for a lot of people. We're involved in the community, charities. I didn't do anything like that during my football years. The Bart Starrs and Carroll Dales did but I didn't. I'm a better person, a better citizen now. I make a good living and I hope I've earned some respect with the things I've done. My years in Green Bay [off the field] were not well-spent, not productive at all. That's not sour grapes. I lived it, I did it so I have to be accountable and responsible for how I acted."

He drank too much. He talked too much. He didn't pay enough homage. He didn't feel the warmth or the love.

If he had it to do over, what would he change? "I would keep my mouth shut and do my best. I would praise Ray Nitschke and say I was lucky to be there."

Carter came to the Packers as a third-round draft pick in 1970 out of the University of Minnesota, where he was a thundering fullback. He was put at outside linebacker to replace ailing Dave Robinson. By the start of the 1971 season, he had won Nitschke's coveted middle linebacker job. The animosity was natural. Nitschke later said, "If I was going to be beaten out, I wanted to be beaten out by somebody who could show me he had more ability than I did." Carter not only replaced a hero, but he didn't show any sympathy when he said that he deserved the job. "I was always popping off about how I thought I was better than Nitschke. Those guys [from the 1960s] didn't give up easily. I probably knew then but just wouldn't admit what a great player he was. The fans loved him. He deserved the accolades. I was jealous," Carter remembered.

Yet 25 years later he still couldn't resist one last opinion, articulated in his booming middle-linebacker voice: "I still think [Dick] Butkus was better."

But it was the 1960s-spoiled fans, not Nitschke, who made Carter's Packer life miserable. With Nitschke on the sidelines, whenever the defense made a mistake the fans booed Carter and called for Nitschke. Middle linebacker, according to Carter, is the position most susceptible to a variety of defensive errors and, thus, the blame. The most poignant moment came in the sixth game of the 1972 season against Atlanta at Milwaukee. Carter hurt his knee and Nitschke came in for several plays. "As I ran onto the field, I heard a big cheer," Nitschke wrote in his biography *Mean on Sunday.* "The Milwaukee crowd was just yelling for old Ray, but Jim thought the fans were cheering because he'd been injured, and it burned him up. Quite a few people wrote him letters to explain they'd been cheering for Nitschke, not against Carter." Even so, Carter still felt bad. "To me it was the same thing. It was like they were cheering because you were hurt. I took it all personally."

The backlash Carter took from fans for replacing Nitschke only "made me a more negative person, more judgmental. I had an alcoholic personality anyway, but it made me party harder and drink harder," he said. It didn't stop him from talking. He had his own television show in Green Bay, live from the bar at the Left Guard. Carter typically would have "a couple of drinks" before the show. He recalled a woman in the audience once asking if he ever would be able to fill Nitschke's shoes. "I said something like, 'Go to hell.' It was a live show. We didn't cut it. It was probably a decent question. I caught hell for that."

Carter made the Pro Bowl in 1973 but admitted not living up to his potential as a player, pointing out, "There's no way you can perform when you miss curfew and are out too late." He recalled a regrettable incident late in his career when, still hung over from a night of drinking, he sought a sexual favor at the Packer offices from a club secretary. The woman complained to coach Bart Starr. The incident was settled internally, Carter said, but not before it got into the news. It was "very bad publicity for me and for the Packers," Carter acknowledged.

Alcohol became a centerpiece of Carter's life. He bought a disco night club in Manitowoc, Wisconsin, near Green Bay, and managed one of Fuzzy Thurston's Left Guard bar and restaurants in Eau Claire. Carter also bought a Left Guard in Janesville, Wisconsin, struggled, and sold it back to Thurston. Carter, who is divorced, gave up drinking on March 3, 1983. It was no coincidence that from then on his businesses began to succeed, he said.

Carter feels that the competitiveness of pro football draws "compulsive type personalities" rather than the game breeding alcoholism. Two of Carter's teammates, kicker Chester Marcol and linebacker Ted Hendricks, also have had drinking problems. A survey by the NFL Players Association found that 13 percent of players from the 1970s, more than any other decade, had alcohol problems during their first three years out of football.

While alcohol may have been the most common vice among Packers in the 1970s, it wasn't the only one. The use of amphetamines as performance enhancers was common among players, including Carter. Players got their jump start in two forms of diet pills, either a tiny pill with a white cross, called White Crosses, or a large pill called a Black Cadillac. Carter took Black Cadillacs. The pills produced energetic feelings of euphoria and heightened alertness—like an overpowering caffeine or sugar rush—in addition to "awful hangovers," Carter recalled. "We never gave it a thought. We felt it was what we needed to do to play well. It gave us an edge. In hindsight, I believe I would have played better without it."

Carter said the team didn't push the use of the diet pills but didn't prohibit them either. It had to be obvious to team officials that players were on some sort of drug because "we all sat there before games with our eyes [wide open], sweating, drinking Cokes, and smoking cigarettes. How could they not know? It was real prevalent. At least half of all the offensive linemen and half of the defensive line took it, some linebackers, some defensive backs."

Offensive lineman Gale Gillingham began taking the diet pills when he arrived in 1966. The team supplied them for players until 1971, he recalled, with few restrictions. After 1971, players got the pills on their own in prescription form—usually pleading fatigue or weight problems—and popped them before games to gain what they thought was a mental edge. Gillingham took the pills throughout his career, but he didn't and still doesn't see it as a serious issue. "What's the big deal? Everybody in the league took it. Truck drivers still take it. It's the intent. It was to help us play better. We didn't take it to get high." The diet pills were a form of amphetamine commonly referred to as speed. Speed was a popular drug—and earned its bad reputation—in the 1960s with California counter-culture groups who took so much of it that they could stay awake for days.

Jim Carter's problems in Green Bay were just a small part of the confusion in the Packer organization after the 1972 season. When the team began losing in 1973, players and officials began taking sides for and against Coach Dan Devine. "The type of conversation was, 'Is he coming or going?' 'How can we get rid of him?' " Carter said. Once, when it was known that Devine's job was in jeopardy, running back MacArthur Lane took a card around the locker room asking players to sign it to show their support for Devine. Carter laughed when he recalled the bizarre situation. He didn't sign the card and neither did about half the players on the team. Carter and Lane became divided on the Devine and strike issues and "didn't get along at all at the end of our time together in Green Bay," Carter said. However, Carter now would like to reconnect with Lane and be friends again because Lane "was an excellent, tough football player and a person who had the courage to speak his mind."

While Carter liked Devine and Devine's family, he didn't think Devine was a good coach. He remembers Devine's first team meeting, when he brought in University of Missouri film to show the Packers how to cover kicks. Carter knew that wouldn't sit well with the players. He turned to Donny Anderson and said, "This is never going to fly." Carter believes Devine "wasn't prepared to deal with the issues that faced him when he came to Green Bay."

Devine himself admitted in a 1990 interview that he was "pretty naive" when he came to the Packers. "I'm not talking about Xs and Os. It was other things, personnel and how you did things." He also said that the lack of support he got from the Packer administration was damaging in 1974. "I had some good players I had to discipline, but they would just go to the seven-man committee and bitch to them and they'd side with the players. You're asking me why I quit and that's one of the reasons."

Devine now lives near Phoenix, Arizona, after retiring recently as athletic director at Missouri. He had hip replacement surgery in 1995, and his wife, Joanne, is wheelchair-bound because of multiple sclerosis. She was diagnosed with the disease when they lived in Green Bay.

The 1974 players' strike over free agency only exacerbated the Packers' confusion and internal disagreements. Devine allegedly offered bonuses to players to cross the picket line, and on July 18, less than three weeks after the strike began, Carter and Larry Hefner crossed the line.

On July 23, Chester Marcol crossed. Carter and Hefner did not get bonuses, but they crossed because they didn't believe in the strike or the leadership of the union under Ed Garvey, according to Carter.

By the end of the 1974 season, when the Packers went to Atlanta for their final game, the players sensed that it was Devine's last game. There were rumors of players boycotting the game. The situation was dismal that rainy day in Atlanta with only a few thousand fans showing up. Carter remembers a reserve Packer lineman filling his water bottle with vodka and drinking it throughout the game. By the end of the game the player was so drunk he "couldn't find his helmet," Carter remembered with a laugh. Afterward, half the Packers didn't fly back with the team, instead scattering to their home towns. Carter and Marcol piled up beer in an empty plane seat between them and drank all the way back to Green Bay.

Carter missed part of the 1975 and all of the 1976 season with injuries. He was back in form in 1977, but after 1978, which saw him become a backup. Bart Starr told him that he wasn't in the team's plans. He retired.

Two years later he was in the car business, ready to put football far behind him. He knew cars. His father owned a Ford dealership in South St. Paul, Minnesota, when Jim was growing up, in those halcyon days when he was a star high school fullback and was recruited by Notre Dame, Minnesota, and other major colleges. He also was a star hockey player, capable of playing pro hockey had he chosen. The world seemed to be his for the grabbing. "I never performed, honestly, at the level I thought I was capable [in the NFL]. When I was in high school I knew I could do things that others couldn't do. I was All-Pro one year. Why not eight years?"

CHAPTER

"Who Am I?"

David Greenwood
Safety, 1986-1987

As a sports agent, Bob LaMonte had seen some of his clients go through withdrawal when they retired. It was common. Then one day former Toronto Blue Jays pitcher Dave Stieb said, "Bob, what do I do the rest of my life?" LaMonte didn't understand at first because he had set up Stieb with an annuity that paid him a half-million dollars annually for 25 years. Stieb told LaMonte, "My wife has something to do; my kids have something to do; but I don't," Stieb, of course, could do anything he wanted, but after throwing baseballs most of his life he had no idea where to begin. That's when LaMonte realized that with all the focus on multimillion-dollar sports contracts, many players didn't know what to do with their money or their time when they retired. For pro athletes, the rewards that come with being young, rich, and powerful are also a prescription for disaster, a "drug lord scenario," according to LaMonte. To deal with the problem, LaMonte started a program called "Invest in Yourself."

His first customer was the Green Bay Packers. When Packer President Bob Harlan bought the program in 1995, he arguably did something that no other head of a pro sports team had ever done: He showed concern for pro athletes after their careers were over. For $6,250 per player, the whole Packer team went though comprehensive habilitative counseling sessions designed to smooth their transition out of the often ivory-tower world of athletics. LaMonte's program could become a standard throughout the NFL and be a model for other pro sports leagues in the coming years.

Football was always a form of physical expression for David Greenwood. At 6'3", 210 pounds, the multi-talented athlete could handle just about any situation. He was big enough to play linebacker, fast enough to play safety, and tough enough to play anywhere. But after seven years in pro football, Greenwood finally found a situation he couldn't handle. At age 30 he retired from the NFL. For the first time in his life he flinched. He was face-to-face with David Greenwood.

Greenwood could no longer define himself by running a fast 40-yard dash, leveling a ball carrier, or giving a receiver whiplash. He had passed from a dream world, as he saw the NFL, to the real world. What a strange new existence it was. It was a world without a six-figure salary, a world that flattens big egos on a daily basis, a world without the only thing he knew—football. "That's what the game does to you. It makes you feel bigger than life, and believe me the world puts you in place," Greenwood said.

For three years, Greenwood and his wife, Julie, saw a therapist to help them deal with the transition that seemed akin to war veterans returning to civilian life. He talked about two former NFL friends who committed suicide and the wife of another NFL friend who did the same. Greenwood said he too fought the incongruous forces of anxiety (about the future) and depression (about leaving his career behind). He had to take days off to sleep. Greenwood was scared for himself, his wife, and their two young daughters. "You look at the suicide and divorce rate among ex-NFL players and it's very high. If I hadn't gotten help I'd probably be divorced." Greenwood had to be deprogrammed because "the whole system, NFL, coaches, media, builds you up as bigger than life.

You're somebody. Then you're out and you're nobody. It's like a death in the family."

Greenwood was far from an anomaly. A 1990 NFL Players Association survey found that of players who left the game because of injury 70.6 percent had emotional problems the first six months. Even if they didn't leave because of injury, 56.2 percent still had emotional trouble. More ominously, within two years of leaving football 78 percent of the players suffered through one or more of three calamitous situations—bankruptcy, divorce, or unemployment.

Greenwood, now 35 and a club golf pro in Florida, spent two years with the Michigan Panthers of the United States Football League (1983-1984), one year with the Tampa Bay Buccaneers (1985), two with the Packers (1986-1987), and two with the LA Raiders (1988-1989).

His biggest adjustment was giving up the NFL lifestyle, one built around pampering and coddling but one that is ultimately cruel, as he sees it. "You're put on a pedestal. It's like teams are playing with you. You're only as good as the last game, then they kick your butt off the field. You've got the big mortgage, the big bucks, then whoa! You've lived a life of fantasy. Then you look at yourself and say, 'Who am I?' "

Despite his success as an athlete, Greenwood realized that at age 30 he was "starting over" in life when most of his high school and college friends had established themselves in their careers. "The therapist sits you down and says, 'Yea, you were great, but now what are you? Nothing. OK.' I never thought I'd have problems in transition. That's what the game does to you."

It did something else to Greenwood: It made him grow accustomed to hurting other people. He's had to fight himself to deal nonviolently with his problems. He remembers being a tough guy while growing up. As early as freshman year in high school, he hit another player so hard that his whole body tingled. "I used to be the one who got the guy on the ground and didn't want to let him up. That's the rage. You try to hurt him. You could use violence. You're used to taking out your problems physically."

But he began to deal with those feelings in 1982 when he became a Christian. He still hit people hard but began to help them up afterward. "I remember when [Packer linebacker] Tim Harris was a rookie. He was a crazy guy. I stuck a guy and helped him up. Harris came over and got in my face and said, 'What are you doing! What are you doing!' I said, 'Listen, rookie, you play your game and I'll play mine.' "

Greenwood plays another game now. While with the Buccaneers in 1985-1986, he joined the Carrollwood Country Club in Tampa and got to know the pro there. "I spent a lot of time there and liked what I saw. I decided golf would be a neat career to follow football." He is head pro at the Magnolia Country Club, a semi-private 18-hole course in Newport Richey, Florida, about a 15-minute commute in his Porsche from his home in Tampa. He works six days a week during the busy spring and fall seasons. He landed the job in August 1994 shortly after earning his Class A Professional Golfers Association card. To get the card, he had to pass two PGA business courses, oral and playing tests, and accumulate credits working as an apprentice pro at East Lake Woodlands, a private 36-hole course in Tampa. "I'm very satisfied where I'm at. I had a goal to be a head pro at 35 and I met it. I'll continue to work at being a good professional," said Greenwood, who not surprisingly says distance off the tee is his forte as a player.

Golf is not new to Greenwood. He played regularly at the local Park Falls, Wisconsin, course while growing up in northern Wisconsin. "My dad taught me [golf] one day. He didn't really know what he was doing, but he showed me how to do it. My best shot that day went through a window. Of course, it was my last shot of the day."

Although Greenwood often played golf all day long during his summers in Park Falls, he never went out for the golf team because of conflicts with track and football. In track, he became the first state athlete to clear seven feet in the high jump. He won six state titles in high school track. He also excelled in the pole vault, and at one time he considered going into track full time, as an Olympic decathlete hopeful, instead of pro football.

Greenwood played football at the University of Wisconsin from 1979-1982, earning All-Big Ten honors his final two years. He also won the Big Ten high jump title in 1982. He was drafted twice in 1983, in the first round by Michigan of the United States Football League and in the eighth round of the NFL draft by New Orleans. He signed with Michigan for $900,000 for four years, a huge contract at the time. He helped Michigan win the 1983 USFL title, and he was named All-Pro. Greenwood's rights were traded, and he wound up in Tampa Bay of the NFL for the 1985 season.

After starting 10 games for the Bucs, he was released spring 1986. That fall, Packers Coach Forrest Gregg made a surprising move, cutting third-year safety Tom Flynn, who had been an NFL All-Rookie team player in 1984. Gregg dumped many of Coach Bart Starr's players after the Packers started the season 0-6. Greenwood signed October 21, 1986 and had two sacks in his first game as a Packer on October 26 against San Francisco in Milwaukee.

He was out with an injury the entire 1987 season—when he expected the strong safety job was all his. The Packers didn't renew his contract for 1988, and he eventually signed with the Raiders for two seasons. With the Raiders, he claims to have been the victim of a racist coach. Defensive backs coach Willie Brown "didn't like white players. It was the first time I saw racism in the sport."

After his experience with the Raiders, he decided to leave pro football. "I got jerked around a little too much the last couple of years and said, 'Well, I don't need this.' I'm a little bitter about the game. Bitter but thankful. I still think of it as a great opportunity, but a player has to deal with it on his own. I've learned how to deal with it."

CHAPTER

The Price of Pro Football

Alphonso Carreker
Defensive end, 1984-1988

Ezra Johnson
Defensive end, 1977-1987

Derrel Gofourth
Center, 1977-1982

Mark Koncar
Offensive tackle, 1976-1981

Bill Lueck
Guard, 1968-1974

By the time you go through your freshman year at a major college *if you don't know it's a damn tough business and a nasty business you're not smart enough to get through college. If you go through the [NFL] ten years, the rest of your life will be changed."*

—Gale Gillingham, former Green Bay Packers lineman

"There are tremendous sacrifices in this game. If you waited until you were healthy to play, you'd play the first exhibition game, the fourth game of the year and somewhere around the 11th you get back in there again. You'd have to stock each team with 250 players. It's all part of the sport. You grow up with it from the time you are in high school—playing with pain, doing it for the team. You think nothing of it."
—Phil Simms, former New York Giants quarterback

In professional football, injuries often are downplayed as simply part of the game. But according to a 1989 survey for the NFL Players Association, injuries are a major part of players' lives. The survey found that 62 percent of players (nearly two out of three from the 1940s through 1980s) suffered a permanent injury because of football. More than half the players (54 percent) had at least one knee surgery in their careers, and 47 percent now have problems with arthritis, the survey found. Among former offensive linemen, 56 percent suffer from arthritis. Since 1970, almost half (46 percent) the players surveyed were driven out of the NFL because of injuries. All the pain was for an NFL career that lasted on average, 4.6 years in 1970 and just 3.2 years in 1986.

Alphonso Carreker

From the time he was a freshman in high school in Columbus, Ohio, until he retired from the NFL in 1993, Carreker always looked to football as his motivation in life. It was his life. Now that he's raising a family in Marietta, Georgia, near Atlanta, he is "excited I can put football behind me." Not, however, without a sack of money, an aching body, and some wonder about what he called the "dark side of the NFL."

He made more than $1 million with bonuses in 1984 when he was the Packers' first-round draft pick. When he went to Denver on Plan B (as a free agent left unprotected by the Packers) in 1988 he got $2 million for three years. "Financially, I don't have to run out and get a job," he said. He owns a three-employee company called Access Medical Supplies and is interested in the restaurant business. "It's a new chapter in my life. I'm taking this on with a more serious approach. Football was more fun. This is a chance to use your mind, not use your shoulder," explained Carreker, a criminal justice major at Florida State.

After back and knee operations caused him to miss the 1991 season and half the 1992 season, Carreker retired prior to the 1993 season because he "wanted to live a normal life." Still, he took from football a reconstructed knee and a left foot that is numb as a result of a slipped disk in his back. He has sought disability income for the injuries but has twice been turned down. He also has a shoulder that has hurt for six years. It was injured in the 1990 Super Bowl when Denver lost to San Francisco, 55-10.

Dealing with injuries and pain is one part of pro football that still amazes Carreker. Some of the strongest men in the world—Carreker, 6' 6", weighed 260 pounds when he played—used pain killers every day to deal with the rigors of the game. Non-prescription brands like Motrin and Advil were readily available to all players in the Packer training room. They are not controlled substances and not addictive. "When I was in Green Bay I took a lot of Motrin. It helped me with my joints. My knees swelled so much. On Sunday nights after the game you'd have to take pain killers just to jog on Monday. The only way you could get up in the morning was if you took Motrin." An anti-inflammatory drug, Motrin was often used by players on a daily basis to help them practice when they were nursing injuries, according to Carreker.

Players in severe pain were given Tylenol 3, a powerful prescription pain killer. Tylenol 3 is classified as a narcotic because it contains codeine, a derivative of opium. It is a controlled substance and can be addictive. Carreker said players had to ask the trainer or team doctor for Tylenol 3, but they always got what they wanted. "You could get ten of those easy. When you get up in the morning and can't walk, you just start popping Tylenol 3s. You take three or four or those and you're in la la land just like anything else. When I had a lot of injuries I would take Tylenol 3s with a beer on the plane after a game. That was just to get you off the damn plane, just to get down the stairs. My knees were swelled so bad, especially if you played on artificial turf."

George "Tiger" Greene, a defensive back in the late 1980s who also lives in Atlanta, agreed that pain killers were "easily accessed. It was a problem. A lot of guys abused the privileges." Greene hurt his shoulder the third week of the 1990 season and had cortisone, an anti-inflammatory drug, injected into the shoulder every week for the rest of the season.

When taken over long periods of time, cortisone can cause the bones to lose calcium. He now has a cyst in the area where the injections took place. That same year he had weekly cortisone injections in his heels. "I'm paying for it now. My ankles, my arm, my knees hurt. My shoulder comes out of joint from driving the car. I take Motrin every day. A lot of times it's the only way I can make it. Every day," Greene said.

Cortisone shots were a staple of the training room in Green Bay, Carreker recalled. Unlike Greene, Carreker refused to take cortisone shots, even though the team "always wanted you to." He knew that cortisone didn't dissolve in the body and ate "the cartilage away so you've got nothing but pain in your joints from then on." His eyes were opened to the reality of the NFL his rookie year when he saw oft-injured quarterback Lynn Dickey get a shot of Novocain—a numbing drug—with the largest needle he had ever seen. "Dickey leaned over a table and they shot Novocain into his back. Thirty minutes later he stood up. He was numbed up, and he went out and played," Carreker said.

When Carreker heard in May 1996 that Packer QB Brett Favre had checked into a rehabilitation center for an addiction to the pain killer Vicodin, he wasn't surprised. For decades players have turned to pain killers, amphetamines, alcohol, and illegal drugs to help them deal with the pressure to perform. "That's where a lot of addictions started. You get used to taking pain killers and pretty soon you get hooked on them. The marquee players, like Favre, face the greatest pressure," Carreker stated. The pressure comes from the coaches and often is applied by the trainers. "The trainers would come up, and you could see the look in their face. They would say, 'Can you go?' You would get frowns from the coach if you didn't play. Forrest Gregg was one of the worst. You would get some big-time pressure in Green Bay. I saw a lot of that in Green Bay," Carreker said.

In his first month as a rookie in 1984, Carreker suffered what he called a jammed neck. "I never had a burner like that before." Although he was leery of playing, Carreker stayed on the field because "I was the Number One draft pick and everybody wanted to see me get in there and play." He was told by the team doctors that he would be OK with some "anti-inflammatory drug to bring the swelling down." Later, he learned he had played the entire season with a cracked bone in his neck.

Carreker believed he couldn't trust the team trainers or doctors, who were loyal to their employer. They were "trained to lie to get players out there [on the field]. Players would get manipulated to play when they knew they were hurt." Domenic Gentile, the longtime Packer trainer who retired in 1992, admitted in a 1995 book, *The Packer Tapes,* that his responsibility to get injured players on the field while at the same time caring for their well-being "was a difficult line to walk."

Former Oakland Raiders internist Robert Huizenga, who worked for the Raiders 1983–1990, wrote *You're OK, It's Just a Bruise,* a 1994 book about the pressure to play with pain in the NFL. Huizenga, now an associate professor of medicine at UCLA, said "You've got owners that cut players who won't play hurt, players who have contracts with incentives to play, and this whole American persona where we want our guys to play hurt. The players' health gets used as a commodity."

All the physical problems caused by football were not worth the big salaries, Carreker believes, but "you go for it because you're doing something you love." Carreker, an All-State football and basketball player while growing up in Columbus, Ohio, was named to the NFL All-Rookie team in 1984. He had 19 ½ sacks in five seasons with the Packers but never became the dominant defensive end they envisioned. His greatest game as a Packer was when he had four sacks against Tampa Bay in the December 1, 1985 "Snow Bowl," when 13 inches of snow fell during the game.

Carreker was delighted to go to Denver because the Broncos were a contending team and Coach Dan Reeves "let you do what you did best." Under Coach Forrest Gregg, Carreker got tired of stepping "the way the coach wanted you to step. When I was first drafted in Green Bay, I was excited about football. The love was there. The first year I saw Gregg he got rid of guys not because of their ability but because he didn't like them. That's when I found out the NFL is a business. It's a cold environment. It's a business system. You have to fit.

"We had animosity between the coach and players. He was screaming at guys for making simple mistakes. He pinpointed you at meetings. I knew guys who didn't want to go to meetings because they knew Forrest was going to ride them all day. He wanted to bring the Lombardi thing back up as far as yelling at players, kicking at chairs." When the Packers started losing under Gregg, the players' morale dropped,

Carreker recalled. "It was survival. The goal was to go out and not get hurt. A lot of guys were there just to get a check. It was worse than miserable."

Ezra Johnson

For Ezra Johnson, the extra effort, perseverance, and all the painful surgeries and rehabilitations paid off. He survived 15 years in the NFL, long enough so that he could retire in style. He's a good example of how the American dream of many a young man—getting rich playing pro sports—actually can come true. Yet what seems to be true and what really is true seldom agree. Early in life, Johnson never dreamed of playing pro football. And now that he's done it, he cautions anyone thinking the NFL is the way to happiness.

Growing up in Shreveport, Louisiana, the middle child of a family of eight, Johnson didn't even play football until his senior year in high school. When he got a football scholarship to attend Morris Brown, a black college in Atlanta, he was the first in his family to go beyond high school. Even then he had no NFL goal, focusing instead on school. Then one day when he was still a homesick freshman, one of the team's best players told young Ezra that someday he could go pro. "I thought, 'You must be out of your mind,'" Johnson remembered.

About a year later, Johnson was excelling at football, yet he couldn't figure out why his father never had come to see one of his games. While home on Christmas break, he noticed his dad watching a pro football play-off game on TV. He mustered enough courage to ask why he would watch the pros but not his son's college games. Ezra said his dad, a cement truck driver, was a big man of few words. "He weighed about 300 pounds and his arms were about twice as big as mine. All he had to do was look at me [to have an impact]," Johnson said. His dad looked at the TV and told Ezra that someday he wanted to see Ezra play on there—on TV in the NFL. Ezra was surprised. Until that moment, he had no idea that he might be able to please his father in that way. "I never had the ambition to do this until my father said that," Ezra recalled.

He went back to school with the NFL on his mind. But the next summer, his father went into the hospital for a broken foot. A blood clot formed and his father died, never having seen Ezra play. But Ezra was intent on fulfilling his father's wish. "It was my motivating force. I always tried to do that little extra. I'd say, 'This is for dad.' "

After the Packers drafted him in the first round in 1977, he quickly became one of the top defensive ends in the NFL. He was All-Pro and was the pride of his family. For a quiet young man who had fulfilled his father's wish and was reaping all of life's pleasures while not yet 25, things couldn't have been better.

While he called playing in the NFL "a blessing, true enough," he soon saw that he was being paid to sacrifice his body for the entertainment and profit of others. The first time he got hurt, he realized that the team's greatest concern wasn't for him as a person but for how soon he could get back on the field. "I figured they liked me because I can sack the quarterback," he said. "I thought, 'Hey, this is serious stuff.' It's not like what I thought. It's an education, and it's a rude and a cruel one." So now when he drives his fancy car to the store and kids idolize his upper-class way of life, "I let them know the reality" of the NFL, he said. He tells them to get an education because "nobody can take that away." In pro sports "you're only as good as your body."

A knee injury caused the Packers to release Johnson after the 1987 season. Johnson is an NFL success story only because he worked hard to overcome 12 surgeries, including three back surgeries and one knee surgery in a 12-month span while with the Packers. Prior to the back surgeries, Johnson played in pain the entire 1983 season with what he thought was a sciatic nerve problem. "I could hardly practice, walk, or dress myself. I made practice one time a week—maybe," Johnson said, recalling that he played only as a pass rusher.

The pressue to play with pain, Johnson said, came mostly from within or from teammates. "I had a great relationship with my position coach, Dick Modzleweski. He didn't pressure me. I made that decision to play with my back. It's something I wanted to do. It's a brutal game, but you're oblivious to it because you want to play so bad. Since the 12th grade I worked out with the mentality that you just suck it up and go. But I have to suffer the residual effects." He still has back problems and tries to keep his weight down to reduce the strain on his back and knees. The 6' 4" Johnson weighs 230 pounds, 30 pounds lighter than when he played.

Johnson recalls seldom, if ever, taking Novocain, cortisone, or pain pills during his career. He figured that if he was in too much pain to play his body was telling him he shouldn't play, and pain pills [because of the codeine] upset his stomach.

He endured the pain and eventually got rich. He received an $80,000 signing bonus in 1977, but his base contract was for only $38,000 a year for five years. In his final season with the Packers, in 1987, he finally began hitting pay dirt. He made $425,000 that year. His final contract, with the Houston Oilers, was $1.1 million split over two years, 1990 and 1991. He also played for the Indianapolis Colts in 1988 and 1989.

He definitely sees the issue of large salaries from a player's viewpoint. The NFL owners have too much control, a Mafia-like domain, and should be paying the players even more for their physical sacrifices, he believes. "People ask me what I think about Deion [Sanders]. I think he's blessed. I think he's smart. I wish it was me," Johnson said of the Dallas Cowboys star, who in 1995 signed a seven-year contract for $35 million.

Johnson is now a defensive end at rest in Fairburn, Georgia, a ritzy suburb southeast of Atlanta where his neighbors include other multimillionaire athletes—boxer Evander Holyfield, former Atlanta Braves star Marquis Grissom, and former Braves standout Lonnie Smith.

Johnson doesn't have to work, so he chooses his activities carefully. He helped coach at his alma mater, Morris Brown, in 1993 and 1994, and he and his wife, Carmen, own a restaurant in his hometown of Shreveport. They have three young children, Carlonda, Dezera, and Ezra, Jr. Johnson said he is focusing now on being a good husband and a father.

Johnson set the Packer career sack record with 84, including 20½ sacks in 1978. He returned to Green Bay as honorary Packer captain for the 1995 game against Detroit, an emotional experience that reminded him of "how much he enjoyed Green Bay and the team," even though moving to Green Bay in 1977 left him with culture shock because of the mostly white town and the cold weather. "I was such an introvert. I had to reprogram my thinking [about white people]." He grew up with the notion that white people were his enemies, he said. "I learned to like country music. I grew and became knowledgeable about life." One time, Johnson laughed, a young white girl in Green Bay, curious about his dark skin, asked him why the paint wouldn't rub off.

One of the reasons Johnson matured was Coach Bart Starr. Johnson believes that playing under Starr, who became a father figure to him, made up for the lack of winning in Green Bay. Johnson still feels partly responsible when he recalls how Starr's relations with the media soured and caused division on the team in the early 1980s. Johnson got into hot water in 1980 when he ate a hot dog on the sidelines during a 38-0 preseason loss to Denver. The media suggested that incident showed how Starr had lost control of the team. Johnson said he ate the hot dog simply because he was hungry—and immature. He and Starr became close friends after that. "I explained to him what happened, and he believed me. He respected my explanation," said Johnson. When Starr was fired after the 1983 season, Johnson was saddened because "they were sacrificing him for whatever reason to save their own behinds."

Derrel Gofourth

Derrel Gofourth is reminded of his NFL career every day. All he has to do is try to button his shirt. "I can't button the top button of my shirt. I can't get that far up." Ten football-related surgeries on his limbs—including four on his elbows—have changed Gofourth's life. "I've been affected by it for sure. I can't do things like play slow pitch softball with the guys or play basketball. I don't lift weights anymore. I can't jog. If I play golf, 18 holes, I still walk but it takes a couple of days for the swelling to go down [in my knees]. I used to play golf three or four times a week, but I play once a week now."

His body is scarred, arthritic, and limited in its abilities. He's just 41 years old, but he has the body of an old man. Gofourth may have made good money playing pro football for nine years, but he paid dearly. "I don't think people realize what's involved in pro football," he said.

Gofourth lives in Stillwater, Oklahoma, where he played collegiate ball at Oklahoma State. Married, with a 17-year-old son, he works primarily as an insurance salesman, selling health insurance, annuities, and mutual funds under the "Gofourth Agency" name. He also owns a small manufacturing company and owns and manages rental property.

Despite the injuries during his career and the way they continue to affect his life, Gofourth doesn't lament his bad luck or his decision to stay in the NFL as long as he did. "I'm not one to look back. Even if I did, I couldn't change it. It was part of the game."

Gofourth was injury-free for his first three seasons with the Packers. Then after the 1979 season he had four surgeries in 13 months. First both elbows went. Then both knees gave out.

"After four surgeries I felt I had hit all four major joints and there wasn't much more to hurt," he recalled. He was half right. One knee and one elbow would go under the knife a second time.

Eventually, he would tear the rotator cuff in both shoulders. Don't ask him to do jumping jacks.

Since retiring, he has had two more surgeries, elbow and knee. The most recent elbow surgery helped a pinched nerve that caused parts of two fingers to atrophy.

Gofourth was on his way up with the Packers when the injuries began. After that he never had a chance to improve as a player but only to rehabilitate and try to regain his previous form. Gofourth, 6' 3", 260 pounds, was the Packers' seventh-round draft pick in 1977. He backed up Larry McCarren at center before transferring to guard. Despite his injuries, Gofourth started 63 straight games from 1978 through 1981, missing the finale in 1981 because of a knee injury. Gofourth was legendary among his teammates for the way he played in pain. He usually waited until the seasons were over to have his surgeries.

After the 1982 season, Gofourth was traded by the Packers to San Diego. The worst part about playing in Green Bay was the losing, Gofourth said. "There were more downs than ups. It was difficult because you didn't want to be in that situation, but unfortunately we were. Somebody has to be the losers. I never did like it, and none of the other players liked it." Of coach Bart Starr, Gofourth says: "I liked Bart as a person. I would have liked to have seen us have better seasons."

Gofourth grew up in Parsons, Kansas, a city of about 13,000 in southeast Kansas near the Oklahoma border. In Stillwater, Oklahoma, he feels at home with many of his farmer clients. "I'm not a big coat and tie guy."

When you can't reach that top button, you don't have much choice.

Mark Koncar

Mark Koncar doesn't need to read old newspaper clippings to bring back memories of the pain he suffered during his pro football career. He is reminded every time he tries to exercise. "I've tried jogging a million times. I say I'm going to get in shape, and I pay for it so damn badly. I used to be able to work out. Lately it's getting tougher and tougher."

Born in Murray, Utah, Koncar lives now in Sandy, Utah, a suburb of Salt Lake City. He is a sales representative for Romic Environmental Technologies. He sells trucking services to large corporations that need hazardous materials transported. Chevron, for example, might need a large shipment of crude oil moved from one city to another. "I put together some pricing. I put the whole ball of wax together, and then I go in and present it. It's a lot of work, but it's a lot of fun and I love it. I really enjoy the business world," Koncar said. He travels three or four days each week as director of sales for the western states.

The cliche "see how the mighty have fallen" is a sad reminder of how big and agile men are reduced to just plain big men many times each year while playing pro football. Koncar, the Packers' number one draft pick in 1976, was one of them. He had a name that sounded invincible, and he was built like a boxcar—6' 5", 265 pounds. He immediately became one of the best young offensive linemen in the NFL, starting every game his rookie season and making the all-rookie squad.

After a minor injury sidelined him for the final game of 1977, Koncar came back in 1978 ready to establish himself as one of the league's top offensive linemen. During the first play of the first preseason game in 1978, he tore cartilage in one knee. He remembers finishing the series of plays then going to the sidelines and noticing his swollen knee. He had surgery and missed the entire 1978 season, when the Packers jumped to a 7-3 start.

He came back strong in 1979, only to miss four games because of knee and ankle problems.

The 1980 season was no better. He spent the preseason and the first four games of the regular season on injured reserve with a badly sprained ankle. He returned in game five, tore an Achilles tendon, and was out the rest of the season.

By 1982 Coach Bart Starr realized that there was little choice but to trade the once-promising titan. "Like I told Bart, I know they didn't want to build around a 30-year-old tackle with bad legs," Koncar recalled. He was sent to Houston for a draft pick the Packers used to take offensive lineman Angelo Fields. After a year and more pain in Houston, Koncar retired.

Along with ankle, knee, and Achilles tendon problems, Koncar suffered and still suffers from a staph infection that he believes happened during his first knee surgery in 1978. "To this day it's very troublesome. That was basically my leg problem." The infection, Koncar said, has eaten way at his knees and caused other health problems.

Koncar regrets only that he didn't get the chance to realize his potential. He has accepted his physical problems. "It would be nice to be able to exercise, if my body would have stayed together. There were lots of risks, but it was worth it. It was one thing I wanted to do." Despite what it did to his body, Koncar calls playing in the NFL the highlight of his life.

Koncar spent two years coaching linemen with Memphis of the USFL immediately after he retired in 1983. He used that experience to "get football out of my system and get ready for the real world." Divorced with no children, Koncar refers to himself as an "old coyote out west." He has kept his weight down to 270 despite his inability to work out. "As a player it's easy, but now it's a battle."

Although he still loves football, on Sundays now he's often trout fishing in Utah on the Green River, one of the best trout steams in the country. It's one sport he can enjoy without having to move fast, twist, and dig in—things he had to swear off years ago.

Bill Lueck

Bill Lueck earned a lot of dividends while playing pro football—money, notoriety, warm memories. Nearly two decades after retiring, he's still paying the price. He'll be paying it the rest of his life.

In 1995, Lueck, the Packers' 1968 first-round draft pick, underwent his fourth knee surgery since returning to live in his home state of Arizona, where he is a cash-crop farmer. Lueck's knee problems have nothing to do with his tilling the soil in Litchfield Park, west of Phoenix. They're all related to his seven years at left guard for the Packers. "Basically I have two worn out knees," said Lueck, who had two knee surgeries while he was with the Packers, giving him a total of six. Lueck, nearing 50, is a "prime candidate" for knee replacement surgery, but doctors tell him he's simply too young for it because artificial knees also wear out.

His biological knees began hurting during the 1974 season with the Packers. Sometime early that fall he unknowingly tore cartilage in his right knee but continued to play the entire season. He wound up having surgery in January 1975. While he was rehabilitating the knee, first-year coach Bart Starr traded Lueck to Philadelphia. Lueck started for the Eagles, but on the Friday prior to the 13th game in 1975 he damaged his left knee in practice. He was on the injured reserve list for 1976, then retired.

Dealing with injured knees has become a way of life for Lueck. He was a competitive tennis player for many years but gave that up after his latest surgery. For exercise, he bikes and lifts weights "intensely" four times a week to help preserve what knee muscles remain. Lueck is slender now, but he has no choice. He stays light to keep pressure off his worn joints. When he needs to stand for long periods of time, he leans against a wall to lessen the pain.

He doesn't bemoan his knee problems, but he is bitter because ex-NFL players have been left to themselves to deal with their damaged bodies. For example, Lueck has borne the cost of his post-career surgeries. He says that "in a perfect world" those surgeries would be paid for by the employer responsible for them, namely the NFL, the Eagles, or the Packers. For several years after retiring, Lueck couldn't get medical insurance because of his knees. "My knees were considered pre-existing conditions. It took me four or five years to get those pre-existing conditions waived," he explained.

Lueck is not alone. In a 1989 NFLPA survey, only 17 percent of former players had football insurance that covered their surgeries; two-thirds used their own insurance. Another 14 percent used personal funds to cover surgery costs. Two percent said they couldn't afford treatment. Almost one-fourth of the players said injuries caused them financial difficulty.

Lueck is active in the NFL Alumni Association chapter in Phoenix. He tells how some members of the chapter who have no insurance have been unable to pay for needed knee or hip replacement surgeries. However, a sympathetic doctor named James St. Ville donated his services. "He does them [knee and hip surgeries] out of the goodness of his heart.

Some players have even come in from out of state [to get surgeries done by St. Ville]," Lueck said.

Lueck, born in Buckeye, Arizona, has been in the Litchfield Park area ever since retiring. He grew up on an area dairy farm, and his father and three brothers are still in the business. He farms 1,100 acres with one full-time employee and occasional part-time help. "That hasn't helped" his knees, Lueck admitted. He has no livestock but raises a variety of crops, primarily alfalfa but also cotton, corn, sorghum, and durum wheat. With the dry, arid climate, he relies fully on irrigated fields and can produce two or three crops annually. "I always had an idea I'd farm," said Lueck, who has two grown daughters with his wife, Mary.

Lueck, whose daughters were born in Green Bay, remembers that when he was drafted by the Packers—the year after their second straight Super Bowl win—the team had an attitude. When he left in 1974 that attitude had been shredded. "We always felt we could beat anybody. [Then] the ball started to bounce the wrong way. Things run in cycles. I think the team had just gotten old. [New Coach Phil] Bengston just caught them at the wrong time," Lueck said. When asked if Bengston was second-guessed by players while trying to coach in Lombardi's shadow, Lueck replied, "I heard plenty of that."

Lueck saw former coach Dan Devine frequently when Devine headed the Sun Devil Foundation at Arizona State University in Tempe. "He basically was a nice man. He was a tough guy to play for, a tough guy to like. That [feeling] was pretty common among the players. It was just his personality. I don't know if he was suited to the pro level. He was out of his element."

Lueck has a special place in Packer history. In 1969 he was the player who replaced one of the most famous and oft-injured left guards in history, Jerry Kramer. Lueck started every game at that position until 1975, the year his knees began to pay the price of playing in the NFL.

CHAPTER

Starr's Stars; Gregg's Rejects

Mike Douglass
Linebacker, 1978-1985

Greg Koch
Offensive tackle, 1977-1985

John Jefferson
Wide receiver, 1981-1984

Paul Coffman
Tight end, 1978-1985

David Whitehurst
Quarterback, 1977-1983

Mike Douglass

Mike Douglass admits that when he played for the Green Bay Packers, he used to cheat—the scales. He weighed between 197 and 204 pounds in his eight years as Packer—almost unacceptably light for an NFL linebacker. But he was listed at 214 pounds because he always weighed in with ankle weights or some other weight secretly attached to his body to meet the coaches' expectations on the scales. "I weighed in with weights for eight years," he said.

Douglass preferred to cheat the scale rather than cheat himself. To Douglass' credit, one of the reasons he was so light was that he didn't use steroids to boost his weight. He saw many of his Packer teammates on steroids and didn't want the problems that the muscle-building drug caused.

A decade after leaving football, Douglass and several teammates admit that steroid use was a problem in Green Bay in the early 1980s. Douglass estimated that 12 to 14 players out of the 45-man Packer roster used steroids regularly. Alphonso Carreker, defensive end from 1984-1988, estimated that 25 to 30 Packers were on steroids. Carreker said "the whole offensive line and the backups were on steroids. The team knew who was on the stuff. They stuck out like a sore thumb."

Anabolic steroids, a synthetic form of the male sex hormone testosterone, help build muscle mass. They were the magic drug in the NFL for two decades. As early as 1969, Packer trainer Domenic Gentile suspected that Green Bay players were bulking up on them during the off season. Defensive back Willie Buchanon, with the Packers from 1972 until 1978, said he saw steroid use in Green Bay, as did offensive tackle Mark Koncar, who played from 1976 to 1981. "I didn't really toy with them, but a lot of people I know did," Koncar said. "It got them big and strong. In a lot of situations it kept a lot of guys in the league for a year or two longer."

It wasn't until the late 1980s that the big crackdown came in the NFL. In May 1989, Atlanta Falcons guard Bill Fralic testified in Congress that 75 percent of NFL linemen were using steroids. The first suspensions resulting from steroid drug tests were announced August 29, 1989. A total of 24 players tested positive that summer, and 13 still on NFL rosters were suspended.

By 1991, steroids were banned from the NFL when their side effects were becoming known. In 1990, the *Detroit News* reported that 1989 Packer Number One draft pick Tony Mandarich was at the center of Michigan State football team steroid usage, although the monstrous, 315-pound Mandarich denied the allegations. Mandarich, touted as one of the best offensive line prospects ever, was a disappointment. He lost weight, developed a thyroid condition, and was cut by the Packers after the 1992 season. In 1991, Steeler lineman Terry Long attempted suicide after testing positive for steroid use. Long had gone from a 160-pound high school player to a 280-pound college player. His Steeler teammate Steve Courson developed heart disease and also blamed steroid use. In 1992, former Oakland Raider Lyle Alzado died of brain cancer at age 43. Before he died, Alzado claimed his many years of steroid use caused his terminal illness.

Many steroid users had injuries directly related to steroid use. "Muscles can't grow that big and stay attached to the ligaments," said Douglass. George Cumby, who played linebacker next to Douglass, agreed that many injuries stemmed from oversized muscles stretching regular-size tendons "like a rubber band. That's not even considering the internal damage steroids cause. I've heard athletes say they would do anything to make the team. One guy said steroids kept him on the team. It's crazy. They were crazy guys."

In addition to making players stronger and faster and thereby helping them make the team, Carreker, who said he did not use steroids, noted that the attraction of steroids was the ego boost when "you're that gladiator that everyone wants you to be. You fit the mold."

Another Packer defensive end, Ezra Johnson, said he easily could spot the players who used—they had acne, their weight rose 20 pounds or more, and they could bench press 600 pounds. Johnson knew the linemen he played against who were on steroids because their bodies were "like a brick. They could stop me with one hand."

The signs were obvious, according to Cumby. "You could tell who was using as far as the cut of their bodies. And their chins and foreheads were a little big, especially if they were using for awhile. They had acne. I had a friend who was a bodybuilder, and he said steroids made him real aggressive minded. He wanted too fight everybody all the time. That's one of the signs."

Douglass believes that part of the blame for steroid problems falls on the NFL owners and coaches, who constantly push for bigger, faster, stronger players. He cited 300-pound linemen who are the norm in the NFL today. Linemen are the players who use steroids most, Douglass and Cumby agreed. "The first thing you say when you look at that [huge lineman] is, 'That ain't real,' and you're right," Douglass said. He called steroid use "widespread and out of control." He said players work around steroid testing. "It's a ton of them, a lot of big-name ball players. It's a big cover-up. It's a shame, but it happens. A lot of guys take the short-cut. What hooks you on it is you get used to being big and you don't like it when you come down."

Douglass didn't like it when he was cut by the Packers prior to the 1986 season. Douglass was not only adamant that he still could play, but he simply didn't want to leave his football home—Green Bay.

In September 1991, for the first time since he left, Douglass returned to Lambeau Field to watch the Packers play Tampa Bay. But it wasn't a sentimental journey. Douglass had a score to settle with his conscience. "I had been having dreams—dreams of getting dressed for a [Packer] game and never playing. I'd have dreams of being in the locker room before the game but I never went on the field, dreams of missing the bus to the game. Anything related to football. In my mind, my time wasn't up when I left Green Bay. So many chapters were left open in my subconscious mind."

So Douglass figured that he needed to return to Green Bay and accept the fact that he no longer was a Packer, no longer a football player. "Mad Dog," as he was called, was introduced along with other Packer alumni before the Packers-Bucs game. But he didn't stay long. "After about a quarter and a half, I said, 'Ah, I don't like this,' and I went back to the hotel."

For a while, the dreams stopped, but a decade since he last put on a Packer uniform Douglass hasn't been able to shake his nocturnal nemesis. He thinks he knows why. "I feel I still have the physical ability to go out and play." At 41, Douglass is no less the physical specimen who made All-Pro, set a Packer tackling record, and who may come back again one day—to be inducted into the Packer Hall of Fame. At 207 pounds, he weighs more than when he played for the Packers, and he is stronger, thanks to a strict exercise and diet regimen that has led him to a new career and propelled him to fame in the bodybuilding world.

Douglass lives in El Cajon, California, near San Diego and operates the Midas Touch Physique health and fitness clinic, one of several business ventures. He opened the clinic immediately after retiring from football. Always a stickler about nutrition, exercise, and appearance, Douglass knew where his interests and expertise lay.

After being cut by the Packers, he played part of the 1986 season with the San Diego Chargers before retiring. He not only went to work immediately, he went to work on himself. "I started from zero—from the toes up. I worked for two years to get myself in top shape." He redesigned his body for posing, not for football, and won the California Natural [or drug-free for life] Bodybuilding Championships five times. He has posed for *Muscle and Fitness* magazine. "People today say I look 20 pounds lighter [than when I played football], but actually I'm three to four pounds heavier. I had 10 to 12 percent body fat then; now it's three to five percent. I'm stronger now than when I played."

As proprietor of Midas Touch Physique, Douglass tries to build up people's bodies and self-esteem. He works with about 70 clients one-on-one, specializing in re-forming their sedentary shapes through proper diet and exercise. He trained members of the Spanish sailing team that competed in the America's Cup, works with NFL players, and has taken paunches off overweight executives of all ages. "I preach lifestyle change," he explained.

Some of his preaching has gone public. He developed a computer software program called BodyPro. For $99, users can define their body type and choose from 150 exercise and nutrition programs to help them reach a goal. On Monday mornings on the San Diego CBS-TV affiliate, he has a one-minute health and fitness spot.

He also has taken his interest in nutrition into the business world, entering into a partnership with a San Diego area Mexican restaurant. He developed a light menu that includes a Mike Douglass burrito. Other items include a low-fat taco salad and a ground turkey burrito with Spanish rice.

His interest in low-fat cooking goes back to his days in college at San Diego State. He often cooked two or three days a week for up to 15 Packer teammates and some coaches, including Forrest Gregg. The players who paid Douglass to cook for them included Gerry Ellis, Mark Lee, Ezra Johnson, Carreker, Paul Coffman, and "just about everybody at one time or another. The Packers would have Arby's or McDonald's catered in. I didn't eat that crap. [James] Lofton and I were roommates for eight years. I cooked for him half the time, even when he was married."

During the early 1980s, while Lofton was the big-play man for the Packer offense, Douglass made the big plays for the defense. In 1983, for example, Douglass twice forced fumbles (two of 30 he forced or recovered in his career) and returned them for touchdowns. Douglass was on the *Sports Illustrated* All-Pro teams from 1981-1983. He had four 100-plus solo tackle seasons, hitting a high of 146 solo tackles in 1981—all after some people said he was too small to play in the NFL. (That's why the Packers were able to get him in the fifth round in the 1978 draft.)

Douglass still wonders why Forrest Gregg cut him after the 1985 season, a season in which Douglass ranked fifth on the team in tackles. Douglass thinks he was cut because he was a "team leader," who stood up for other players. "When Gregg took over, he wanted more players he could control. We were Bart Starr's players and he wanted his own players. He said he was tired of 8-8, but what happened the year after Bart left?" The Packers were 8-8.

Douglass and Gregg had a "couple altercations." One occurred after a game against the Colts when Gregg accused Douglass of missing an assignment. "We had words. He accused me of not turning the play up inside. My job was to not let the play go wide. I denied it. He was acting on what another coach had told him." The next day, after the team reviewed game films, Gregg apologized to Douglass in front of the team. "I think that didn't sit well with him. I think it was important to let players know who was standing up for them. I was a team leader. I don't think they wanted that kind of player," Douglass said.

Douglass, who with his wife, Olga, has a young daughter, Marisa, is hoping to become a member of the Packer Hall of Fame. He has a satellite dish and still watches all the Packer games. "Nobody duplicated what I did," he said, referring to three straight seasons with 100-plus tackles. "Not Ray Nitschke. No one. Now I can't wait until the Packers put me in the Hall of Fame. I look forward to the time when they recognize what I've done. That would be my greatest reward."

Maybe then the dreams will stop.

Greg Koch

When the loquacious Greg Koch played for the Packers he was nicknamed by one reporter the "Texan with the 10-gallon mouth." He always was ready with a good quote or story and never ran out of opinions about the NFL, Green Bay, the Packers, or his teammates.

Those opinions were the by-products of a busy mind. He wasn't just a big Texan blowing hot air. While playing for the Packers, he also was attending St. Norbert College in adjacent DePere, finishing up the bachelor's degree in chemistry that he started at the University of Arkansas. He was planning ahead. After football, he would go to law school. He wanted more than a B.S. degree.

When his football career ended, he returned to school at Arkansas in 1989. Three years later, in 1992, he became a lawyer, graduating 19th in a class of 132. He was the commencement speaker and—having been successful in one career—was chosen most likely to succeed.

Koch recognized early that pro football was a temporary job and believed that one of the few guarantees in life was "you will be an ex-athlete." And "you can't live on glory the rest of your life."

Thus he talks for a living now, and people not only are listening, but they're paying him Texas-sized hatfuls of money to hear what he thinks. Koch, 41, is a partner in the Houston, Texas, law firm of Porter and Koch. He worked for a short time with a large Houston firm but set up his own firm in 1993 with a friend, Jim Porter. They deal mostly in civil lawsuits. For example, they engaged in a $15 million lawsuit involving one oil company that sold a pipeline to another company but continued to use the pipe. "You have to become an expert at something in a short period of time. You do all the legal research and what legal precedent there is. Our clients stay with us. We do pretty well for them," Koch said.

After making good money for 12 years in the NFL, Koch could have settled back into a low-profile job, but he chose to work at a professional level equal to the NFL, where the demands and the pressure are cutthroat every day. He also knew that in the "real world" he wouldn't have people asking for his autograph or patting him on the back when he went to work in the morning.

When he came out of high school, up to 50 colleges recruited him. In college, he lived a pampered life on a football scholarship. In Green Bay, he got discounts, for example, at a dry cleaners simply because he was a Packer, even though his salary was six figures. "That's kind of skewed. I didn't think I'd ever say it, but sports are way out of whack now. They put guys on a pedestal because they can dribble well or shoot well. That can change you a little bit. You can get caught up in that. Coming out of college if I had $20 in my pocket I'd be happy, then all of a sudden you've got money. You live in this false world."

He admitted that he succumbed to pressures and tried to look and act the part of an offensive tackle in the NFL, meaning he got the "image of a bad ass" and now wishes he had been nicer to the people around him. "I'm not proud of a lot of things I did," he recalled.

During the season "everything in my life revolved around football." During the off season, he worked out four hours a day while dreaming of making the Pro Bowl. He thought he had his best year in 1982, when the Packers made the strike-altered playoffs, and when he made only All-Pro second team he was depressed for six weeks.

Koch came to the Packers as a 6' 4", 265-pound second-round draft pick in 1977. His upper-body strength—he could bench press 500 pounds—served him and the Packers well as he became one of the guardians of oft-injured quarterback Lynn Dickey. Koch does not regret one part of his career that he has kept silent about: His use of steroids when he played for the Packers. While he didn't openly admit to using steroids, he didn't deny it. "When you get to the level of a professional athlete, you're like a gladiator in an arena. If there's a way to safely use [steroids] and not abuse, would I say use? Yes. I looked at it as a personal choice. You've got to look at the motivation of players. If you look at a guy who's a 230-pound lineman and he can get up to 260 pounds [using steroids], the difference is 30 pounds and $200,000. Steroids are like any drug. If you abuse them they can hurt you. You can take it a safe way. Anything you hear is about people abusing them," Koch said. He didn't bear the trademarks of a heavy steroid user in the NFL. His weight didn't fluctuate wildly. He was listed at 276 pounds during his final years as a Packer. Also, he didn't develop the joint problems or other maladies that often showed up in heavy steroid users and kept them on injured lists. He moved into the starting lineup ahead of Dick Himes in 1978, and from that time through the 1985 season he missed only two of 120 possible starts.

His NFL career ended on his terms. After being cut by the Packers in 1985, Koch played with the Miami Dolphins in 1986 and the Minnesota

Vikings in 1987. The Vikings wanted him on their 1988 team but he turned them down. In 1987 with the Vikings, Koch had started all but three games, including the NFC title game loss against the San Francisco 49ers, his last hurrah. But Koch never considered himself a Dolphin or a Viking. "I wish I could have finished my career in Green Bay. It was harder [switching teams] than I thought it would be because I really wanted to be in Green Bay. It was harder in one sense because my zest for the game was diminished somewhat. I always told myself that once that left I wasn't going to be one of those guys who hang on for the sake of making money."

What he didn't like was the way Packer Coach Forrest Gregg cleaned house in 1984, 1985, and 1986. Gregg, who was named coach in 1984 to succeed Bart Starr, cut many Packer veterans in an attempt to rebuild the club with young players. Koch was among those cut. He remembers being suited up ready for practice one day when he got the word from Gregg that he had been released outright. In other words, Gregg gave Koch away for nothing. Koch was signed by Miami, and the Dolphins got two fifth-round draft picks for Koch when they traded him to Minnesota. "I don't think he was particularly fond of me. A lot of [cutting veterans] he did out of personal spite. I had probably four more years left. That spite cost the Packers two fifth-round draft picks," Koch said. "It left somewhat of a bitter taste in my mouth that an individual in a certain position of power could come in and interrupt nine-tenths of what you had been doing."

While Koch seemed to bond with one irascible and infamous Packer coach, offensive coordinator Bob Schnelker, saying Schnelker had a "brilliant" offensive mind, Koch didn't share the same feelings for Gregg. He disliked Gregg's Lombardi-esque way of singling out players for criticism at team meetings and thought Gregg was outdated in the way he approached issues that affected players. On the other hand, he thought that Starr had progressed from an average coach in the late 1970s to, ironically, a "great" coach when he was fired.

The irony of pro football was never lost on Koch. There was the time when Gregg learned that several players had tested positive for using marijuana. Gregg called a team meeting and asked the players if they remembered the hippies of the 1960s. Gregg told the Packers that those male hippies joined communes and eventually grew female breasts as a result of their vice, a story that was greeted by players in attendance with sideways glances and smirks. Koch remembers the tradition of a big cake being set out in the locker room when it was a player's birthday. Once, the table was set but the birthday boy had been cut from the team the night before and was long gone. A coach simply scraped off the player's name and everyone ate cake anyway. Another time, the son of country singer Charley Pride was trying to make the Packer roster. An assistant coach cozied up to the player, said he loved his dad's music and would like to get some tapes. Pride's son said he'd try to oblige. The coach walked away and joked that he hoped the tapes showed up soon because the player was about to be cut from the team.

The memories, experience, and lessons are what stick with Koch and give him feelings of power, confidence, and destiny even today. He can't forget the 48-47 Monday Night Football win over the Super Bowl champion Washington Redskins in 1983. The Washington game is indelible to him because "we should have lost." Redskins kicker Mark Moseley missed a 39-yard field goal on the last play of the game. A poignant picture of a triumphant Koch, holding both arms and his helmet above his head after Moseley's miss, was printed in newspapers around Wisconsin and around the nation the next day.

When he was in college, Koch remembers his father saying that he should play for the Packers. Koch's dad was a Houston salesman for the giant Kimberly-Clark paper company, which employs 6,000 people in factories near Green Bay. Eventually, Koch knew that he was meant to be—and always will be—a Packer. "I'd never want football to be what defines me, but certainly it's an integral part of who I am. Now my life is geared to the kids growing up in a good atmosphere and being good people," he said. Koch has deprogrammed himself from the life of an athlete. He spends his free time with his wife, Renee, taking their young children, Zach and Victoria, to Little League games, playing golf, or lifting weights.

John Jefferson

Ask Packer fans what memory of John Jefferson is frozen in their minds and they may say his ubiquitous smile, the Red Baron-type goggles he wore, the rousing high-fives he joined in mid-air with teammate James Lofton, or the feeling of excitement he brought to Green Bay like no one since Paul Hornung. Or the sight of him downfield waving his arms, wide open and waiting for a pass.

A decade has passed since Jefferson shelved his pads and cleats, but his magnetic personality has endured. He still draws an admiring crowd at his University of Kansas office in Lawrence, Kansas. He does much more than work 40 hours a week handling housing, travel, and other aspects of KU athletics. As assistant athletic director, he cherishes the chance to deal one-on-one with athletes who need a pat on the back or some advice. "My door is always open, and my office can get pretty full at times," Jefferson said with a chuckle. "I guess kids just like me. I have a teenage daughter so I still can talk the hip-hop language. It's one of my strong suits. There's not a very big gap between me and these kids."

After coaching wide receivers at Kansas for three years, Jefferson changed jobs in 1994 so that he not only would be home more with his wife and children but would be able to help students. "Pregnancies are one of the biggest problems. I try to get them to take responsibility. That's the main thing I try to teach them."

With the school year winding down on a balmy May day, Jefferson talked about how he would like to be an athletic director some day, how he is sincere about fighting for the rights of the student athletes.

His people-first philosophy is an extension of what he learned in pro football. He always took time to sign autographs, he said, because he didn't want to let down the people who showed an "amazing love" for football. He always drew strength from the people he played with. The experience, not the statistics, was what kept him motivated. "I always compared it to being in the military. The bonds you had with teammates were unbreakable."

He admits that life in the office at a university is mundane compared to playing in the NFL. That's OK with him because he knows that high-five careers can't be duplicated. "No matter what you do when you get out of football, there is no more exciting experience. Not too many people get to walk out of the tunnel with 60,000 or 70,000 people cheering. I feel fortunate. I know what it's like."

He remembered how he spent one year after he retired in 1985 just trying to put some distance between himself and pro football, watching games on TV and knowing he still could play. He started his post-Packer career selling commercial real estate in his hometown of Dallas. Then he began coaching full time as an assistant at Southern Methodist University under Forrest Gregg, for whom he played with the Packers. When a local paper picked up the story about Jefferson coaching, suddenly he had job offers from several other colleges, including Kansas. "I was kind of skeptical at first. Forrest talked me into coming up for an interview. It was a nice college town and a peaceful atmosphere. My family loved it."

Some ten years earlier, the situation was far different. Jefferson was an all-pro receiver arriving in Green Bay from San Diego. To get Jefferson, the Packers gave up wide receiver Aundra Thompson, a number one draft pick, and two number two draft picks. Jefferson left San Diego unhappy with his salary. He "knew the system was different in Green Bay" and that he might not catch as many passes as in San Diego, where he "was spoiled" with a surfeit of passes. In Jefferson's three seasons as a Charger (1978-1980), he caught 56, 61, and 82 passes. He was the first receiver ever to gain 1,000 yards in each of his first three NFL seasons. Jefferson was a first-round draft choice by San Diego in 1978, the 14th player drafted. Lofton went to the Packers on the sixth pick of the first round.

With Jefferson's talent, people talked of titles and remembered the 1960s, the last time the Packers truly had a reliable offense. With Jefferson and James Lofton at wide receiver, fans thought the Packers could fly. They almost did. The Packers went 5-3-1 in the strike-shortened 1982 season. "One of my goals was to get the Packers in the playoffs. It was a good accomplishment, even though it was a strike year," Jefferson said. In the playoffs, the Packers met St. Louis in their first post-season appearance at Lambeau Field since the 1967 "Ice Bowl" game. The Packers won 41-16. It was a "JJ" day. He caught a 60-yard TD pass and totaled 148 yards receiving, both Packer post-season records. The next week, the offense again did its job, amassing 466 yards, but the Packers lost in Dallas, 37-26.

After the 1982 season, Jefferson's first full one as a Packer, the dream team of Jefferson-Lofton lasted two more seasons. The Packers went 8-8 in both 1983 and 1984. Jefferson remains surprised that Bart Starr was fired after the Packers' 8-8 season in 1983. "I thought we came off a pretty good season. I was surprised. Had we beaten the Bears [23-21 loss in season finale] we would have gone to the playoffs the second year in a row. Things were starting to come together, I thought."

Despite his enthusiasm, Jefferson often was rumored to be unhappy in Green Bay because he shared the limelight with Lofton. Jefferson was referred to as an expensive decoy for Lofton. Often, Jefferson was the wideout who would run the much-hated routes over the middle while the speedier Lofton would take the deep glamour patterns. Ron Cassidy, a backup wide receiver from 1979 through 1984, said that "when JJ came to Green Bay that first year, he had the clutchest hands I had ever seen. On third down, that first year, if I had to take JJ or Lofton, I'd take JJ." Lofton, however, was known for working out harder and coming into camp in better shape than Jefferson, offensive tackle Greg Koch recalled.

In Green Bay, Jefferson's best year was 57 receptions in 1983. He caught 36 TD passes in San Diego and 11 in Green Bay.

After the 1984 season, Jefferson asked to be traded, and Gregg sent him to Cleveland. He retired after one season there because "my body told me. I was in the training room longer than on the field. Your body lets you know."

Jefferson admitted that he asked to be traded because he felt he wasn't getting the ball enough. "A lot of times anybody with talent in certain situations wants the ball to help the team. I felt they could have utilized the passing game better by spreading it around more to different people. The passing game had become too predictable." He was happy with offensive coordinator Zeke Bratkowski but grew bitter while playing under Bob Schnelker, who became the offensive coordinator in 1982. In 1984, Jefferson played in 13 games, starting 12, and caught just 27 passes.

Jefferson believed he was open and wasn't getting thrown to enough. Several times he admonished Schnelker, to no avail. "I got tired of telling people I was open. It got pretty bad. I started to feel like it was a personal thing [between me and Schnelker]." In retrospect, Jefferson said the problem was one of communication. He didn't explain his displeasure to Gregg. "Now I wish I had approached Forrest with the problem. He could have enlightened me."

After retiring, Jefferson went back to Arizona State and finished his bachelor's degree in history. Other than football, he said he never gave much thought to what he wanted to do with his life. One of six children, his father was a supervisor at a steel fabrication plant and his mother a beautician. John was pulled along by the power of his athleticism, knowing as early as his sophomore year at Dallas' Franklin Roosevelt High that he had pro potential. He was so good that Cowboys Coach Tom Landry said Jefferson could bypass college ball and jump right into the NFL. "That makes you feel pretty good," Jefferson said.

He remains in many ways the John Jefferson who can't be stopped. "When I get an assignment I attack it, just like when I got an assignment in football." He remains the John Jefferson who makes people happy. "It's amazing how kids come to you with their problems. It makes you feel young."

Paul Coffman

Paul Coffman always looked forward to fall because he could enjoy his favorite pastimes—football and hunting. Now there's another reason why he loves the change of colors. He's anxious to find out how his corn and soybean crops have done. Once one of the top tight ends in the NFL, Coffman has circled back to his roots. He grew up on a farm in Chase, Kansas, population 600, where his dad raised wheat. He has returned to the area, and he and his wife are raising cash crops and four children on 80 acres near Kansas City. Coffman's new address is Peculiar, Missouri, although there's nothing peculiar about that to him. His college degree is in grain milling. "I always thought I'd have an acreage some day."

The Coffmans bought the land in 1990 and went to work planting seeds, stocking three ponds with fish, and fixing up the old farmhouse they live in now. "I tell my wife it's going to take all our time and money, and all we're going to have is an old home. It's pretty neat, but it's a lot of work. There's a lot of mowing and fixing. There's pasture land, plus I've got a lot of deer and quail on the land." He leases his land to another farmer, who does the actual planting and raising of crops; the two parties then split the harvest profits in a sharecropping arrangement. The Coffmans also have a hired hand on the farm because Paul doubles as a sales representative in Kansas City for an industrial chemical supply company,

Russ Meyer Lab. Between his farm and his sales job, Coffman is one happy Kansan. "I have a flexible schedule and there's no coat and tie. That's just not me."

But there's one aspect of Coffman's life that neither he nor any of his 1980s Packer teammates would have expected. He's become a committed Christian. That may shock people who knew Coffman as a free-spirited prankster when he played with the Packers. It's even more of a shock to Coffman. "I remember sitting in the locker room and making fun of Rich Campbell [former Packer QB who now is a minister] and his beliefs," Coffman said. Several years later when the two met, Coffman "spent about 20 minutes apologizing to me," Campbell recalled.

"It's funny. I'm like a lay pastor now. Six years ago there was no way I ever thought I'd have anything to do with the Lord. I only went to chapel because I thought it was a good luck charm. I went once and had a good game. I was always happy and fun-loving. I don't know if there's a whole lot of change there, but I can see now that everything before was for self. If it didn't please me I didn't do it. I can see where God turned my heart away from myself and toward my family," Coffman explained.

Coffman, 40, came to a "personal relationship with God" just before he was cut by the Packers in 1985. He says he was influenced by hearing others giving testimonies about God helping them. What happened after Coffman accepted God? "I got cut." Coffman's career continued unceremoniously in Kansas City for three seasons before he retired, but he's still putting his NFL experiences to work. Coffman, a member of Fellowship of Christian Athletes, works with Prison Power Ministry in the Kansas City area. His role includes organizing a group of athletes to play softball games against convicts in Kansas and Missouri prisons, such as the Johnson County Correctional Facility or the Lansing State Penitentiary. He's hoping to get the ministry into Leavenworth. "It's amazing how God has opened the doors for me."

Coffman sees himself as a changed man. His greatest joy used to come from dragging three defenders into the end zone. His personal affirmation came from accolades and statistics. His ego swelled and he sometimes was a "jerk" because as a young man he wasn't mature enough to handle the attention. "I was 24 and thought I was an adult. You go through a period when you think you're invincible."

Because he was a Packer in a town where "people knew what you put in your grocery cart" he was patted on the back and told "what a great guy" he was wherever he went. Football was his security blanket. "Everybody has the need for acceptance and significance in life." All that faded away like a soft Sunday afternoon when he retired. He felt fortunate that he had begun to see past football. "When I go in to make a sale now, nobody cares if I played for the Chiefs or Packers. I look back at football now and it was fun, but what good is it? Pretty soon people forget. Somebody else comes along to break the record. You're still judged by how you treat other people.

"I'm probably more at peace now. The joy I find is from raising children, seeing them come out of the womb, holding them in your hands. This is what life is all about." He's so committed to his role as a father that, *a la* Kevin Costner in the movie *Field of Dreams,* Coffman is tearing up a section of his farmland to put in a baseball field for his three boys and one girl, ages three to nine. A neighboring farmer is growing the sod; the backstops will come from an old church field. "Build it and kids will come," joked Coffman, who coaches his nine-year-old son's youth baseball team. The left-field "fence" will be a soybean field.

Although Coffman's life is more complete now, he forever will cherish football for the memories and for what the game taught him, specifically accountability. On the football field, every move you make is filmed, he said. There are no excuses for mistakes. Players have no choice but to be accountable for their actions, which is one of life's most basic tenets. "Football correlates a lot to life" said Coffman, who is still tall, lean, and angular but whose hair no longer is dark and curly but short and graying.

The Packers signed Coffman almost by mistake. When assistant coach John Meyer showed up at Kansas State in 1978 to try out Coffman's All-American linebacker roommate, Gary Spani, Coffman tagged along. Coffman started two years at Kansas State (making second-team All-Big Eight one year) but wasn't being scouted by the NFL. Coffman got signed by the Packers, he figures, because they needed another body in camp. When he arrived in camp, he was listed seventh out of seven tight ends. "They gave me a number in the 90s. Those are usually the guys who get cut. I took the attitude that every day could be my last. It was determination."

Coffman was admired by Packer fans for his blocking, sure hands, and up-field running. He caught 322 passes, ranking him fifth in the Packer record book. He is the Packers' all-time tight end reception leader, well ahead of Rich McGeorge (175 catches). He averaged 13 yards per catch and scored 39 touchdowns. He was inducted into the Packer Hall of Fame in 1994.

During a period when the NFL was loaded with great tight ends (including Todd Christianson, Kellen Winslow, Steve Jordan, and Mark Bavaro), Coffman went to the Pro Bowl three straight years beginning in 1983, when the Packers had one of the most prolific offenses in the league with Lynn Dickey at quarterback.

At 6' 3", 225 pounds, Coffman never was known for his size or speed, just his ability to produce week after week. "I always said that the long grass and the cold weather always brought everybody down to my level so that's why I could play in Green Bay." After getting cut by Forrest Gregg in 1985, Coffman returned home to Kansas and played for the Chiefs in 1986 and 1987. He finished his career as a backup with the Vikings in 1988. "After Minnesota, my head wasn't in it anymore."

While playing with the Chiefs during the 1987 strike season, Coffman caused a stir one afternoon on the picket line when he and two teammates showed up in Bill Maas' souped-up pickup brandishing unloaded hunting rifles and yelling "Where's the scabs!" Coffman later recalled. "We didn't know how big of a deal it would be. The cameras were all on us. Everyone laughed, but when the reporters wrote it up they added some spice and it got on CNN, like violence had erupted in the strike in Kansas City." With the Packers he could be found playing pranks constantly, things like cleaning out the lockers of teammates who were on the edge of being cut from the team. "It was cruel," he now admits. Or he would secretly pour a slow stream of soap on the head of a showering teammate who was trying to rinse.

Coffman will never forget one of his last days in Green Bay in 1985. It will always remind him of how at one time in his life football got all the attention. "Lynn [Dickey] and I had both gotten cut, and I was riding with him over to his house to get his playbook. He was going too fast and a cop pulled us over. Lynn told him that he was having a bad day, that he had just been cut. The cop couldn't believe it. He went back to his squad car and started telling everyone. He forgot all about the ticket."

David Whitehurst

More than a decade has passed since Charles David Whitehurst, once a protégé of Bart Starr, retired from pro football. So what would you expect from someone who "loved almost every minute" of an up-and-down seven-year NFL career to be doing these days when he wants a little fun? Playing football, of course.

David Whitehurst still plays quarterback—minus the pads—for a Fulton County recreation league team near Atlanta. It's only flag football, but Whitehurst still loves spinning an orb on a straight line, timing a pass, splitting a defense, hitting the open receiver. The thing is, he hasn't lost his touch. "At times I amaze myself. I throw it better than when I played with the Packers. . . . But I can't run very well. My body isn't young anymore." His gridiron experience is important in his new life. For the past three years he has coached his son Charlie, 13, in football. Charlie Whitehurst's teams are 32-9-1 in that time, including one state championship and one second place.

Whitehurst, 40, lives in Duluth, Georgia, a suburb north of Atlanta, with his wife, Beth, and their four children. He owns David Whitehurst Homes Inc., which he started in 1985, the year after he was cut by the Packers. He is a one-man operation, overseeing the construction of his clients' homes through subcontractors, a job not unlike a quarterback's. He learned the trade through his father, also a builder, and with a former partner, but the feelings of accomplishment now are all his. "There's a great deal of satisfaction when a house is completed and when a buyer is happy," he said. Whitehurst, who grew up in nearby Decatur, Georgia, builds about six homes a year just north of Atlanta in the Duluth-Roswell area of Fulton County. Prices range from $400,000 to $700,000 for 3,800 to 5,000 square-foot homes.

Whitehurst was the Packers' offensive rookie of the year in 1978, the same year he became a starting quarterback because Lynn Dickey had been injured. In 1979, Whitehurst was voted the team's most popular player, a reflection of what he calls his "affection for the fans" in Wisconsin. "We were playing for the team which had the richest tradition and the best fans in the league. I still believe that, of all the cities to play football in, Green Bay is the greatest," Whitehurst said.

The aspects of Whitehurst's career that stand out now don't center around how many games he started or won, his completion percentage, or any other statistics that prove his abilities. "Today when I look back, I realize they were some of the best years of my life. I was 22 and Bart Starr was my coach. He was my childhood idol. There's nobody who was a better role model than Bart," Whitehurst recalled. "He was patient. He was kind of like your dad. He was a great leader. He is a man who always commanded your respect and admiration, and no one ever doubted his complete integrity and commitment to every member of the team and their families."

Under Starr the Packers never became Super Bowl contenders (except for making the playoffs in the 1982 strike-shortened season), but Whitehurst said "team morale and unity was extremely high. Although our record was not fabulous, the experience was."

Whitehurst, 6' 2", 205 pounds, the Packers' eighth-round draft pick in 1977, was from Furman, a South Carolina college not known for producing NFL players, especially not NFL quarterbacks. He came in the year after Dickey had established himself as the team's number one quarterback.

However, in the ninth game of 1977, Dickey suffered a broken leg in County Stadium on the final play against the Los Angeles Rams. The next week, with the Packers playing Washington on Monday night on national TV, Whitehurst made his first start. He completed 12 of 24 passes for 140 yards with three interceptions, and the Packers lost 10-9. However, most people—including ABC analyst Howard Cosell—gave Whitehurst high marks for his poise. The Packers won two of their last four games in 1977 under Whitehurst.

Then the Packers started 7-2 in 1978, only to finish 8-7-1 and miss the playoffs by a game. "I think probably my lack of experience hurt [in 1978]. I don't think I was as talented as a lot of quarterbacks in the league. I think that surfaced, and I didn't play as well at times. We were a young team. We just couldn't win the big ones down the stretch."

Dickey's injury kept him out for almost two years. He didn't return until late in the 1979 season. Whitehurst admits he had an ideal opportunity to show his talents. He started 34 straight games. He completed more than 50 percent of his passes in that stretch but had far more interceptions (35) than TD passes (20). "I felt it was an opportunity to do what I had been wanting to do all my life. I probably didn't take full advantage of that opportunity. At one point I was finally throwing the ball well—after 1980—and was understanding how to play. And I never had the opportunity to play again," said Whitehurst, explaining that he threw very little in college and was inexperienced as a passer. "This may sound strange, but my problem was I couldn't grip the ball hard enough to throw it as hard as I wanted. I couldn't deliver the ball the way I wanted to."

After Dickey returned, Whitehurst was strictly a backup—but a good one. In 1981, the Packers were struggling at 2-6 but recovered to finish 8-8 with Whitehurst's help. During a three game November winning streak, he started two games and relieved Dickey in another. "I helped turn the momentum in our favor," he recalled of that season. "Even though I started only 39 games [in my career], I was called upon often in a backup role, and for the most part performed well."

The positive atmosphere in Green Bay began to change on May 31, 1982, when Judge Robert J. Parins was elected the team's first-ever full-time executive. By the end of the 1983 season Starr was gone, coldly fired without explanation by Parins. Early in the 1984 training camp, Whitehurst was gone too.

"There was a certain amount of power Bart lost as general manager; it was stripped of him when the judge came. From a player standpoint, the atmosphere was not as good," Whitehurst said. "The game changed and the situation in Green Bay changed. My first couple of years I was just happy to be there. Then you see things happen to people you don't agree with. It becomes a business. I wasn't hungry like I was, and when you're not hungry you lose your edge." Some of the bad feelings in Green Bay surfaced in the media in the 1980s. Stories began to attack Starr and his lack of success. The negative reporting didn't sit well with Whitehurst, so much so that he quit paying attention to what the media said. "It left a sour taste in my mouth for most people in the media. When you read some negative things about you—these people attack you personally. I didn't like it and I don't know anybody who does like it. Emotionally it was hard to handle. Part of football is confidence and these people are saying you're no good. Who are they? I quit reading the papers to keep my sanity."

Although Whitehurst was cut in Forrest Gregg's first training camp in 1984, he believes his fate was sealed before the camp began because of a poor performance the year before in a game against Detroit. White-hurst relieved an injured Lynn Dickey but completed just six of 17 passes for 33 yards with two interceptions. The Packers squandered a 20-3 half-time lead and lost in overtime. Whitehurst never threw another pass for the Packers. "It was the worst experience of my life. I played horrible. I fumbled the snap on the first play, and they recovered. It was one of those things. It shouldn't have happened, but I share the responsibility for it. I share it, but I took the heat for it." He explained that center Larry McCarren snapped on Dickey's cadence, catching Whitehurst off guard.

Although the Packers switched coaches from Starr to Gregg during the off-season, they retained offensive coordinator Bob Schnelker. That's why Whitehurst's debacle against Detroit the year before meant so much. Schnelker wasn't a Whitehurst fan. "I was not his choice of quarterback. I always felt I was playing the opposing team and him. I felt like he wasn't on my side . . . but don't get me wrong. I probably learned more football from him than anybody else."

When Whitehurst was released, he was picked up by Kansas City and spent part of a season there before being cut again and retiring.

He's glad that time has separated him from a few painful memories, including once failing to move the offense and being booed by 50,000 people, an event that "made a man out of me. I handle my career now better than I used to. Some of the negative things have moved away in my mind. I had a decent career and I'm proud of it." Despite playing full time only about two seasons, Whitehurst ranked in the top ten all-time in several Packer passing categories, including total yards and passing accuracy, when he retired.

Those aren't the things Whitehurst singles out for posterity. He'll take to his grave the joys of having played to the best of his ability, having played under Bart Starr, and in front of the Packer fans. It was, in many ways, the best time of his life. It's why you can wander out to suburban Atlanta and still find Charles David Whitehurst fading back.

Second Comings

Rich Campbell
Quarterback, 1981-1984

George Cumby
Linebacker, 1980-1985

Ken Ellis
Cornerback, 1970-1975

Rich Campbell

When family-room discussions and bar-room arguments get around to famous Packer personnel mistakes, there's plenty to talk about. There was the debilitating 1970s trade for John Hadl, the bypassing of Joe Montana (for tackle Charles Johnson) in the third round of the 1979 draft, the loss of Number One pick Bruce Clark to the Canadian Football League in 1980, and the 1990s disappointment of lineman Tony Mandarich.

Sure to come up in the conversation is the choice of Rich Campbell, the Number One selection in the 1981 draft. Touted as a franchise player,

Campbell unimpressed his coaches with a weak arm, throwing just 68 passes in his Packer career. To put his selection in perspective, the Packers passed on drafting defensive back Ronnie Lott, who finally retired in 1996 after 15 seasons and a record-tying 10 trips to the Pro Bowl.

Packer fans may think of Campbell as a wasted draft pick. Bart Starr once called drafting Campbell a "colossal blunder." When Campbell thinks about his football career now, he calls it a "minor disappointment."

Don't count Campbell among those interested in Packer forensics. Ronnie Lott may wear four 49ers Super Bowl rings and be headed to the Pro Football Hall of Fame, but Rich Campbell long ago won something that to him is much more important—perspective.

When he was cut by the Packers, Campbell admits that a lifelong dream died. But he knew which road to take next, and soon after another dream began to evolve when he chose a career as a minister. In 1985 he enrolled at Western Seminary in Portland, Oregon. "It was especially enjoyable after four years of wilderness in Green Bay," he remembered. In 1990 he graduated with masters degrees in divinity and theology.

After years of study, thought, and personal growth, Campbell no longer ached for what could or should have been in Green Bay. The Reverend Campbell simply saw what had passed. "I look back now and it's in perspective. I see how really insignificant football is. I feel I'm doing what I'm supposed to do." He had been interested in the ministry ever since his days as Santa Theresa High School in Oakland, where his friendship with basketball coach Glen Miller led to a "strengthened relationship with Christ."

After graduating from Western Seminary, Campbell worked for five years at Fellowship Bible Church in Little Rock, Arkansas. He was one of 12 ministers for a congregation of 3,000. During that time he began to do in-house inspirational writing for the church.

In 1995, the second coming of Rich Campbell on a national level began. With well-known Christian evangelist Robert Lewis, he co-authored a nationally distributed book called *Real Family Values*. It was well-received by critics, Campbell said, and quickly went into a second printing. Before 1995 was over, he and Lewis wrote another manuscript, *Modern Day Knighthood: Helping Your Son Grow to be a Man,* and he began helping write a third, *A Call for Family Reformation: Restoring the Soul of America One Family at a Time,* with national radio evangelist Dennis Rainey; that book was published in 1996.

In December 1995 Campbell took a job with a Little Rock-based national ministry called FamilyLife, which is headed by Rainey. Campbell also writes and speaks for another Little Rock-based national group, Dad, the Family Shepherd. In 1996, his career changed again when he became editorial page editor for *The American,* a daily newspaper in Hattiesburg, Mississippi. Campbell, 38, and his wife, Janice, have a daughter and a son. In football parlance, it could be said that Campbell finally has found his arm.

To Campbell these days, the thought of pro football now "almost seems like another life. I remember dressing out for games and thinking this would be the biggest moment of my life, and ten years later no one remembers the game."

Ten years later some people don't even remember his name. He played in the Vince Lombardi charity golf tournament in Milwaukee and found his name misspelled on his bag tag. Then he introduced himself to his playing partners, and they couldn't remember who Rich Campbell was. While that indicates Campbell never was famous, it speaks volumes to him about how important we perceive football to be and how unimportant it really is.

The emphasis put on pro football in the United States, with the huge player salaries, intense media coverage, and spectator fanaticism, indicates something is missing in the lives of many Americans, Campbell believes. "In some ways pro sports and football in general are a reflection of despair in our society. Our infatuation with sports might show how empty our lives are. They fill a void."

The Packers were trying to fill a void in the 1981 draft, looking for someone to eventually replace aging QB Lynn Dickey. They thought they had a future star in Campbell, who had set season (70.7 percent) and career (64.5 percent) NCAA records for passing accuracy at Cal-Berkeley. In six previous drafts under Bart Starr, the Packers had not made a QB their number one pick.

Campbell was called a "franchise-type player" at the time by Atlanta Falcons personnel director Tom Braatz. The Packers had the sixth pick in the 1981 draft. Some of the players still available when they took

Campbell were Ronnie Lott, Mel Owens, Neil Lomax, and Keith Van Horne, who all became NFL stars.

Campbell appeared to have it all. He was 6' 4", 215 pounds, intelligent, and had played in a pro-style offense in college. When it came the Packers' turn to pick, Starr said then that there was "No hesitation. We feel we took the best player at the time to help our team." Years later Starr recanted, recalling how his instincts had told him that he should draft Lott because he was concerned about Campbell's "short-armed" throwing style.

In his rookie season, Campbell played in two games, completing 15 of 30 passes. He did not throw a pass in 1982 or 1983. In 1984, he played in four games, completing 16 of 38 passes. Campbell's career totals were 31-for-68 for 386 yards, three TDs, and five interceptions.

Was Campbell simply not good enough to play in the NFL or didn't the Packers give him a fair chance? Although many people said Campbell had a weak arm, he says that wasn't the reason he failed. "No. There are a number of players in the NFL who don't have strong arms but who are more than adequate," he insisted.

Asked if he thinks the Packers gave him a fair chance, he said, "No. I still think things could have been different. If my attitude had been different and I had been handled differently." Campbell said that he let the problems associated with lack of playing time affect his confidence and "once you lose that whatever hopes I had of becoming a starter were undermined." Campbell pinpointed his problem at Green Bay as "my relationship with Bob Schnelker." The respected but highly opinionated Schnelker became the Packers' offensive coordinator in 1982. Campbell declined to talk further about Schnelker, saying, "It's a dead issue."

The highlight of Campbell's career isn't hard to determine. There was only one—the pass to Phillip Epps that beat the Chicago Bears 20-14 late in the 1984 season. With 40 seconds to play, Campbell underthrew a long pass to Epps, who came back to get it and circled his defender for a 43-yard TD. Campbell finished the game 9-for-19 for 125 yards with two interceptions. Campbell came into that game to replace Randy Wright, whose knee was injured in the first half.

Campbell hasn't been back to Green Bay since he was cut. The last time he picked up a football was when he played a pickup game at a church summer camp. "I was so sore afterward I decided that I didn't want to do that again." It was an experience much like his NFL career.

Yet four frustrating years in the NFL are something he wouldn't give back. "The one positive thing it gave me is a better understanding of who I am. Football has a way of exposing a person's character. When football was over, I understood myself."

George Cumby

It was October 1985 and there had been rumblings that Chicago Bears coach Mike Ditka would use William "Refrigerator" Perry, the 320-pound defensive lineman, to block for Walter Payton. The Bears were playing the Packers on Monday Night Football, and it seems the whole country saw or heard about Perry flattening 224-pound George Cumby—twice. Perry was the ramrod blocker for two Payton TDs that night, and Perry ran for a TD himself against the red-faced Packers.

"Nothing like that had ever happened to me," Cumby said from his home in Houston, Texas, incredulously recalling his place in Packer history as he simultaneously shuffled his three young sons off to bed. "He was so much bigger than me. Once he hit me it was over. It was just a matter of where I was going to fall. My message machine was so full that night [after the game]. All the Oklahoma players called and said how I let them down, how I let the university down. The Packer coaches didn't want to be around me."

Cumby was the Packers' second pick in the first round of the 1980 draft after earning All-American honors at Oklahoma. Although his first year was hampered by a knee injury, he came on strong as one of the Packers' leading tacklers in the early 1980s. His knee trouble (five surgeries in seven years) eventually caught up with him by 1986, when Forrest Gregg released him. Cumby played in 1986 in Buffalo.

Cumby started professing his faith during his Packer career. He was one of about seven Packers, including Rich Campbell, who during the early and mid-1980s met for Bible studies and openly professed their Christian faith. Cumby and another linebacker, John Anderson, would pick through the letters sent to the Packers' speakers bureau and take all the church assignments. He also worked with FCA and Athletes in Action as a Packer and gave testimonials in homes around the Green Bay area.

Several years after retiring, Cumby, now an ordained minister and youth worker, thought about the "Refrigerator" incident and asked God why it had happened. Then one Sunday he was a guest preacher at a small church in Cleveland, Texas. "It was an all-white church, full of old people. It was like they all were dead," said Cumby, who is black. He knew he needed something to wake them up. One memory came to mind immediately. "I started telling the 'Refrigerator' story. They knew it. It's something about that story—it seems everybody saw it," said Cumby, wondering how even a group of senior citizens would know of his infamy. Within moments, Cumby had the congregation alive, smiling and in the palm of his hands. They were sharing his pain. Suddenly, they could relate. From that day on, Cumby no longer questioned why God had a Goliath flatten him in battle while the world watched. "Since then, every place I go to speak I tell that story. It breaks the ice. Now, I'm glad it happened."

Cumby has been a minister since 1988. He was ordained in 1991 at the Wheeler Avenue Baptist church in Houston and began working for the Fellowship of Christian Athletes (FCA) in Houston. Prior to that, he worked as a speaker for SportsWorld Ministries, which at that time was headed by former Packer lineman Mike McCoy.

Cumby hopes to return to school to get a divinity degree and eventually be the minister of his own church.

Cumby believes that working for the FCA is part of his calling because his background as a football player makes him a role model, a job he gladly accepts. He helps set up Bible studies, or "huddles," as he calls them, for middle schools, high schools, colleges, and pro sports teams in the Houston area. One week might find Cumby talking to teenagers, speaking to the University of Houston football team, and then doing a pre-game chapel for the Astros. In 1992, he gave a pre-game chapel service for the Packers before they won an important late-season game in Houston. In the spring of 1995, he read the Gospel at the funeral of former Packer tight end Mark Lewis, 32, who played from 1985-1987 and died suddenly, apparently of a heart attack or a brain aneurysm while living in Houston.

When it comes to working with youth, Cumby knows all about peer pressure and faith. He was called a Jesus freak and a holy roller when he came into the NFL and faced pressure to socialize with teammates whose values differed. "When they realized you weren't going to do what they wanted, they respected you. When you're in that type of environment you would hear a lot of stuff." Cumby was proof—and he wanted to be—that a good football player didn't have to drink or swear to succeed.

Not surprisingly, Cumby respected Bart Starr, who was fired as coach after the 1983 season. Starr also openly acknowledges his Christianity. "He was such a great person to play for because he treated you like a man, not like you were an animal. That got him in a little trouble at the end. Some players were causing trouble, and he [didn't deal] with them in a way some of us wanted him to."

Cumby began to get serious about his faith about the time the Packers drafted him, saying "That's when my life began—when I went to Green Bay." He remembers going to his Oklahoma dorm room one day after receiving one of his many honors. He looked at all his awards and felt something was missing in his life. "I sat in my room for about an hour and tried to figure out what was wrong. I felt depressed and not worth anything." His older brother, Mac, who played for North Texas State, happened to call minutes later and asked to see him the next day. So George drove to see Mac, and Mac revealed he had asked Christ into his life. George, a churchgoer since he was a kid, realized he hadn't completely committed his life to Christ. The next day, George went to church, followed in the footsteps of his brother, and began to follow the Lord. "I was letting George run my life. I had to let go of George and let God be in control."

Ken Ellis

Ken Ellis likes to tell people that when he played for the Packers he relied on a lot of "God-given talent." When Reverend Ken Ellis goes to work now at Bethany World Prayer Center near Baton Rouge, Louisiana, he likes to say that he gives his talent to God. "People now don't look to me for my athletic ability, but now it's for my ministering ability."

It's a way of life that began beckoning Ellis in 1971. He was a rising star in the NFL, but he lacked what he called an inner peace. A native southerner, he was in culture-shock when he found—to his amazement— bar signs on seemingly every corner in Green Bay and Milwaukee. He got drunk, did things he normally wouldn't, and felt ashamed. "A war was going on inside of me. I knew something was missing." It also was the same year his father, a blue-collar worker who never finished high school, died in a factory explosion in Georgia.

Ellis was at a crossroads. He noticed something admirable about the way big defensive tackle Mike McCoy carried himself. McCoy began telling Ellis about the need for a personal relationship with God. After the 1971 season, McCoy invited Ellis to a Pro Athletes Outreach Conference in Dallas. It was there that Ellis "sold my heart to the Lord."

After the Packers traded Ellis to Houston in 1976, he bounced around to five teams—the Oilers, Miami, Detroit, Cleveland, and the LA Rams—in the next five seasons. After tearing a muscle during the 1980 training camp in LA, he knew where he was headed. For several years he had been speaking during the off season for SportsWorld Ministries, where McCoy worked. Ellis saw his future in the faces of the teenagers he spoke to. "At that time I was moved and touched by what I saw when I stood in front of high school kids and told them how Christ came into my life. I saw the impact it had on young kids. I saw I was putting something into people's lives that would last and help people."

Ellis became a full-time member of the Bethany clergy staff in 1983. He calls Bethany a non-denominational charismatic church, along the lines of the Pentecostal church, where the non-traditional, upbeat services draw people out of their seats to clap and dance in the aisles. Ellis was ordained with the church in 1985 but worked only part time until 1988. Since completing a Minister Training Institute program in Baton Rouge in 1991, he has been firmly committed to his new vocation. "You're able to see a life change, a life that was headed to destruction. To be able to minister to those people and set them free . . ."

He preaches on occasion at Bethany World Prayer Center, which has 10 pastors and draws 5,000 parishioners each Sunday. But much of Ellis' time as associate pastor is spent at a church counseling center, working with church groups and reaching out to the community. He often goes to the 5,000-inmate Angola State Prison and the federal Dixon Correctional Institution to counsel and lead Bible studies. He officiates at weddings, funerals, "the whole nine yards." As the oldest of eight children, he has been a father figure in his family, especially two years ago when he officiated at the funeral of a younger brother.

As an ex-pro football player, Ellis knows that people will listen to him, that he has a forum. "It's helped get me into doors and helped me to share how the Lord has helped in my own life. Even though I've been out of football for many years, when I tell people I played pro football their eyes just light up," he said.

He told of going to a state hospital and helping a teenage drug user, to the eternal gratification of the teen's mother. "She said I was the only person who could get through to him. My main function is a lot of evangelism. As you know, you can always find someone who has a problem, who is sick, who needs to be encouraged, who needs a shoulder to cry on."

Ellis often gets asked about drug use in the NFL. He tells them what he saw—and what he did. "I say I saw teammates using drugs. As far as illegal drugs, I experimented with them but I did not use them on a regular basis." He admitted seeing players, including Packers, use amphetamines to stimulate their performance. The drug most commonly used among Packers, Ellis said, was alcohol. "My drug of choice was alcohol. In Green Bay, we used to go out and do a lot of things as a team. One of them was drink together." For example, beer was provided by the team, he said, on the bus trip home after games in Milwaukee.

Ellis was a wide receiver and punt returning standout at Southern University in Baton Rouge when the Packers drafted him in the fourth round in 1970. His rookie year he played wide receiver behind Carroll Dale for the first two weeks of Packer training camp. But when Herb Adderly was traded away, Ellis moved to cornerback. Coach Phil Bengston noticed that Ellis liked to bump and run so the staff thought it seemed natural that Ellis try defense, Ellis recalled. "I could stay with any wide receiver in the league." By the opening game in 1970, Ellis was starting. As a testament to his world-class speed, Ellis once caught receiver "Bullet" Bob Hayes from behind, recalled ex-Packer linebacker Jim Carter, who added he'd never seen anyone else do that.

Ellis was all-pro from 1972 through 1974 and played in the 1973 and 1974 Pro Bowls, the jerseys of which are displayed—along with other Packer mementos—in a special room in his house.

Ellis and his wife have two grown boys and a girl who, taking after her father, in 1995 was named Louisiana's outstanding track athlete after winning the 100- and 200-meter dashes. While he has declined to compete against his daughter, Ellis is a svelte 175 pounds—15 below his playing weight—thanks to jogging 25 miles a week, playing racquetball, and weight lifting.

He would like to line up just one more season, he said, to make a six- or seven-figure salary. "One season, that's all I would need." He laughed when he remembered that in 1970 he got a two-year contract, $16,500 his rookie season, $18,000 his second season, and a $10,000 signing bonus. In 1975, he wanted a $60,000 contract from new coach Bart Starr. He walked out of camp twice, was fined and suspended. He figures that contributed to his being traded away with John Hadl in the deal that brought Lynn Dickey to the Packers.

None of that concerns him now because he has moved from his days as a somewhat self-centered football player to a selfless, higher existence. "I never liked the idea of people catering to me. Jesus came to serve, not to be served. I just get a joy out of serving people and helping people."

CHAPTER

The Quarterbacks of Dan Devine

Scott Hunter
Quarterback, 1971-1973

John Hadl
Quarterback, 1974-1975

Jerry Tagge
Quarterback, 1972-1974

Jim Del Gaizo
Quarterback, 1973

In his four seasons as coach of the Green Bay Packers, ten quarterbacks threw passes for coach Dan Devine. Two of them, Bart Starr and Zeke Bratkowski, retired in 1971 after distinguished careers. In the next three seasons, Devine tried desperately to find a quarterback who would match the expectations Starr and Bratkowski had set. He tried trades, draft picks, and the waiver wire, but Devine could not find a savior, not Dean Carlson, Jack Concannon, Jim Del Gaizo, John Hadl, Scott Hunter,

*Charlie Napper, Frank Patrick, or Jerry Tagge. Ironically, when Devine
left the Packers to coach Notre Dame, he helped tutor Joe Montana, who
became one of the best quarterbacks in NFL history.*

Scott Hunter

Scott Hunter played only a third of his pro football career in Green
Bay, but those first three years left some indelible marks. Hunter, 49, who
since 1980 has been sports director at WKRG TV in Mobile, Alabama,
still refers to Green Bay as a "special place. Being a Packer is truly a
love. The rest of pro football is a business."

Much happened, both good and bad, when he played for the Packers during one of the most unusual periods in their history. The players
and front office experienced the joy of a Central Division championship,
the divisiveness of a strike, and the departure of a coach during Hunter's
three seasons.

Early on, it all was good to Hunter. With new coach Dan Devine trying to rebuild the Packers, Hunter became the QB halfway through his
rookie season in 1971. In 1972 the job was all his. He responded by leading the Packers to a 10-4 record. Although he completed only 43.7 percent
of his passes, Hunter had only nine passes intercepted and threw 13 for
touchdowns. He appeared to be the field leader the Packers needed to
replace Bart Starr, who had retired the year before. Hunter was the youngest QB to lead a team to the playoffs since the Cleveland Rams' Bob
Waterfield in 1945. "It all fell to me," Hunter said. "Having played at
Alabama for Bear Bryant, I was used to pressure. That didn't bother me."

But he was bothered by the 1972 divisional playoff game against the
Washington Redskins in the capital. Washington won 16-3 behind its five-
man defensive front that held John Brockington to nine yards in 13 carries. The real story wasn't Washington's defense; it was Green Bay's
coaching, Hunter said. The Packers knew that Washington might use the
five-man defensive line, and assistant coach Starr had prepared Hunter
for the possibility. Early in the game, with Starr calling the plays, the
Packers used audible calls by Hunter to get a field goal. "I thought, 'If
they stay in this [five-man front] we'll kill them,' " Hunter remembered.
"They only had two linebackers. We knew we could hit the back coming
out of the backfield."

But on the next series, the Packers ran three straight dive plays and got nothing. Hunter was confused. A short time later, two different plays were sent in to him simultaneously. He couldn't figure out what was going on. Then he realized. Devine had started to overrule Starr on play-calling. Hunter looked to the sideline. "Bart and Devine were 50 feet apart. They weren't talking." The Packers continued to try to run against the five linemen, passing only in predictable situations, and they didn't score again.

Ken Ellis, a cornerback on that team, agreed that the five-man front isn't what beat the Packers, even though that's what got all the media attention. "Devine tried to take over and start calling the plays during the game. Bart had prepared Scott for the five-man front. Bart would call a play and Devine would change it. We just got outcoached," Ellis said. Starr said in his book *Starr: My Life in Football* that the only disagreement he ever had with Devine was during the Washington game "when I fought to permit Hunter to pass more."

Brockington remembers that about three weeks before the playoffs, a media report said that the Packers had three coaches, Devine, Starr, and Dave Hanner, the defensive coordinator. "That was the point [Devine] started getting involved in the offense. [Devine] had a tremendous need for power," Brockington said. Against Washington, Hunter was ready to audible pass plays to get around the five-man front, but Devine began calling a "30 dive" play that kept getting no yards, according to Brockington. "By the third quarter, Bart was totally disattached from the game; he was down at the 30-yard line. It was Devine's play; he got outcoached and it was not a pretty sight." At the Pro Bowl that year, Brockington met Washington defensive lineman Chris Hanburger. "[Chris] said they never intended to get into the five-man the whole game. They never expected us to keep running the ball at that defense. He said, 'When you didn't attack it we stayed in it,' " Brockington quoted Hanburger.

The playoff game aside, 1972 still is Hunter's favorite year of pro ball. "That was the epitome for me in the NFL. It was one of those years when all the guys came together. There was a oneness with that team," Hunter recalled. Hunter remembers thinking that if the Packers could get past Washington and Dallas in the playoffs they would have had a psychological edge against the unbeaten Miami Dolphins in the Super Bowl.

"We were the last team to beat the Dolphins. We beat them [14-13] in the exhibition season."

By 1973, the square-jawed, confident Hunter was in Devine's doghouse. The Packers opened the 1973 season with a 23-7 victory over the New York Jets. The next week, during what ended as a 13-13 tie against Detroit, Devine pulled Hunter and put in another young QB, the inconsistent Jim Del Gaizo. "Devine pulled me for whatever reason. Then things got all muddy." Soon Hunter, Del Gaizo, and Jerry Tagge were moving in and out at QB and the Packers finished 5-7-2. "That team was one where the chemistry was so important. When you tinker with the chemistry, that's when the problems start," Hunter said.

During the 1974 preseason, Hunter was traded to Buffalo for tackle Steve Okoniewski and running back Pete Van Valkenburg. Del Gaizo was sent to New York about the same time. Tagge was the Packer QB, but within months Devine went shopping again—unbeknownst to virtually everyone in Green Bay, including the Packers' executive committee—and made the infamous trade for aging QB John Hadl.

Hunter thinks the Packers used the 1974 strike as a reason to trade him. Hunter stayed out of camp during the July walkout, and the Packers probably didn't like that "because I was in a team leadership role. I came to camp and wondered if I should break the strike or not. I called Bear Bryant and asked him what to do. He said, 'What's your offensive line doing?' I said, 'They're out.' He told me to stick with them." Hunter said players were offered money to cross the picket line—he was offered more than $10,000 by Devine to cross. "I told coach I'm the quarterback and it would kill me with the other guys if I crossed. Coach Devine treated us like we were striking against him."

Hunter spent the 1974 season with Buffalo. He didn't play in 1975, deciding instead to return to Alabama and run for a county political office. He lost the election but got a job out of it anyway. Former Packer personnel man Pat Peppler was with the Atlanta Falcons and saw a story about Hunter losing the election. He sent a box of balls to Hunter and told him to start throwing. Hunter played with the Falcons 1976-1978 then wound up his career in 1979 with Detroit, where he suffered a severe knee injury.

The closest Hunter gets to a football now is when he does interviews at Auburn and Alabama or does pay-per-view analysis for Alabama games. Since leaving the NFL in 1980 he has been at WKRG, a CBS affiliate in Mobile. He is the sports anchor and sports director, overseeing a small staff in the nation's 50th largest market. Although most sports anchors work in the evenings, Hunter works mornings. The Gulf Coast has a large blue-collar labor force—a large audience of early risers. Often during the football season when he's done with his morning shift, he pilots his Cessna airplane to report on the Crimson Tide or flies to their games on Saturdays.

Hunter, who is married with three children, including a budding quarterback son in high school, regularly jogs and lifts weights. His arm is stronger now than when he played for the Packers, he said. "I wish I knew then what I know now about strength and conditioning. [Packer trainer] Domenic Gentile tried to tell us, but I wouldn't listen." Hunter had a strong arm, but he didn't bring it with him when the Packers drafted him in the sixth round. "In the fall of my senior year [at Alabama], I separated my shoulder. I never really got time to bring it back. When I was in college I could throw the ball as far as I wanted to," he recalled.

Hunter broke most of Joe Namath's passing records at Alabama. When he got to Green Bay, he's not sure if the right people in the Packer organization knew that his arm was hurting. The injury didn't keep him from playing, and he found ways to "compensate for it" by getting the "ball down field with whatever it took to do it. When I look back I know I was doing the best I could with everything I had."

John Hadl

When John Hadl heard that the Los Angeles Rams had traded him to the Packers in 1974, he was dumbfounded. Why would the Rams trade him as he was coming off one of the greatest seasons of his career, one that included leading the Rams to a 12-2 mark and a division title?

It was October 22, 1974. Hadl remembers it well. "They had started Jim Harris at quarterback the week before. I had been around long enough so I knew something was up," said Hadl, 55, who is associate athletic director at his alma mater, the University of Kansas, in Lawrence, Kansas, the same city where he grew up. "[Rams Coach] Chuck Knox took me out of a meeting and told me they had traded me to Green Bay. I said, 'Chuck, what the hell do they want around here? We're 12-2, division champs and I'm out of here?'"

Then Knox told Hadl what the Packers had given the Rams in exchange for the 34-year-old quarterback: The Packers' first, second, and third-round draft picks in 1975 and the Packers' first and second-round draft picks in 1976. "I said, 'I can understand now,'" Hadl remembered. Much of the NFL, and most Packer fans, were shocked at first, saying it was a horribly high price to pay for one aging player, albeit an NFL star. Coach Dan Devine thought the trade was the answer to the Packer woes. The lack of a seasoned QB had hung like a millstone around the neck of Devine's Packers since he took the job in 1971. Devine, in a 1990 interview, stood by his trade, saying Hadl "could still play" and that the price wasn't exorbitant because "at the same time Philadelphia traded to get Roman Gabriel and San Francisco traded to get Jim Plunkett. And both paid more than we did."

After a few weeks in Green Bay, Hadl knew he would not be a savior, not when he saw the Packers' low level of talent. "They were weak in other areas. Up front. And they didn't have a lot of speed. [John] Brockington was a good back, but they didn't have the real speed. Devine was a little desperate at the time. He had a little pressure on him. He had to do something that year. He probably didn't care too much about what he had to give up to get it done. It was a lot to give up for anybody."

In Hadl's second week, the Packers went to Minnesota and beat the Vikings 19-7. "We got back in the race for a while. Devine was pretty popular that week," Hadl recalled. Even though Hadl led the Pack to three wins, the team lost its last three games of the season. He couldn't save Devine. On the contrary, the fact that Devine made the widely criticized trade without consulting other front-office personnel probably contributed greatly to the pressure on Devine to resign.

Was short-term success—and that was all Devine could hope for from a 34-year-old quarterback—worth the long-term price the team was going to pay through lack of draft choices? The deal is universally castigated as one of the worst in Packer history, so famous that the phrase "The Hadl Trade" is synonymous with "bad judgment" in the minds of Packer fans.

Two months after the trade, Devine resigned under pressure as the Packer coach. The Packers lost their last three games of the 1974 season to finish 6-8. Hadl especially remembers the last game of that season, a 10-3 loss in Atlanta. "We got about 10 inches of rain in three hours that day. [In the locker room], I had gotten word that he had gotten fired. I was getting ready to go back to California. I said 'Coach, I'm awfully sorry.' He said, 'John, I appreciate that.' And then he said he was going to be the next coach at Notre Dame. I just about fell out of my socks."

Devine actually hadn't been fired at that point, but it appears that he was expecting—or hoping—to leave Green Bay. That night, he called Green Bay from Atlanta and requested that the Packer executive committee meet and determine his fate for 1975. The committee hadn't been planning such a meeting but went ahead at Devine's insistence. So the next day, December 16, the committee met, agreed that they didn't want Devine back, and Devine agreed to resign. However, he got the Packers to pay the final year on his contract. With that money in the bank, Devine succinctly informed the surprised committee that he had taken the Notre Dame job, according to John B. Torinus, a former committee member and author of *The Packer Legend*. Devine thus got paid two salaries for 1975, galling the Packer brass.

If Devine told Hadl about the Notre Dame job in the Atlanta locker room, then it's true Devine knew well before he resigned—well before he forced the committee's hand—that he had other employment. It was a fitting end to a four-year coaching reign that began with Devine breaking his leg in his first game in 1971 when a sideline play toppled him, alienating Packer fans in a *Time* magazine story that was critical of Green Bay, making one of the worst trades in NFL history and, finally, duping the team's executive committee. (Devine was an outstanding college coach. At Notre Dame 1975-1980 he had a record of 53-16-1 and won a national title in 1977. In 16 seasons at Missouri and Arizona State before coming to Green Bay he was 119-41-8.)

In 1975 Hadl was the starting Packer QB under new coach Bart Starr. He completed 54 percent of his passes for six TDs. But he also was intercepted 21 times. In 1973 with the Rams, Hadl hit 52 percent of his passes and threw for 22 TDs with only 11 interceptions. He made the Pro Bowl. By April 1976 the Hadl "era" in Green Bay was over. Hadl was traded to Houston, but he didn't fetch nearly the price the Packers paid for him. In order to get Lynn Dickey, then a backup quarterback to Houston QB Dan Pastorini, the Packers gave up Hadl, young starting cornerback Ken Ellis, and two draft choices (fourth and sixth rounds) in the 1976 draft. So for just 22 games of Hadl's service, the Packers gave up seven draft picks and two starting players (Hadl, Ellis) to get one starting player, Dickey.

Many people contend that Starr was handicapped by "The Hadl Trade" in his first three years as Packer coach. Starr didn't have his first winning season until 1978. Devine begs to differ. "The team I left at Green Bay was a Super Bowl-type team. What happened to it after I left, I don't know. They had Ted Hendricks and Fred Carr—the two best linebackers in the conference. The secondary was sound. The offensive line was good. Brockington and Lane were good backs, and Hadl was a great quarterback," said Devine, who now is retired and living in the Phoenix, Arizona, area.

After he was traded by the Packers to Houston, Hadl played backup to Pastorini for two years before retiring. During his 16-year career, which began in 1962 with San Diego, he became one of the NFL's all-time leaders in passing yards and TD passes. When he looks back at the trade, Hadl is matter-of-fact. "I had nothing to do with it. It was just a business deal, and I could do nothing about that."

Despite the pressure, the 6'1", 214-pound Hadl found a pleasant atmosphere in Green Bay and total support from the fans. "They were loyal, hearty people. I couldn't believe in training camp when people from all over the state would come in. I really did enjoy it when I got there." Hadl especially remembers turning a corner once in Green Bay, looking down the street and seeing "about 20 Budweiser and Stroh's signs in one block. It's a hearty bunch." Although a star, Hadl fit in well with the Packers because he would go out and drink beer "more like an offensive lineman," said linebacker Jim Carter, who to this day said he thinks "the world" of Hadl.

After Hadl retired from the NFL, he returned to Kansas as offensive coordinator from 1977-1981. Then he was Rams offensive coordinator for one year under Ray Malavasi before coaching in Denver under Dan Reeves. Hadl helped tutor John Elway in Elway's rookie season. Hadl also was head coach of the Los Angeles Express in the USFL for two seasons. He returned to Kansas in his current position in 1987.

As associate athletic director, he raises money for the school's athletic scholarship fund and for the department's development and building funds. "We raise $3 million a year for scholarship athletes," he said, adding that Kansas has more than 400 such athletes. He goes to all the KU football games and often travels to KU alumni events around the country. Hadl's office is across the hall from another ex-Packer, assistant athletic director John Jefferson.

Hadl has seen Devine once since 1974. Did he and Devine discuss the trade? "No," Hadl said. "Not really."

They didn't need to. Enough already had been said.

Jerry Tagge

Jerry Tagge attended Green Bay West High School, the same school that produced Arnie Herber, the Packer passing star of the 1930s who made the NFL Hall of Fame. When Tagge was chosen in the first round of the 1972 draft, the comparisons were made and giddy talk abounded. Tagge grew up hawking popcorn at Lambeau Field, had made it big at the University of Nebraska, and was coming home to honeymoon on the field of his dreams. It was all so supposed to be so neat and sweet.

Now a middle-aged man, Tagge lives in Omaha with his wife, Betty, and two sons, ages 17 and 12. Almost 25 years after rocketing into the NFL on the strength of leading Nebraska to back-to-back national titles, Tagge is all but isolated from his former life in the lights, although one son, a defensive end, helped lead his Omaha team to the Nebraska prep title in 1995, and his youngest son is an aspiring quarterback.

Tagge is a partner in Tagge-Rutherford Group, an Omaha-based investment firm that sells a variety of financial services statewide. He started the business in 1993 after working for New York Life Insurance and a stint as vice president of an office furniture business. Rooting around for a new career is the down side of playing pro football, said Tagge, because "You've got to start at the bottom of the totem pole. I tried to get back into mainstream society and everybody had a 10-year start on me. It wasn't an easy experience for me."

Tagge hasn't been to Lambeau Field since the Packers cut him during the 1975 preseason. It's not surprising that he wouldn't want to return, he said. The football phase in his life is long gone; the Green Bay phase of that isn't worth his remembering. He gets to Green Bay about once a year but only to visit his parents. He has almost no contact with former Packer teammates, and was not even aware that his former roommate, Chester Marcol, had attempted suicide. In Tagge's new life, football isn't even on the field. "I'm really content where I am right now. I enjoyed my career, but it's over. Sales—it seems more real. No matter what you say about football, it's still a game. I'm in control of my destiny now. When you played football you weren't. But all the lessons I learned in football, I still use them. So football has done more for me than I could do for football."

Tagge's best football memories are pre-Green Bay. He was MVP of the 1971 and 1972 Orange Bowl games, which gave the Cornhuskers national titles. He was inducted into the Orange Bowl Hall of Glory in 1990. He regularly attends reunions of Nebraska national title teams and uses his name recognition in the state—where Cornhusker football is king—to help his business. "The people in Nebraska don't even know where Green Bay is. I've almost forgotten my Packer days. Out here I never, ever get a question about the Packers."

His professional career produced no everlasting Packer fan adoration. Even though an alumni gathering for Packer players is held each season, hometown boy Tagge has never attended. Tagge's college career was fun; his pro career wasn't. "Pro ball was an eye opener. Coming off two national championships [at Nebraska], everybody was gung-ho. Then I came to a place [Green Bay] where everybody was unhappy. They didn't like the town, the players, the facilities, the weather. I was all fired up and I was a minority," Tagge remembered.

Tagge figures he landed in Green Bay at the wrong time. From 1972 until 1975, he saw the aging Packers weed out player after player as they tried to rebuild. "I suppose I could have done better, but it wasn't a good situation for me. I was pretty young at the time. I was a young player on an old team. I was expected to do a lot. I wasn't ready. I've never been able to walk into anything and be an instant success. I didn't have enough talent. I didn't have the quickest release, and I wasn't the fastest. My strengths were knowing my teammates, reading the defenses, and being more of an astute-type player. I think I could have gotten there."

Coach Dan Devine said as much after the 1972 draft, saying he took Tagge for his intangibles, not his talent. Devine had seen Tagge perform in pressure Big Eight games without making mistakes. He had risen from number eight quarterback as a freshman at Nebraska to number one as a sophomore. As a senior, Tagge completed about 60 percent of his passes. "I knew Jerry wasn't rated too high," Devine said after the draft. "He figured to be about a third or fourth round draft choice. If he would have had an arm like [Jim] Plunkett or speed like [Archie] Manning or [Dan] Pastorini, he would have been rated much higher. It was pretty much my decision [to take him No. 1]." In an interview 15 years later, Devine said: "I always thought, and Bart did too, that Tagge could play in the NFL. It just proves we were wrong. He was just a hair away. I don't know what it was."

Scott Hunter was the starter in 1972, but in 1973 Tagge emerged as the starting quarterback in the ninth game of the season when Hunter, Jim Del Gaizo, and others failed. Tagge completed 56 of 103 passes and went into the 1974 season number one. But he didn't hang on to the job. After starting the first six games of 1974, he was replaced by Jack Concannon.

Tagge remembers the 1972, 1973, and 1974 seasons as "totally confusing to me. It was crazy. I look back at it and I wonder how anybody survived. You never knew where you stood. You never knew where the coach stood. Pro ball was a disappointment to me. I never expected all that."

When the Packers gave up five high draft picks to get John Hadl in October 1974, it was all over for Tagge. "Once John Hadl got there I never took another snap. We used to rotate snaps but when he came in I went by the wayside. John wanted every snap [in practice] and he got them." Tagge was cut during the 1975 preseason by Starr, the rookie head coach; Starr gave no explanation, according to Tagge.

If anybody had told Tagge after draft day in 1972 that his greatest memories as a pro football player would come while playing in Canada, he probably would have laughed. But today, Tagge is thankful his career didn't end in Green Bay. After the Packers cut him, Tagge played with San Antonio of the World Football League in 1976 before the league folded during that season. Tagge resurfaced in 1977 with the British

Columbia Lions of the Canadian Football League (CFL). He started for three years, led the team into the playoffs two years, and was MVP of the Western Division in 1979. He suffered a career-ending knee injury in 1979 when the Lions were 11-1 and about to enter the playoffs. With the Packers, Tagge completed 48.4 percent of his passes. With the Lions, he completed 57 percent. "When I got to Canada a light switch went on in my head. I could see the whole field, the coverages. I had the experience." Tagge's greatest memory of the CFL? "It was fun."

Jim Del Gaizo

When the Packers needed a quarterback in 1973, the fans thought Dan Devine had acquired a winner in Jim Del Gaizo, a swashbuckling, black-haired, mustachioed southpaw whose cocksure style spawned the giddy bumper sticker, "All the Wayzo with Del Gaizo." He may get credit for the most unusual bumper sticker in Packer history (better even than "Forrest will set the Pack on Fire," and "We are Guided by Devine Inspiration") but Del Gaizo did little else worth remembering.

When Devine traded for Del Gaizo from Miami in August of 1973, he had shown promise in 1972 as an understudy to Dolphins QB Bob Griese. That explained the high price—number two draft picks in 1974 and 1975—that Devine gave up.

Del Gaizo retired in 1976 after a second stint with the Dolphins and now works in financial services near Boca Raton, Florida. Never short on opinions, he blamed Devine for his career stalling in Green Bay. "All of us had the misfortune of playing for Dan Devine. He impersonated a coach. He, personally, was one of the worst things that happened to my football career. He knew nothing about football. The players just despised that guy. As a football coach, he was without a doubt—and I'm speaking at any level—the most incompetent coach I played for. He dismantled that program."

Devine may have felt the same way about Del Gaizo when he traded him to the New York Giants early in 1974. When given the chance to start in 1973, Del Gaizo responded poorly, going 4-for-14 passing for 36 yards in one of several unimpressive starts. For the season, he completed 27 of 62 passes and had six intercepted. Once, Del Gaizo completed three straight passes and didn't get a first down. "A good quarterback can go his whole career and not pull a stunt like that," Devine said. By midway through the 1973 season, Del Gaizo was all the wayzo on the bench, having never fulfilled expectations, much like all of Devine's quarterbacks.

CHAPTER

Glory Forever

Bart Starr
Quarterback 1956-1971
Assistant coach 1972
Coach 1975-1983

Ray Nitschke
Linebacker 1958-1972

Bart Starr

He utilized everything God gave him. He rose to the challenge. His *best games were in the big games.*"—**Ray Nitschke, teammate**

"*I'll never forget the effect Bart Starr had on me. He was totally involved in community. I used to think he did it for whatever reason. Then it dawned on me that he likes this.*"—**Francis Peay, teammate**

"*I loved him as a man. He was a tremendous leader and had a tremendous amount of class and dignity, something I would always try to be like and never could be like.*"—**Rich Wingo, linebacker**

"There's nobody who was a better role model than Bart. He was patient. He was kind of like your dad. He was a great leader. He is a man who always commanded your respect and admiration, and no one ever doubted his complete integrity and commitment to every member of the team and their families."—David Whitehurst, quarterback

"When Bart came in [as coach], there were not any great players. When he got fired he really had the team on the threshold to compete well and probably win it. I got the feeling sometimes that he did not have the power to get the people he wanted. I felt like he didn't have total freedom, and he was supposed to have that power. If Bart had any drawback, he was too nice. Sometimes people take advantage of that."
—Lew Carpenter, teammate (1956-1958), assistant coach (1975-1983)

Bart Starr. Crisp, rhythmic, and poetic, the monosyllabic words roll off the tongue smoothly and beautifully the way the nose end of a spiraling football spins through the air. Almost mesmerizing. And that last name—Starr—is so pretentious, so full of good connotations that it challenges, almost burdens, its owner with responsibility. It's a name you have to live up to.

When he played for the Green Bay Packers, Bart Starr was the living embodiment of his name. He always did the right thing, said the right thing, rose to the occasion at the right time. MVP. All-Pro. Hall of Famer. Christian. Community leader. Willing role model. Successful businessman. Winner. The only shadows Starr walked in after taking over as quarterback in 1960 were those cast by the adoring fans, business agents, and media who constantly were at his feet with their scraps of paper, memorabilia, pens, contracts, and microphones.

Then he became coach of the Packers. He ignored his instincts and the advice of his friends to take a job that he wasn't prepared for and in a situation that wasn't conducive to winning. But it seemed to him the right thing to do—try to put the Packers back on top. From 1975-1983, for the first time in his life, Bart Starr was a failure. He lost almost 60 percent of his games and never got close to another Super Bowl. The same people who saw him as invincible as a player questioned his ability as a coach. The media tested his mettle and occasionally got him to boil over when they criticized his decisions or tested his temper, for example, by eavesdropping on closed practice sessions. A joke booklet with the title, "All I Know about Press Relations, by Bart Starr," began circulating. The inside pages were blank. When some fans began booing in 1981, a humbled Starr made a public appeal for team support.

He was fired on a Monday morning, December 19, 1983—about 16 hours after losing to the Chicago Bears to end the season. A win would have put the Packers in the playoffs and preserved his job, but a last-minute, stake-in-the-heart field goal by the Bears sent Starr into the dark. He closed the door to his office and cried that Monday when he no longer was a Packer.

He went into the real estate business in Phoenix and began working with a group trying to get an expansion NFL franchise. Starr would have been team president. When the St. Louis Cardinals moved to Phoenix, it killed the chances of the group Starr was with. Starr's final NFL dream flared out and he eventually returned to his home state, Alabama, to continue in the real estate business.

On a fine Friday morning in September 1995, Bart Starr stood outside a new Electric Ave. & More store in Wisconsin and said the good things you'd expect Bart Starr to say. As he spoke, hundreds of Packer fans snaked almost a quarter-mile through a mall parking lot waiting for their chance to say hello and have those two great words, Bart Starr, scribbled on a mimeographed photo of him in sport coat and tie. The "fair-haired" boy, as former teammate Gary Knafelc called him, showed mostly gray on his 62-year-old crown, but the boyish smile with which he greeted every fan was original vintage.

Bart Starr, who in 1968 was named one of the 10 outstanding young men in America, who is associated with winning more than any other quarterback, still strives to succeed. He lives in Birmingham, Alabama, with his wife, Cherry, and is chairman of HealthCare Realty Management, a company that owns, leases, or manages 60 medical buildings across the country. Not surprisingly, he goes about his job supervising some five dozen employees in what he calls a "wonderful team environment." Not surprisingly, he still gets up every morning to do his best and live by the motto that his father instilled in him, "Trust and respect must be earned."

Under the layers of Bart Starr's 1990s business persona are the favorite son of one Packer generation and the troubled father of another. No one has to tell the boss at HealthCare Realty Management about staying ahead of the competition. He's been there, done that, and knows what to do tomorrow. "There's a great deal to be learned from my background. If you don't truly seek to excel someone else will beat you," he said. But after all the success he's tasted, why is he hungry for more? "What drives me is I do have a lot of personal pride. There's a lot to be achieved out there. I dearly love to come to work every morning," he said in the soft Southern accent that seems a hybrid of Jimmy Carter and Bill Clinton.

His typical week he describes as "full of work," although he usually finds time to work out at a gym in his home. He travels frequently in his job and gets plenty of offers to make appearances and speak. The public adoration he continues to receive—such as the line outside the electronics store—is a "real thrill. It touches you a great deal." He was "delighted" to see a line of fans, even though he had seen carbon copies of that line thousands of times. "You shouldn't expect anything. Life treats you commensurate with your efforts," he said.

One of Starr's former teammates, roommate and still close friend Gary Knafelc, said Starr's celebrity status is "an amazing thing. I traveled with Bart a lot. He's as big now as he's ever been, bigger. He's as big [a name] in the United States as he is in Wisconsin. He's very well known no matter where he goes."

Americans remember Starr the player far more than Starr the coach. Ditto with Starr, who tries to not dwell on his coaching days. When asked about it, he paused then said, "It's past . . . I've moved on. It bothered me that I didn't win. I had never failed at anything. It's a burr under my saddle." He is proud of the many friendships he made with players while coaching the Packers and was pleased to think he may have set a good example for them to follow. Numerous players continue to speak highly of Starr's integrity and commitment to winning. They simultaneously bemoan his firing, just when he had become a good coach.

Far more painful than losing games was the loss of his son, Brett, who grew up while Bart was coaching the Packers and who appeared to have overcome his drug addiction before relapsing in 1988. Brett, 24, had been using cocaine when he died at his home near Tampa, Florida. Bart found the body. "It changed our lives dramatically. It's one of those things you have to live with all your life," Starr explained, gazing at a picture of Brett in his office. Right next door in his office building is the office of his other son, Bart Jr. It was Bart Jr. who persuaded Bart and Cherry to move back to Birmingham after Brett's death. "He said we needed to be closer as a family. He was right," Starr said.

Through his highs and lows, the name Bart Starr has held up to public scrutiny because Starr has. Knafelc saw Starr come down from the pinnacle of his playing days but never saw his character waver. "He has been down many, many times," Knafelc said, "but he has a very strong character. He's very strong within himself."

Knafelc, a Packer tight end from 1954-1962, roomed with Starr for six years. Now the Packer public address announcer, Knafelc recalled how Starr came to Green Bay in 1987 to sign copies of his autobiography, *Starr: My Life in Football*. When the lines at the book store grew too long, Starr had all the unsigned books—hundreds of them—boxed and delivered to Knafelc's house, where Starr was staying. For two days, Starr signed every book, "each one with something personal," Knafelc recalled. Starr then took all the books back to the store.

Who is Bart Starr today? He hardly seems to have changed because he still does and says the right things, such as, "The strong common denominator in anything is directly attributable to attitude." And he gets up each morning still trying to earn trust and respect. Bart Starr. The name is magical not because of its poetic properties but because of the person. "If there's anything that depicts Bart, it's consistency. Since 1957 he's changed very little," Knafelc said. "He's the most honest guy I've ever met."

Ray Nitschke

When Al Pahl was editor of the Packer Report *for nine years in the 1980s and early 1990s, one of his jobs was to call Ray Nitschke after every Packer game, interview him, and ghost-write Nitschke's column, which appears on the inside cover of the publication Nitschke began in the early 1970s. During those nine years, the two became friends and Pahl learned that the man with enormous hands and shoulders also had a huge heart. Pahl saw Nitschke always live up to his image when in*

public, never refusing to say hello, shake hands, or sign his name with
a smile. One time Pahl received a phone call from a man whose father
was dying of cancer. The man wanted to know if somehow Nitschke
could call the sick man, a stranger, with a few words of encouragement.
Nitschke called.

Pahl's favorite Nitschke story concerned a chance meeting at a mall
between Nitschke and an acquaintance. The acquaintance had remar-
ried a woman with several children. The man's relationship with his
stepchildren was like "oil and water," Pahl recalled. As the man walked
through the mall with his stepchildren, he ran into Nitschke and they
began to talk. Nitschke knew nothing of the personal weight on the man's
shoulders but good naturedly built him up in front of the children, saying
he was a fine person and that the children always should listen to and
respect their father. The wide-eyed children were impressed their new dad
not only knew Nitschke but that Nitschke thought he was a swell guy.
Almost miraculously, from that day forward, the man's troubles with his
stepchildren faded.

Ray Nitschke ambled toward the door of a Perkin's restaurant on
Oneida Street in Green Bay, and before he made it to the vestibule, wide-
eyed hostess Vicky Peterson said to anyone nearby, "Here comes Ray
Nitschke." Indeed, there was no mistaking him. No less the imposing ter-
minator figure than when he played for the Packers, he was broad shoul-
dered, square-jawed, and at age 59 looked ready to stop a train.

More than twenty-five years after he tackled his last ball carrier for
the Packers, the legend of Ray Nitschke has not faded. Credit his fame if
you like to his famous hairless pate, his "Greatest Middle Linebacker of
All Time" tag, or the Oldsmobile, Miller Lite, or Wisconsin Lottery commercials he's done, but one thing is for sure, Nitschke remains famous —
even in death. When he died unexpectedly at age 61 on March 8, 1998 of
a heart attack in Venice, Florida, thousands of fans grieved. His death was
news across the country, and ex-teammates, along with NFL dignitaries,
filled a Green Bay church for his funeral. He was buried in Green Bay.

When a man at Perkin's said Nitschke was his all-time favorite,
Nitschke grinned, said, "Aw, you're kidding," and went over to shake
hands. And his legend grew. The wide-eyed man turned out to be Richard

John Brockington—the Packers took away his best play.

Top: Jim Carter (50) closes in on Chicago running back Walter Payton in the mid-1970s. Left: Carter, 1996, at Jim Carter Ford, Eau Claire, Wis.

Photo: David Joles

Chester Marcol at the 1995 Packers reunion. The Polish
Prince in Green Bay, the Polish Fisherman in the Upper
Peninsula

No. 83 John Jefferson—
under Forrest Gregg and
Bob Schnelker, often
open, seldom hit.

Photo: *Eau Claire Leader–Telegram* files

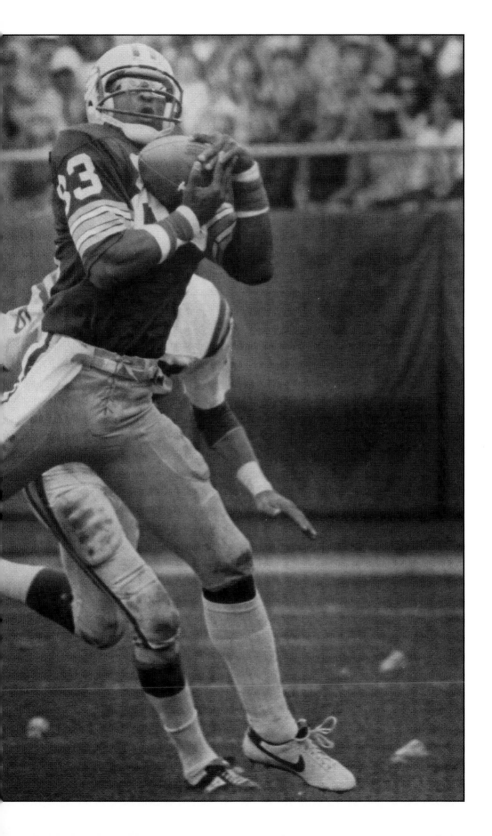

Top left: Greg Koch in the 1970s. Top Right: Fuzzy
Thurston in the 1960s. Above: Thurston with Greg's
son Zach at the 1995 Packer reunion.

Photo: Steve Kinderman, *Eau Claire Leader–Telegram*

Bart Starr—the perfect role model as a Packer player, did he come into an unwinnable situation as a Packer coach?

Photo: Steve Kinderman, *Eau Claire Leader–Telegram*

Photo: Michael Klein

Above: No. 84 Steve Odom as a kick return specialist in the mid-1970s. Left: Odom in 1996, at the Berkeley, California, Police Department.

Peterson, the middle-aged husband of the wide-eyed restaurant hostess. "He was really taken by Mr. Nitschke," Vicky Peterson said later of her husband's reaction to finally meeting his hero. "To [Richard] nobody was ever equal to Ray Nitschke. First, he has a really nice personality. He's such a down-to-earth person. He acts like anybody else. Second, he was just a fine football player."

No doubt Richard Peterson told all his friends that he finally met Nitschke, and that, yes, his hands were HUGE! and he seemed like a really nice guy, and he looked just like he does on TV. The legend of Nitschke never faded because Nitschke never got tired of being Nitschke. He never had an identity problem. "Not a day goes by that people don't bring up Number 66 or Lombardi in my life. So I think I'll always be Number 66," Nitschke said. He thought of himself at times as two people—the Ray who played football and the Ray who didn't—but then he glanced at the expensive, leather-sleeved Packer letter jacket and the green Lombardi Classic sweatshirt he wore and said "everybody relates" to him as a Packer.

He lived in the Green Bay suburb of Oneida. The area was his home ever since the Packers drafted him—but in any given week he could be found around the country doing what he did best—acting like Ray Nitschke. He wrote columns for the *Packer Report*, was an America's Pack fan club spokesman, made appearances at hardware shows for the Newell company's Easy Painter product, did the banquet circuit, and endorsed clothing for Champion and NFL Throwbacks.

He and his wife, Jackie, raised three children who all live in the Green Bay area. Jackie had a cancerous lung removed in May 1995 and had a cancerous brain tumor removed in April 1996. She died that summer. "It wakes you up. She's in God's hands," said Nitschke, whose ascension to the ranks of the NFL elite coincided with the stabilizing effect of his marriage to Jackie. She was credited with smoothing the edges of his sometimes rough personality and, one Christmas when she gave him a Lincoln Continental, moving him to tears. For more than 20 years of their nearly 40 years together, they were the honorary leaders and successful fundraisers for the Cerebral Palsy telethon in Green Bay, making them one of the city's favorite couples, as inseparable and well-known as another famous Packer couple, Bart and Cherry Starr.

When he was home, Nitschke walked three miles a day with his Siberian husky, Butkus, and played to a five handicap at the Oneida Golf & Riding Club, where Jackie also was an avid golfer. He knew it was a life that even money often can't buy. "I'm one of the lucky few to make a living doing what I wanted to do," he said. "The phone is always ringing. I remember Paul Hornung saying that Ray Nitschke got more out of football than anybody who ever played. I think he's right. Every place I've gone I've been treated well." The debt of gratitude Nitschke felt toward football was repaid in his dealings with the public. "I want to treat everybody well," he said. "The game has been so good to me I could never give back what's been given to me. I want to return it."

He often went out of his way to make a good impression. Two days after Bart Starr appeared at an Electric Ave. & More store opening in Wisconsin, Nitschke appeared. While Starr wouldn't sign personal items (only store-provided pictures) for fear of people using his name for profit, Nitschke signed everything people brought. What impressed him most about the long line of fans were the parents who had brought their children. "They probably met me once and thought enough of me to bring in their kids. It's the greatest compliment."

Nitschke especially enjoyed being around children, possibly because he remembered the pain of growing up without a father (killed in an accident when Ray was three) then having his mother die when he was 13. But just when everything seemed to be going wrong in his life, all the right things began to happen. Ray grew into a 6' 3", 235-pound physical specimen, and football gave him a direction. "It kept me in school. It taught me to utilize my time properly. It's really a character building game." Without parents, football became his family and gave him the blessings and love that said he was OK, that he was somebody.

When asked what he would have done in life without football, he answered that his two brothers became a beer truck driver and a sheet metal worker. "I went to the right high school [East Proviso in Maywood, Illinois], the right university [Illinois], went to the right place in Green Bay with the right coach. The [coaches] all influenced me. They all gave me encouragement and helped me to succeed. I've got to be the luckiest guy in the world."

He played quarterback in high school and was a fullback and line-backer in college, an all-around gifted athlete who could throw a foot-ball nearly 100 yards and a running back nearly as far. "Sometimes he would play quarterback in practice," former Packer linebacker Bill Forester said. "I remember seeing him throw the ball 100 yards in the air. That sounds like Texas bull, but it's not. The problem was he would throw the ball with the same velocity if it was a 10-yard hook, and nobody would want to catch it." Nitschke never played offense in the pros because "my temperament suited me to play defense."

Nitschke was accorded nearly every accolade possible in his career. After playing on five Packer championship teams, he was elected to the Pro Football Hall of Fame in 1978, had his Number 66 retired by the Packers, and was named the best middle linebacker in the first 50 years of NFL history. He was a Packer for 15 years; only Bart Starr played longer (16 years). Their lockers are side by side in the Packer Hall of Fame. After he retired, his fame grew. He wrote the story of his life, *Mean on Sunday*, was in two movies ("The Longest Yard" and "The Head" with the Monkees), and became a product pitch man. "I'm [more famous] now than when I played. I don't know what it is," Nitschke said. He and Starr were voted the two most recognizable faces in Wisconsin. He "seriously" considered coaching, but "nobody ever asked."

He was proud of being part of a team that changed NFL history and in some ways American culture. "There will never be an era like we had. It's unbelievable what we did, not only for the Packers but for the league. It's incredible how those teams have influenced football." In the 1960s, football became America's favorite spectator sport partly because of the success of the Packers, he believed. If there's one thing about modern football players that bothered Nitschke, it was their lack of knowledge about NFL history and how players from decades ago laid the groundwork for the huge salaries of the 1990s.

One of the first things Nitschke did after retiring from football was join the Oneida Golf and Riding Club. On the golf course he could keep alive his competitive flame—if only for personal pride and small bets. It was also an outlet for his aggression. "I took it out on the golf ball. That certainly helps. I went about football totally. Hopefully you had to knock me out to get me out of there. After an adjustment, I got to know that life goes on after football." He wasn't necessarily a long hitter anymore in golf because tightness in his back limited him to a three-quarters swing. The back problem and one leg that was shorter than the other because of an old knee injury were the only limiting physical problems he had from football, he said.

Nitschke owned 10 Packer season tickets and attended every home game when he was in town as well as some road games. He didn't attend Packer practices; you don't blow barbecue smoke in front of an old bear. At least once a year, however, the fire in the old warrior was rekindled when he attended the annual alumni gathering and his name was announced at halftime. "The only time I miss the game is when I get introduced at halftime. It's unbelievable what goes through my mind when my name is announced and I run off the field," he said, his blue eyes squinting and his hands outstretched as if ready to pull down a ball carrier. "It's an unbelievable feeling I have being in that stadium. I was comfortable there. That was my stage. Fifteen years of playing out there. That was my place, my field."

Ray Nitschke's stage was wherever he went. His bald head, his ambling walk, his Packer clothes, his gruff exterior, and his kind gestures—they all said Nitschke, they all said football. "I've really had a wonderful life because of the game of football."

CHAPTER

Lombardi Lives

Jerry Kramer
Guard, 1958-1968

Doug Hart
Defensive back, 1964-1971

I *will demand a commitment to excellence and to victory, and that is what life is all about.*

". . . the quality of a man's life has got to be in full measure to that man's personal commitment to excellence, to victory, regardless of what field he may be in."—Vince Lombardi

Jerry Kramer

In the summer of 1958, Jerry Kramer and University of Idaho teammate Wayne Walker were on their way to play in the College All-Star football game. Kramer had been drafted by the lowly Green Bay Packers, a team that hadn't come near a championship since World War II. Walker had been chosen by the Detroit Lions, the defending NFL champions. It was a long ride to the game for Kramer, and for all he knew at the time it might be an even longer trip through the NFL in Green Bay. Kramer, a blue-eyed, crew-cut, all-American farm boy from Sandpoint, Idaho, had to be excused if he sunk down in his seat a bit while his buddy gloated. "He was giving me crap about going to Green Bay," Kramer recalled. "He said, 'I'm going to the world champion Deeee-troit Lions with Bobby Layne!"

After he got to Detroit, however, Walker must have been the one feeling less fortunate. Across Lake Michigan, it was apparent Jerry Kramer had gotten the luck of the draft. In 11 years with the Packers, Kramer was fitted for five championship rings—including two diamond-encrusted Super Bowl rewards, while the Lions were regularly beaten by the Packers and never won another title. "You've got to have a gram of luck to be there. It certainly was good fortune," Kramer admitted.

It was more than good fortune, rings, and gloating rights for Kramer and his cohorts. It meant more even than the endorsement and business opportunities that came with fame. Beyond the adulation accorded the players and their fans, a generation later fans everywhere are still are drawing good vibrations from a '60s phenomenon called the Packer Glory Years.

The legacy of the '60s Packers isn't turning out to be wins and titles. It's turning out to be inspiration. Just ask Jerry Kramer. He still is uncovering the Packers' '60s influence, 35 years after their first title. He's the guardian, or right guardian if you will, of the Packer legend, the intuitive right guard who wrote four Packer books, including best-sellers *Instant Replay,* a diary of the 1967 season, and his last book, *Distant Replay*, which is based on a 1984 reunion of the 1967 team. People often wonder why the Packers and Packer stars of the 1960s still are so popular. Kramer knows that on the surface the reason is three straight titles, which no team has accomplished since. The real reason the glory of the 1960s hasn't faded? It's intangibles; it's all about influence.

Kramer remembers once meeting a man from Chicago who said he watched all the Packer games of the 1960s. Kramer wondered why because the man was a Bears fan. It was simple. "I just enjoyed excellence," the man told him. And there was the letter Kramer got from New York financial guru Alan Greenberg with the statement, "I have always dreamed that someday my team would be known as Greenberg's Packers."

The legacy of the 1960s at its most basic level is the success stories—of which there are many—of the players themselves. It wasn't surprising that people like Bart Starr, Ray Nitschke, Willie Davis, Bob Skoronski, Max McGee, and others carried their wills to succeed into the business world. All they did in football was win. It was the only way they knew how to operate when they left football behind.

At its most esoteric level, the reason people still talk about the '60s Packers, why people like Kramer and his cronies still are sought-after speakers, has everything to do with the lessons about commitment, pride, sacrifice, courage, will, determination, perseverance, faith, family—the cornucopia of values that was Vince Lombardi. It has everything to do with Lombardi, his disciples, the examples they have set and the lessons they have passed down.

"We don't know how many people we inspired," Kramer said, and then he mentioned Lombardi fan and famous automotive executive Lee Iacocca. In his autobiography, Iacocca explained how he applied to business the three things Lombardi told him were essential to winning at football: Fundamentals, discipline, and love. "I've gotten so many letters from people who say we had an impact on them," Kramer added.

Kramer's role as a chief Lombardi spokesman has much to do with his four Packer books, including his personal favorite, *Lombardi: Winning is the Only Thing*. The book peeled away the layers of Lombardi's persona while adding to the legend of the man. It wasn't the biggest seller of the four, but more than the other books it captured his spirit through interviews with people who knew him best.

Not the least of those affected by Lombardi have been the children of players like Kramer, who can see strong Lombardi-esque traits in at least two of his successful sons. Kramer tells how in 1995 he gave his youngest son, Jordan, a Lombardi-like pep talk. Jordan was a sophomore running back on his high school football team in Idaho. "I told him he needed some fire and intensity." The next game, Jordan ran for 256 yards on eight carries. Jordan wound up being all-conference and gaining almost 1,000 yards for the season. He made dad proud.

But the long-lasting Lombardi influence is far more than familial. Not long ago, Kramer received a clipping from an article about Tommy Lee Jones, who was an All-Ivy League football player but went on to become an actor. Jones won an Oscar for his role in the 1993 film *The Fugitive.* In the article Jones was asked who his hero was. "Jerry Kramer of the Green Bay Packers," Jones replied. "Those positive things just keep happening," Kramer said. In January of 1997, the day before the Packers' Super Bowl win over New England, Kramer faced disappointment when his nomination to the NFL Hall of Fame was rejected by the Veterans Committee.

Kramer once received a letter from a man whose goal was to become a professional golfer. Inspired by the Packers, he put everything he had into making the pro tour. He succeeded and was a respectable 37th on the money list one year when he suffered a career-ending injury. He was heartbroken but rather than pity himself he went back to the tenets of Lombardi. "I knew if I quit that you and the coach would be disappointed in me. So I went back to school and became an orthopedic surgeon," the man wrote.

The benefits of such testimonials, of course, do much to make aging a graceful process for Kramer, age 60, and his former teammates. Kramer never has to look far for affirmation. But more than that, if there's a story beyond *Distant Replay,* beyond the fact that the players' success and love for each other hasn't abated over the years, it's that the influence of Lombardi lives. Kramer always is amazed that a man who died at age 57 in 1970 continues to affect peoples' lives, that one person was strong enough to affect untold numbers by who he was and what he accomplished.

Certainly the Lombardi legend benefited from good timing. When the Packers were kings of the football world, television was just becoming the medium of the masses. And in the socially unstable 1960s, the Packers were a rock of traditional values when "there really was not much quest for excellence. We stood for high standards when the world was blowing flowers, looking for no distractions, kind of a happy medium," Kramer said. "Lombardi taught us that the intangibles in life are what's very critical. It's great to have education, etcetera, but if you don't have the need, the want, the burning desire. . . . They were the basic reasons for our success," Kramer believes.

Lombardi may have taunted, raged, and demanded souls like a devil in training camp, but he took on God-like qualities—and often was the subject of deific jokes—in the eyes of many around him because he displayed no serious weaknesses. He had a triune belief in God, Family, and Profession, in that order. After the Packers won Super Bowl II in 1968 for their third straight title, one of the first things Lombardi did was lead the team in the Lord's Prayer.

So Lombardi's disciples—not the least of which is Kramer—have spread the gospel out of admiration for their departed leader. "We want to share that formula" for success, Kramer said, acknowledging that much of his life and what he has to say verify his respect for Lombardi.

It's a life that has had its share of twists, turns and bumps. Kramer had so many surgeries from childhood and football accidents that he was known as the "Zipper" by teammates. He was so well known for recovering from injuries that he was one of the subjects of a 1968 sports book titled *Winners Never Quit*. He experienced great financial gains and losses in the business world as well as in his personal life, which has been marked by two divorces. Wink, the woman to whom he dedicated *Distant Replay*, has been his ex-wife since 1993 but still is a good friend. The two spend time together with their three children, but "we just don't seem to be able to live together yet." Jordan and another son, Matthew, a 6' 5", 225-pound defensive end at the University of Idaho, take after their dad in football. Kramer has three grown children from his first marriage as well as several grandchildren.

After spending the 1970s chasing his dreams in his personal "brave new world," as he called it, Kramer re-prioritized his life to focus less on material wealth and more on his relationships with his children, in essence coming back to the basic values taught him by his parents and reinforced by Lombardi. A turning point came one day soon after his business partner and former Packer teammate Urban Henry died suddenly. Kramer picked up a book called *Life after Life* in which people relate their near-death experiences. One man said he encountered a being that asked him, "What have you done with your life you want to show me?" Kramer stopped reading, went over to a mirror and posed the question to himself. He initially thought of all the earthly "junk" he had accumulated. Then he realized that the only things worth salvaging are the intangibles, such as God and family.

Living in slow-paced Parma, Idaho, has helped him keep his focus, he said. He doesn't regret turning down television and Hollywood business offers that would have relocated him in New York or Los Angeles. Parma, in the state's southwest corner near the confluence of the Snake and Boise rivers, has 1,735 people, "a lot of cowboys and cattle people, a lot who don't care about football," Kramer said. He has lived there for 25 years, and although he is one of the most famous residents in the region, he can go to the local store and still get asked for identification. Kramer has a 620-acre ranch near Boise, Idaho, that he leases out, but he maintains the "hunting, bragging, and driving around rights."

He golfs from a seven to twelve handicap, hunts ducks, fishes trout, and takes four-mile walks when he feels pudgy. Physically, he isn't limited by football injuries other than by "aches and pains and some back trouble" that require him to keep Advil handy. He takes part in Packer Fantasy Camps and agonized when the Packers couldn't repeat '60s history and beat the Cowboys to get to the 1996 Super Bowl. He gives motivational speeches to groups and corporations and does commercials for InterMountain Gas of Idaho, a job that has earned him the dubious nickname "The Gas Man." "I do whatever the hell I feel like at the moment," said Kramer.

He now has two business interests. He is a partner in Single Source Telecommunications, a small company in Kansas City. Also, he and former teammate Bob Skoronski are two of three partners in Agristar, a vegetable brokerage business in Nampa, Idaho, 20 minutes from Kramer's home.

Kramer's friendship with Skoronski is an example of the theme in his book *Distant Replay*. The bonds between the two grow stronger as the years go by. "Our friendship has grown over the last five to ten years, even greater than when we played," Skoronski said. He views Kramer as an "extremely bright guy" who has "mellowed a lot. He sees life a little different than he did 15 to 20 years ago." (Skoronski spends winters in Florida and is building a new home near Madison, Wisconsin.)

While it's been 12 years since the 1984 reunion that inspired *Distant Replay*, Kramer remains close to his teammates, even if he sees them only occasionally. "It doesn't seem to matter whether I see them or not. That warmth and emotion doesn't seem to fade. There's no awkwardness. When you spend 10 or 12 years with these guys, in a very real sense they're almost like family."

Many of the players are approaching or past 60—Skoronski is 62, semi-retired and looking for his first Social Security check—so football is no longer the focus of their lives. "It seems like a faint dream, but it seems like yesterday at times," Kramer mused. As he watches today's bigger and better players, he eschews sentimentality for an odd sort of comfort in the knowledge that "you're not the end product of the evolutionary process." Packer players of the '60s thought they had re-set the standards of the Johnny Bloods and Buckets Goldenbergs of the old Packer teams. They thought they were the greatest players in the world, Kramer said; they were for a few years. The level of individual talent in the NFL may be higher now, but no teams have taken the place of the 1960s Packers, who set the standard of excellence for teamwork and whose timeless values still inspire people. Said Kramer, "It was a wonderful trip. I'd take it again in a heartbeat."

Lombardi's last game as coach of the Packers was Super Bowl II, the Packers' third straight NFL title. After the game, Lombardi was carried from the field on the shoulders of Forrest Gregg and Kramer. A famous photo of the moment shows Lombardi with his arm around Kramer's helmet and patting Kramer on the cheek in a instant that's a mixture of pure elation, affection, and appreciation. Their eyes are locked onto each other. "It's a wonderful picture. Look at my eyes and look at his eyes. It was a love affair," Kramer recalled. The love affair hasn't ended, not with Kramer, Packer fans, or the Americans who still look to a team and a coach as an inspiration. Vince Lombardi lives.

Doug Hart

For many Packers of the 1960s, success didn't end when they hung up their jerseys. One of the enduring fascinations with the players from those teams is how they applied Vince Lombardi's principles beyond football, elevating their Packer days to a life-changing experience.

Meet Doug Hart, 57, president and chief operating officer for Satellite Industries Inc. of Plymouth, Minnesota, a western suburb of

Minneapolis on the edge of the prairie. Since rising to the top position in 1984, Hart has seen his company become the world leader in the manufacture of portable restrooms, those chains of blue cubicles that are parked at construction sites, concerts, and athletic events. Satellite does business in 50 countries, including China. Hart has managed a new division of the company, Satellite Shelters, which accounts for one-third of Satellite's business. The new division manufactures and leases mobile offices and modular buildings. "We're working on becoming a world-class manufacturer, and we're coming right along with that," said Hart, who lives a short drive from work in Long Lake, Minnesota.

On a sunny May day, Hart stood outside the beige brick Satellite factory wearing a striped shirt open at the collar, reading glasses hanging from his neck, and awaiting a call from Germany. The Super Bowl II ring was on his right hand, and he explained how bits of the green tourmaline stone under the three diamonds had chipped off and needed repair. The other championship rings, he explained, were in a safe deposit box.

Hart acknowledges that Lombardi's coaching philosophy has made a big impact on his football afterlife. "I would be a much different person today if I hadn't gone through then what I went through. It was an overhaul in my way of thinking. Just having played for Lombardi and listening to him talk about things for five years—it becomes your way of thinking. My concentration level was so high, even for a couple of years after I played."

Lombardi's tenets have become so ingrained that Hart is in some respects a shadow of his former coach. For example, Hart often talks of the philosophy about how "in the final analysis we're judged by performance." That's Doug Hart talking, but echoing Lombardi's voice. "I mirror him in many things that I do. I never had a crossroad when I wanted to emulate him, but I heard the wisdom and value of what he had to say. Some of the things come back and you take them on as your own thoughts, but you know what the source is."

Hart, his once-black hair now streaked with gray, laughed easily when reminded of Lombardi's legendary temper and how Lombardi wasn't very good at telling jokes, which made him seem comical but endearing. Hart remembers Lombardi one time bellowing at him, "Douglas, Douglas, you're the ugliest!" and then roaring with laughter and walking away.

Hart was hired by Satellite in 1979 after spending seven years with Arctic Cat Snowmobiles. He first became associated with Arctic Cat during his playing days, ran a distributorship in Neenah, Wisconsin, in the mid-1970s, and became a corporate vice-president in 1976. When his playing days were winding down, Hart considered a career in broadcasting. He co-hosted the Packerama TV show for five years with several players, including Bart Starr, Dave Robinson, Jim Carter, and Fuzzy Thurston. "I did give [TV] a lot of thought, but I had in my mind before my football career was over that I wanted to be the president of a company. I had been looking forward to it."

Now he's the coach, so to speak. At least three times a day, he walks through the plant and talks with workers, a Lombardi-like trait of knowing how to push and how to be a friend. Hart occasionally puts in long hours—whatever he needs to get the job done. He learned by example; his father was in the permanent rather than port-a-potty business—a plumber. "You go from an individual performer to someone who manages other peoples' behavior. There are those times when you really feel successful when you accomplish something. You've got to be forward-thinking—one, two, three years out on what you want your company to be doing."

Hart, who with his wife Marilyn has three grown children, still enjoys bird hunting. When he was a Packer, Hart and former teammate Carroll Dale regularly went grouse hunting on Mondays. On Sunday afternoons now, he listens to football on the radio while driving through the woods of Minnesota or Wisconsin en route to a hunting site. He follows the Packers and the Minnesota Vikings, but not religiously. "One of the things you think about when you're playing is what everybody else does on Sunday afternoons. It's kind of nice now," Hart said.

For 10 years, Hart's Sunday afternoons were anything but relaxed. Year after year, he believed he had to prove himself, and year after year he did. "I spent nine years thinking that one year it would be over. I just kept making cuts."

A native of tiny Handley, Texas, near Fort Worth, Hart wasn't a shoo-in pro player. He signed as a free agent out of the University of Texas-Arlington in 1963 with St. Louis. The Cardinals cut him, but the Packers picked him up. "I was really surprised when I was called by the Packers," Hart recalled. The fact that Lombardi wanted Hart in itself gave Hart confidence, Jerry Kramer recalled. "The Packers had high expectations. Hart knew they thought a lot of him because they wanted him, and because of that he thought more of himself."

Hart spent 1963 on the Packers' taxi squad. Then in 1964 he made the team and started five games, making the first of his 15 career interceptions. In 1965, the 6' 1", 190-pound Hart became the starting right cornerback. An injured foot prevented him from playing in the NFL title game win over Cleveland. "Bob Jeter came in and played really well," Hart recalled. Jeter won the right cornerback job in 1966 and in 1967. But in 1968, the speedy Hart returned to the starting lineup as strong safety, where he remained until he retired.

That comeback of sorts was an example of the diligence he learned from Lombardi, a trait Hart retains to this day. "If there's something we decide to do at work, I'm not easily swayed off of it. During a recession period, you have to make your company succeed. Sometimes just your will makes you succeed."

Lombardi couldn't have said it better.

CHAPTER

The Green Bay ex-Packers

Fred "Fuzzy" Thurston
Guard, 1959-1967

1995 Alumni Reunion

Tony Canadeo
Fullback, 1941-1944, 1946-1952

Finding *former Packer players in the Green Bay area isn't difficult, much as it's easy to get a glimpse of movie stars whenever you're in Hollywood. Just turn on the TV or the radio to hear them at work in Green Bay, open the telephone book white pages to find their phone numbers, buy a newspaper to get their opinions, attend a charity fund-raiser to see them in person or . . . go for a beer to reminisce.*

Fred "Fuzzy" Thurston

Drive out of downtown Green Bay on Monroe Street, along the Fox River, and you'll find Fuzzy's Shenanigan's bar next to Allouez Liquor in a modest residential area. If a big car is parked outside, chances are there will be a big man inside, 6' 1", 250-pound guard Fuzzy Thurston, surrounded by walls nearly papered with historic photos from the Packer glory years. There's Fuzzy leading a sweep. Fuzzy and Hornung. Fuzzy and Bart. Fuzzy and Vince. Fuzzy and nearly every one of the 1960s Packers. And Fuzzy and Mike Holmgren.

There's Fuzzy in the flesh at the bar as beef sizzles on a nearby grill. Still a bull-like man, he has mountainous shoulders and a square, low-set head that looks like it either was designed for ramming or simply was rammed many times. An amiable, teddy-bear shaped man, he's more than an old hero in Green Bay. He has become a cuddly figure of a Packer era that fans won't let go.

He owes his popularity largely, of course, to having played for Vince Lombardi's five title teams. Yet Fuzzy, who grew up in Wisconsin in the tiny west-central town of Altoona and who understands the significance of Packer nostalgia, has cultivated his own cult-like following in recent years with his undying loyalty to Green Bay.

He hasn't left since arriving in 1959 in one of Lombardi's first trades. At age 61, he is more involved than ever with the Packers, selling package weekends to Packer games through his bar, working for Packer Fan Tours as an ambassador for road games, attending Packer Fantasy Camps and making charity appearances. He can't get enough of the Packers, and vice versa. "People seem to be for some reason impressed with the '60s more as we get older. I think people realize they want to say thank you one more time," Fuzzy theorized.

Of course, the 1960s afterglow helps his bar. Filled with Packer memorabilia, it has become a Mecca for fans from around the country. Chances are you'll see Fuzzy in person too if it's the night before a Packer game. On September 16, 1995, the eve of the Packers-New York Giants game, he was still at the packed watering hole near midnight signing shirts and hats with big sweeps of his meaty arms. Empty beer cans lined the brick window ledge outside as rock music blared into the crisp fall night. A female bartender wore a smile and an oversized Packer shirt that read "Love, Fuzzy" on the shoulders. Behind the bar serving with Fuzzy were two other Packer greats, Willie Davis and Willie Wood, who came to town for the annual Packer NFL Alumni gathering. It was nirvana for Packer fans. Ditto for Fuzzy, who dearly loves the combination of a beer and a

Packer crowd. "We had fans [that night] from Nebraska, Oklahoma, Michigan, Minnesota, Indiana . . . We get them from Europe. We opened 11 years ago, and it's now very, very popular," he said from behind the bar, which is managed by his son, Mark.

"I love coming down here. I love this business and love people. Everybody knows me like the guy next door. I'm not a big celebrity type, and people appreciate that. I never turn down an autograph, and people appreciate that too."

If Fuzzy seems down to earth despite the six NFL championship rings he owns (five with Packers, one with the Baltimore Colts), it's because he had humble beginnings and some humbling experiences. His success is a tribute to his resiliency. More than ever in his life, Fuzzy is showing with his resurgent popularity and perseverance that he still has the mettle of a champion. Maybe that's why Packer fans love him so, even though he wasn't one of the marquee names of the 1960s like Starr, Nitschke, Kramer, Hornung, or Taylor. "Lombardi said everybody falls a couple of times," said Fuzzy, who was All-Pro in 1961 and 1962. "The main thing is to get up."

In 1992, he had two hip replacements because "I ran a lot of sweeps." He walks five miles daily to keep his new joints working, saying he finds it easy to obey his doctor's rehabilitation regimens. Why? "I played for Lombardi."

In the early 1980s, he suffered a double blow that would have put most people down for good. First, he was diagnosed with throat cancer and had his voice box or larynx removed. Once an entertaining dinner speaker and leader of many a party and team chorus, he now forces a gravely whisper. "That was tough. I was one of the loudest on the team. I would sing a lot, party a lot, be crazy." Rather than hide from public appearances, which he said many people do after his type of surgery, Fuzzy now makes more than ever.

Next, his 20-year-old chain of 11 Left Guard restaurants in Wisconsin went out of business. The first one had opened in Neenah, Wisconsin, on Mother's Day in 1961, with Fuzzy serving the first meal to his mom. In the long run, success was the enemy. "We had too many of them, that was the problem," he said. Fuzzy lost his home and many other personal possessions. "There were a lot of difficult days. The only thing I had left was my attitude," he recalled.

Fuzzy was tested early in life too. His father died of a heart attack one night after playing pool at a local pub. Five-year-old Fuzzy woke up the next morning fatherless, his mother struggling to raise seven children on $40 a month. With money short, Fuzzy spent one summer as a teenager in Florida loading so many watermelons onto trucks that he said he never wanted to see another one. Now he owns a home in Florida and spends winters there.

He has carried his nickname since birth. A sister saw his crop of fuzzy black hair and started calling him Fuzzy. Oddly, this was the same way Earl Lambeau got his nickname "Curly." And like Curly Lambeau, athletics changed Fuzzy Thurston's life. As a standout guard on the Altoona High School basketball team in 1951, he got a scholarship to Valparaiso University in Indiana. As a junior, he took up football when the coach spotted his expanding, muscular frame. By his senior year he was a team captain and a small college All-American lineman.

Altoona High School's football field now is named after him, although the school didn't have football when he attended. Once, when visiting his hometown with Paul Hornung, Thurston took Hornung past the field and said, "Hornung, you may be great, but you don't have a field named after you."

A fifth-round draft pick of Philadelphia in 1955, he kicked around with several teams before landing with the champion Colts in 1958. Thurston was on his way to Canada to play in the Canadian Football League in 1959 when Lombardi tried to reach him. Thurston's stepfather got in touch with officials at a U.S.-Canada border crossing. Thurston was intercepted, told he was wanted by the new coach in Green Bay, and returned home to Wisconsin to become one of the famous pulling guards for the Packer sweep of the 1960s. After the Packers won Super Bowl II in 1968 for their third straight title, Fuzzy retired at age 33.

In 1994, his wife got a call one night at home from Meatloaf, the nationally known pop singer. Meatloaf had grown up a Packer fan and loved to watch Fuzzy play. He invited the Thurstons to his concert in Milwaukee, where they had front-row seats and where Fuzzy got a special introduction from Meatloaf during the show. "He said I was the best, I was his idol," Fuzzy remembered. "He liked the sweep and the way I played." Impressed with the music, he loaded up his jukebox at Shenanigan's with Meatloaf records. Now when business is hopping before or after Packer games and when someone pushes the right musical buttons, Fuzzy gets behind the bar and does his best Meatloaf impersonation.

The good times are back in Fuzzy's life—the Packers are winning, business is good, and the 1960s Packers still are in vogue. No wonder Fuzzy feels like singing again.

1995 Alumni Reunion

Thurston, Lombardi, and eight other players were inducted into the Packer Hall of Fame in 1975. That class had a 20-year reunion and homecoming in 1995. Thurston, Jerry Kramer, Ron Kramer, Willie Davis, and Jim Taylor were among nearly 80 ex-Packers who came to Lambeau Field for the game against the Giants. In a pregame ceremony, a bronze bust of Henry Jordan, another member of that 1975 class, was presented to his widow. Two months earlier Jordan had been posthumously inducted into the NFL Hall of Fame.

The Packers beat the Giants 14-6 before a record Lambeau Field crowd of 60,117. The feeling of history in the air was unmistakable. The Packers were playing the Giants for the 49th time (including five title games) since their rivalry began in 1928. When Lombardi came to coach the Packers, he left behind an assistant's job with the Giants. When the Packers rose to power in the early 1960s, they beat the Giants for championships in 1961 and 1962. In the December 30, 1962, game Taylor forever endeared himself to Packer fans by taking a beating from linebacker Sam Huff and the Giants defense but still running a playoff record 31 times for 85 yards and a TD in a 16-7 win. Jerry Kramer scored all the other Packer points in that game with three field goals and an extra point.

As the Packers went through pregame drills, the ex-athletes gathered in a corner near the end zone and got within smelling distance of pro football again. Some of the men stood silently on the very edge of the field and looked longingly at how near they were to their youth—and really how far away they were. Just over the white line was the world they once knew and loved—full pads, full contact, camaraderie. They watched with some wonder and probably jealousy the agile Reggie Whites, Ken

Ruettgers, George Teagues, and Edgar Bennetts who had taken over the jobs they once held. Realizing their dream had been spent, they turned away and gave fellow ex-Packers hearty welcomes, took pictures, and told stories.

Before the game, Chester Marcol escorted a young boy of about six onto the field, getting autographs from Hall of Famers. Marcol had just met the boy's parents in the stands; he enjoyed using his celebrity to bring joy to the ever-appreciative Packer fans. From the alumni gallery, former linebacker Dave Robinson, admired by his ex-teammates as one of the great students of the game, kept up a running commentary throughout the first half, at one point animatedly complaining that defenses no longer block the tight end at the line of scrimmage. He pointed out a Giants tight end roaming free after a snap. "It's sacrilege," he howled.

All of the former players were accorded a ceremonious moment of glory at halftime when they heard their names announced like the old days at Lambeau Field. Loud cheers went up for players like Thurston, Kramer, Taylor, Wood, Robinson, Coffman, Marcol, and others as they gave fleeting waves and crossed midfield to the sidelines, something they had done hundreds of times before, only not in sport coats, Dockers pants, and pullover shirts and not with their stomachs soft, their hands smooth and clean, and their muscles fresh.

Of course, there were recent Packers who still looked like they could play, including Jessie "The Body" Clark, a still pumped-up 1980s running back who now has a corporate car-washing business in Phoenix; Kansas prairie farmer Paul Coffman, still trim and limber; and svelte Ken Stills, the ex-safety who is assistant general manager for the Milwaukee Mustangs of the Arena Football League and a sports agent. Others, like Willie Wood, would have angered Lombardi by reporting to Green Bay overweight.

Mostly it was a gathering of large, graying men who had come to see how Green Bay, the NFL, and their teammates had changed and how to re-measure the yardstick—football—that defined their lives as young adults and to a degree always will.

The night before the game, a reception at the Packer Hall of Fame was a history book brought to life as ex-players, their families, and VIPs drank and ate and told stories. Hall of Famers lingered in front of displays of themselves and other Packer greats. Old teammates hugged each other and got down in three-point stances, paired up, and disappeared into the fall night for one more evening on the town. Coffman, still the prankster, showed up with a pink neon cap that had a long, gray ponytail attached to the back. More than a few people were taken aback until he took it off, and there was relief that Coffman hadn't flipped out and adopted a biker gang image. Then the hat found its way onto various heads, including distinguished septuagenarian running back Tony Canadeo, the former Packer vice-president, who laughingly brushed the pony tail away from his face, clearly enjoying again the friendship of fun-loving football men. Canadeo stood only inches from his Hall of Fame locker display, which featured his old leather helmet and retired Number 3 jersey.

The aura of football greatness swirled throughout the room like an electric current. By the time the night was over, there was even a rumor that Johnny "Blood" McNally, the 1920s-1930s star back, had been in attendance. He was, but only in a static, museum form. He had died years earlier.

When the alumni weekend ended, the men had bonded again: They had partied, gone to a football game, gone to a gala dress-up dinner downtown after the game, and played golf for charity together on Monday morning. They revealed to friends and strangers who they had become. They re-connected themselves to football and to Green Bay.

For some players, the connection to Green Bay was never interrupted.

Turn on the television in Green Bay and two familiar faces beam forth from local stations. Brian Noble, the linebacker who suffered a career-ending knee injury in 1992, reports sports and outdoors for the ABC affiliate, WBAY. Former center Larry McCarren has been sports director for seven years at the CBS affiliate, WFRV. In the fall of 1995, McCarren joined the Packer radio broadcast team of Max McGee and Jim Irwin. McCarren also writes a column (as does city resident Ray Nitschke) for the *Packer Report* weekly fan newspaper.

Asked why the Illinois native stayed in Wisconsin after his playing career ended, McCarren said "I played 12 years here. This is my home now. It was a fairly easy decision to make." Now he's part of the city's social fabric. "I'm a Green Bay-ite. It's amusing when I hear kids get drafted and say, 'Green Bay?' When they get up here, most of them stay.

There's an awful lot about Green Bay to like. It was a privilege to play in Green Bay. The players stick together. They don't go to 10 different suburbs after the game."

After their careers ended, roughly 26 living ex-Packers stayed in or near the city, according to John Biolo, who works with the Green Bay chapter of the NFL Alumni Association and organizes the player homecoming game each September. Many former Packers, such as TV announcer John Anderson, live in the Milwaukee area. Biolo himself is a former Packer, having played guard on the 1939 championship team. He didn't stray far from Green Bay after 1939 either, acting as a player/assistant coach in 1941-1942 for the Kenosha (Wisconsin) Cardinals, who were coached by Johnny Blood. Biolo then settled down to coach and teach at nearby St. Norbert College in DePere and at Green Bay West High School before retiring.

Other ex-Packers who played and stayed in the Green Bay area include three 1950s era ends, Jim Temp (insurance), John Martinkovic (retired from auto sales), and Gary Knafelc (businessman). Knafelc has been the Lambeau Field public address announcer since retiring in 1964. Temp is on the Packer executive committee. Then there are 1960s tackle Bob Skoronski (Appleton businessman), 1970 kicker Dale Livingston (teacher), 1970s linebacker Paul Rudzinski (sales), 1970s lineman Steve Okoniewski (principal at Luxemburg-Casco High School), 1970s running back Eric Torkelson (sales), 1970s-1980s safety Johnny Gray (teacher), 1980s linebacker John Dorsey (Packer scout), and 1980s fullback Gerry Ellis (sales). Ken Bowman, 1960s center, practiced law in Green Bay for about 20 years before moving west.

Forty miles northeast of Green Bay on the Door County peninsula (Wisconsin's thumb) in Sturgeon Bay, Wisconsin, are 1960s linebacker Jim Flanigan and 1960s-1970s tackle Dick Himes. Flanigan runs Flanigan Distributing, a Budweiser beer wholesaler, and lives along the waters of Green Bay, where he also runs a campground. He has one son, talented Jim Jr., playing the defensive line and occasionally fullback and tackle eligible receiver for the Chicago Bears. Jim Jr. does not share his father's love of the Packers. Another of Flanigan's sons plays football at the University of Wisconsin. A few miles away, Himes and his wife, Sylvia, operate the wooded, well-kept Jellystone Park campground, complete with three pools, a rec hall, and a big orange statue of Yogi Bear at the gate. They have worked 14-hour summer days since Dick's retirement in 1978. Dick, who fills up the front seat of his minivan like you'd expect of an old lineman, often spends summer evenings around the pool or campfire telling tales about his younger days, when he stood toe to toe against the biggest, meanest men in the land.

Tony Canadeo

Tony Canadeo's greatest season was 1949, when he rushed for 1,052 yards. The feat is all the more amazing considering the circus atmosphere surrounding the Packers that season. They were the worst team in the NFL, struggling to a 2-10 record and finishing last for the first time since the NFL began in 1921. In addition, there was controversy over the status of longtime coach Curly Lambeau. Not the least of the distractions was the team's financial condition. Cash flow was so bad that the players held an intrasquad game on Thanksgiving Day to help keep the club afloat. Evan Vogds, a guard who played in 1948 and 1949, had vivid memories of that fund-raiser. "It snowed in the morning and we played at 2:00 p.m. A lot of merchants came out and sold fruit. There were door prizes. It was $2.50 admission, and it was packed at City Stadium. We raised almost $50,000 from an intrasquad game. That's unbelievable." Vogds, born in Johnsburg, Wisconsin, and a University of Wisconsin football star in 1941-1942, remembered that all 34 players took part. But not all was serious. Ex-Packer great Don Hutson, then in his fourth year as an assistant coach, put on a uniform again and caught a few passes at halftime. Quarterback and team comedian Ted Fritsch entertained the 15,000 fans, including doing some fake wrestling with mammoth Ed Neal, all 6' 4", 290 pounds of him. With the intrasquad game money, the Packers' financial problems began to fade. It was the Packers' last appearance at home that season. With all the distractions, it was probably to Canadeo's advantage that the team's final three games were on the road as he closed in on the defining moment of his career.

Tony Canadeo wobbled past the Lombardi Room at the Midway hotel in Green Bay, cut a couple of corners without losing speed, and finally came down in the lounge. The grand old man of Green Bay football had completed another run, and he didn't need the morning sun to highlight the sparkle in his eyes. A long football career and 20 years of kidney medication had weakened the muscles in his once marvelous legs, but he still moved with force and determination. And his voice still sounded sharp and youthful. If you closed your eyes you could imagine him, one fist clenched, shouting marching orders to linemen as he rounded a corner on a Packer sweep 50 years earlier.

He was and still is a presence. Tony Canadeo was known as the Grey Ghost of Gonzaga. He's been reincarnated as the Grey Ghost of Green Bay, a quiet, silvery, seemingly omnipresent figure. For more than half a century and parts of six decades, Canadeo has influenced the fortunes of the Packers, first as a star player and then as a member of the team's executive committee. He was there in the 1940s, playing offense and defense, *sans* face mask, and buying Packer stock for himself and his children to help the financially troubled team.

No one can claim a longer association with the Packers. Curly Lambeau helped start the team and was part of it for 30 years. Canadeo has been there for 56 of the Packers' 78 years, a marriage he is very proud of. He was on the Packer board of directors beginning in 1955 and did much to see that a new City Stadium (now Lambeau Field) was built in 1957. He traveled with the team for many years as a television commentator with Ray Scott, bringing fans the 1960s championships. He was on the team's executive committee from 1958 to 1993 (ascending to vice-president in 1982). At age 77, he remains on the board of directors. He takes part regularly in Packer festivities, goes to most games, and can be found on Lambeau Field during fantasy camps.

A seventh-round draft pick in 1941, his Packer legacy began when he helped the Packers win the division title by tying the Bears. He remembers the team's reception upon returning from Chicago. "There were flares along the tracks from DePere to Green Bay. There were so many people we could hardly get off the train."

Two of Canadeo's best years were given to his country, but he didn't lose sight of football after he went in World War II in 1944. He flew home from Fort Bliss, Texas, during the middle of the Packers' 8-2 championship season in 1944 because his wife was about to give birth to their son, Bob. Canadeo played three games that season while on furlough, playing his finale against the Bears, a 21-0 Packer loss at Wrigley Field on November 5. He didn't know the Packers had won their sixth NFL title until about a month after the December 17 title game. He had been sent to Europe and read in the *Stars and Stripes* newspaper that the Packers had beaten the New York Giants, 14-7, before 46,016 fans at the Polo Grounds in New York. When he got back after the war, Canadeo found out the Packer players had given him a half share of the title money, worth $800 to the new father.

Canadeo was in the Navy and Army, serving in the latter as a corporal in an anti-aircraft division when the war ended in 1945. He was "behind a lot of the fighting" but was in Germany on V-E Day. He also helped coach an Army football team while in Europe but didn't play himself for fear that injury might interrupt his pro career.

When he got back, he was 25, Don Hutson had retired (Hutson day was October 22, 1945) and the Packers were a new team. But they had a familiar look with their gray-haired leader once again doggedly pounding out yardage. Canadeo never was fazed when others thought he was old. He had gray hair before he was 16 at Steinmetz High School on Chicago's northwest side. He was dubbed the Grey Ghost of Gonzaga when he played for that state of Washington college near Spokane. Once an NFL referee saw Canadeo on the bottom of a pile and wondered if Canadeo were too old to be playing. Canadeo shot back: "I may be a little old, but I can still run a hell of a lot better than you can see."

At 5' 11", 195 pounds, Canadeo was an average size back, but he had Hall of Fame desire, often refusing to let opponents help him up after a tackle and occasionally thumbing his nose at them. And he wasn't just a back. He passed, punted, played strong safety, and returned kicks. All of his numbers were good. He averaged 37 yards as a punter, had nine career interceptions, averaged 11.1 yards on punt returns and 23.1 yards on kick-off returns. He was All-Pro in 1943 when he ranked fifth in the NFL with 489 yards rushing. That same season he shared single-wing passing duties with Irv Comp after the retirement of Cecil Isbell. Canadeo's throwing career included 16 TD passes and 20 interceptions. When the Packers switched to the wing-T in 1946, Canadeo settled in at halfback.

Canadeo retired after the 1952 season. The opportunity to remain a part of the Packers after his playing days, while making a living in the steel business, delighted Canadeo. "It always kept me close to the thing I liked best. The smartest thing I ever did was not go into coaching. The best thing was I had a chance to go with a steel company, Production Steel, in 1952. They allowed me to play one year while I still worked for them," recalled Canadeo, whose wife, Ruth, was born in Green Bay. At age 60 he started his own business, Canadeo Metal Sales, and operated that for nine years before retiring completely in the early 1990s.

Being part of the Packer executive committee was rewarding, Canadeo said, even through the team's ups and downs. "The only time it changes is when they're winning. When they're losing everybody knows who's on the board, and when they're winning nobody knows who's on the board. There have been good years and bad years like everything else. Over the years I wouldn't change the operation of the Packers for one minute." His loyalty to the organization was obvious. He tactfully sidestepped numerous questions about controversial people and team decisions, refusing to stick any burrs into a relationship that has been one of the centers of his life.

He takes medication daily because of a kidney transplant operation in 1972, but his health has remained good. The kidney was donated by his oldest son, Bob. In 1973, he was named to the Packer Hall of Fame. Then in 1974 the unsuspecting Canadeo was selected to the NFL Hall of Fame. "It was a shock. The greatest thrill of my life," he said at the time. "I'm just overwhelmed. You know, you never think you're going to make it, but you always dream of it anyway." Canadeo's Number 3 is one of four numbers that have been retired by the Packers. The others are Don Hutson's Number 14, Bart Starr's Number 15 and Ray Nitschke's Number 66.

Three was an appropriate number for Canadeo. In 1949 when he rushed for 1,052 yards he became the third NFL rusher to reach that milestone. Beattie Feathers did it first with 1,004 for the Chicago Bears in 1934, followed by Steve Van Buren's 1,008 for the Philadelphia Eagles in 1947. Van Buren took some of the shine off Canadeo's accomplishment by rushing in 1949 for 1,146 yards. Canadeo is third on the Packer all-time rushing list with 4,197 yards, behind Jim Taylor (8,207) and John Brockington (5,024).

He hit it big in 1949 during the low point in team history. Canadeo averaged 5.1 yards per carry, but the Packers' 2-10 record was their worst ever. He topped the 1,000-yard mark in the final game of 1949, rushing 14 times for 77 yards in the mud and fog in a 21-7 loss at Detroit. He joked that he didn't get the game ball because "the Packers couldn't afford it." Canadeo made $8,500 in 1949 and got a raise to $10,000 after his big season. He gained yards that season the hard way, too. The season was just 12 games, he had just 12 yards in one game against the Redskins, and he also played defense at times. He was also 30 years old and probably past his prime.

The game when Canadeo topped 1,000 yards turned out to be Curly Lambeau's last. Lambeau resigned on January 31, 1950. The team had financial trouble partly because the competing All-America Football Conference was back in business after the war, and competitive pressures raised salaries. The Packers' troubles were partly blamed on Lambeau. He was called the "Early of Hollywood" after he began spending winters in California in the late 1940s. He sometimes spent games sitting in the press box and left the coaching to his assistants. "He was a good person, but he liked to win above everything," Canadeo recalled. "He was a dedicated football man, a motivator. He had great ideas and was ahead of his time. He set up the 5-4 defense. He was one of the first to do that." Lambeau died of a heart attack in Door County in 1965, after which City Stadium was renamed in his honor.

Like Lambeau, the name Canadeo has become synonymous with Packer football. Someday, something in Packerland will be named after him, a road like Canadeo Way or Canadeo Drive. The Grey Ghost of Green Bay deserves as much. As someone who has spent most of his life helping and watching the organization move forward, there always has been and always will be—or so it seems—the name Tony Canadeo in Green Bay.

CHAPTER

Frozen Memories

Jim Grabowski
Fullback, 1966-1970

Chuck Mercein
Fullback, 1967-1969

Jim Grabowski

The frigid day of December 31, 1967—the Ice Bowl—arguably stands as the greatest in Packer history, but it is also crystallized in Jim Grabowski's memory because it was so inglorious for him. While the Packers were playing their way to the pinnacle of success, Grabowski was on the sidelines enjoying the game only as much as one can when his future suddenly is in doubt. "I was thrilled for my teammates and for myself being part of the team," Grabowski said, "but it was bittersweet."

The 6' 2", 220-pound second-year player was scheduled to start at fullback. But shortly before the game, Grabowski, Number 33, was running a warm-up pass pattern. While running that route, Grabowski made a cut. His right knee gave out. The turf at Lambeau Field, frozen solid despite heating coils in the ground, didn't cause the injury. That had happened two months earlier when he tore knee cartilage during a game. He had been playing on the wounded knee ever since. When it buckled in warmups, Grabowski knew immediately that his day—and possibly much more—was over. But he didn't leave; he stood on the sidelines and "froze my tush off. I wasn't going anywhere." The cold was good for one thing—he didn't need to go into the locker room to get ice for the knee.

Now Grabowski knows that afternoon was the beginning of the end to his once-heralded NFL career, a career that some say could have been as great as Jim Taylor's or Jim Brown's. Three knee surgeries later, in 1971, the former first-round draft pick and half of the "Gold Dust Twins" (with Donny Anderson) was cut by the Packers. "It always affected my play," Grabowski said about his knee problem. "My leg was never the same. I couldn't get any drive off that leg. If it happened today I'd be fine. In those days there was no arthroscopic surgery. If I have any regrets, it's that the medical advice wasn't the best at that time. But I never dwell on it."

As an understudy to fullback Jim Taylor, Grabowski gained just 127 yards in 29 carries his rookie season in 1966 as the Packers won their first Super Bowl. He began to shine in 1967 after Taylor's departure to New Orleans. In the first half of the season, he set a club record with 32 rushing attempts against the Bears. "I felt I was just starting to play as a pro. I was just getting to know the game," Grabowski said.

Then in the eighth game of the 1967 season, Grabowski's right knee suffered its first injury. The Packers were playing the Colts in Baltimore. "It was a fullback option outside and as I took it outside the cornerback, Bobby Boyd, tackled me and I felt [the cartilage] pop right there. I was right next to the sidelines so I crawled off the field. At first it didn't look like it was much, but it was serious enough." On the previous series, the Packers had lost halfback Elijah Pitts with a torn Achilles tendon, Grabowski recalled. The Packers wound up losing the game 13-10.

Grabowski didn't go on injured reserve. He continued to try to play. "I felt like I was obligated to hang in there, but I kept reinjuring it," said Grabowski, who like most of Vince Lombardi's players grimly tried to follow their leader's command to ignore pain. He reinjured the knee two or three times, suffering more extensive damage as a result. Grabowski had surgery a week after the Ice Bowl. The injury helped make an Ice Bowl hero out of backup fullback Chuck Mercein, who made several big plays on the game-winning drive.

Grabowski's legs always will have a place in football history because he broke Red Grange's running records at the University of Illinois. Grabowski, who grew up in Chicago, set six Big Ten records while running for 2,878 yards at Illinois. He had 1,258 yards in an All-American senior year.

With halfback Paul Hornung and Taylor both aging, the Packers were looking to the future. They drafted halfback Donny Anderson on the first round in 1965 as a future selection (Anderson didn't play until 1966). In 1966, they got their fullback, Grabowski (after trading Ron Kramer to Detroit to get the Lions' first pick). Grabowski spurned the advances of Miami and the New York Jets of the then-rival American Football League to sign with the Packers. "I never regretted it. I was thrilled to be a Packer." And the Packers were thrilled to have him. With burgeoning television contracts, the Packers had a fat wallet and opened it for Anderson ($650,000 contract) and Grabowski ($350,000), much to the surprise of established players who were used to five-figure contracts that they had to fight Vince Lombardi for, even after championship seasons. For example, 10 years earlier Paul Hornung was making just $15,000 a year. The Packers had an unheard-of $1 million backfield; the "Gold Dust Twins" were born.

A big portion of Grabowski's contract was deferred so that he made just $15,000 in salary his rookie season. However, that same season he also got a $9,400 players' share from the NFL title game and a $15,000 players' share from Super Bowl I. "I'll never forget practicing the week before [Super Bowl I]. Fuzzy Thurston said that $15,000 was three times what he made the first year in the league, and Forrest Gregg said it was two times what he made his first year," Grabowski remembered.

While Anderson and Grabowski showed signs of meeting the high expectations brought on by their big contracts, they didn't bring any more glitter to Titletown. Grabowski led the Packers in rushing in 1967 with 466 yards, despite his knee injury. He gained a career-high 518 yards in 1968, but his production fell the next two years and Dan Devine cut him prior to the 1971 regular season. He still riles at the thought of how his association with the club ended. It was customary when a player was cut to inform him at night when few other players were around. Grabowski came to practice, suited up, and was on the field when an assistant coach took him aside and informed him he had been cut. Devine, in his first year as coach, never did talk to Grabowski about the decision. "It was classless the way [Devine] did it," Grabowski said, although he doesn't dispute Devine's decision to cut him.

Grabowski played with the Chicago Bears in 1971 then retired. He gained 1,582 yards as a Packer, which for many years ranked him among the top 20 team rushers of all time. Anderson played two more years than Grabowski, wound up with 3,061 yards (seventh best all time) and was inducted into the Packer Hall of Fame in 1983. Grabowski is not in the Packer Hall. Grabowski and Anderson were roommates for five years, and they remain close friends. Anderson lives in the Dallas, Texas area.

Grabowski, 51, lives in Palatine, Illinois, with his wife and has two grown daughters. He is a principal owner of Great Lakes Telecommunications, a 75-employee company that sells long-distance telephone services at a discount to businesses, taking advantage of tariff laws that allow his business to sell AT&T service cheaper than AT&T can. "We can go anywhere AT&T goes. You still get your AT&T bill but with a 22 percent discount," Grabowski explained, adding that the hardest job is getting customers to believe this is possible. An Academic All-American, he has put his business administration degree to good use.

Grabowski, who alternates wearing his Super Bowl rings, also learned lessons from football and Vince Lombardi that guide him at work and in his personal life. Those years shaped his present attitudes about such moral directives as perseverance. When he finds himself in difficult business situations, he still can hear Lombardi saying, "If you believe it's going to happen, it will happen."

On fall weekends for almost 20 years, Grabowski has announced University of Illinois football games, most recently with Neil Funk, who also is the radio voice of the Chicago Bulls. Grabowski enjoys golf and lifts weights regularly, still displaying impressive biceps and shoulders. There is one activity he doesn't try anymore. Knee surgeries in 1968, 1970, 1971, and 1973 (after he retired), put an end to what Grabowski loved to do most—run.

Chuck Mercein

Jim Grabowski's injury before the Ice Bowl changed the life of one other person—his backup, Chuck Mercein, who was one of the stars of the game and who was pictured on the cover of *Sports Illustrated* the following week.

Yet that night after the Ice Bowl, Grabowski was happy for his teammate. "We went to dinner after the game," Mercein said. "[Jim] was very gracious about it. He said he knew he couldn't have done any better. He was not resentful or bitter at all."

The Ice Bowl was the crowning moment of Mercein's six seasons in the NFL. Now 52, his long business career has taken him to the position of manager of over-the-counter institutional stock trading for the Wall Street firm of Furman Selz Inc. He also is owner of *Chuck Mercein's Giants Xtra,* a New York Giants fan newspaper he started in 1990. Mercein, a 1965 second-round draft pick by the Giants, oversees the publication of 30 issues a year.

Mercein was born in Milwaukee and attended school in suburban Shorewood until fifth grade, when his family moved to Chicago. He was high school All-State in Illinois before attending Yale, where he was All-Ivy League. He is one of just three Yale alumni to play for the Packers, the others being tight end John Spagnola in 1989 and quarterback Brian Dowling in 1977. Dowling became a symbol for political cartoonist Gary Trudeau, another Yale graduate, in the nationally syndicated *Doonesbury* strip. Trudeau and Dowling attended Yale in the late 1960s. Trudeau often uses the character B.D. (ostensibly, Brian Dowling), who always wears a helmet, usually a football helmet.

Mercein recalls vividly how he became a Packer. He was trade bait because he feuded with Coach Allie Sherman. When the Packers lost Grabowski and Elijah Pitts in the same game halfway through the season (leaving only Donny Anderson healthy in the backfield), a nervous Lombardi saw a third straight title slipping away. He got on the phone to Giants owner Wellington Mara. The sharp-eyed Lombardi remembered Mercein, who will never forget the feeling of being wanted by Lombardi himself. "It was arranged between Lombardi and Wellington Mara. I'll never forget when Coach [Lombardi] called. Other teams were pursuing me. I was about to go to Washington. I was sitting in my house on a Sunday night, the phone rang and it was Lombardi. I said, 'Yes sir.' And I told my wife to unpack the car, we're going to Green Bay. I was very impressed. I was flattered. It was humbling. Also, I was going virtually from the outhouse to the penthouse. [The Giants] were terrible," Mercein remembered.

Although he never became a Packer star and doesn't have any statistics that rival the 1960s heroes, Mercein won't be forgotten. He accounted for 35 of the 68 yards in the 12-play final drive of the Ice Bowl, which culminated with Bart Starr's 1-yard sneak with 13 seconds to play to give the Packers a 21-17 win over Dallas.

Mercein, a 6' 2", 220-pound fullback, recalled the two key plays that he made. First, he caught a 19-yard pass in the left flat from Starr to take the ball to the 11-yard line. The pass came on a first-and-ten from the 30-yard line with 1:35 to play. "I told Bart in the huddle that I was open. He remembered," Mercein said. When recounting the drive years later, Starr remembered Mercein's key suggestion and called him a "perceptive" player. On the next play, Mercein got the call on a "give or sucker play" and powered his way down to the two yard line. "I thought I was going to score, but I couldn't cut on the ice," he recalled.

Two hand-offs to Donny Anderson failed to put the ball in the end zone but gave the Packers a first down at the one yard line. Starr then called a 30-wedge play, which meant Mercein would get the ball. However, Starr fooled nearly everyone when he took the snap, waited for the hole to open between Jerry Kramer and Ken Bowman, and pushed through for the winning TD. A classic end-zone photo of the play shows Starr on the ground with Mercein above him, his arms outstretched in what appears to be a TD signal. However, Mercein actually was holding up his arms to show the official that he wasn't pushing Starr in; thinking he was going to get the ball on the play, Mercein was right behind Starr.

Still banged up from the Ice Bowl, Mercein played only "a little" in the Super Bowl win over the Oakland Raiders, but his place in Packer history was secure. He still has copies of the *Sports Illustrated* Ice Bowl issue sent to him to autograph. "It was some thrill to come to the Packers and play in the Ice Bowl. God has smiled on me with my timing. I was never with as many men I admire as with that team. There have never been so many great men assembled on one team."

Midway through the 1969 season, Mercein was placed on waivers by Coach Phil Bengston. He went directly to Washington at the behest of Lombardi and spent the rest of the season on the Redskins' inactive list. When Lombardi died prior to the 1970 season, Mercein said he and other ex-Lombardi players were cast aside by the Redskins. He spent 1970 with the New York Jets before retiring.

When Lombardi was dying of colon cancer, Mercein and teammate Vince Promuto were the last two players to see him alive. They left training camp on September 2, 1970, to visit Lombardi in the hospital. "There was just small talk. I thanked him for everything he had done, and I just said good-bye. I remember how terribly sick he looked. I was shocked because he did have that aura of strength, gruffness, toughness about him. It was hard to see someone fail that quickly. When I got outside the room, I started to cry and I kept crying."

Lombardi died at 6:12 a.m. on Thursday, September 3, 1970. He was 57. He had gone into the hospital for the first time on June 27 that summer to have part of his colon removed. He returned to the hospital in late July.

Lombardi's "Commitment to Excellence" speech still hangs on the wall of Mercein's Park Avenue office. A picture of Lombardi hangs in his New York City apartment. And Mercein is wearing out his Super Bowl ring, the one that has three diamonds (for three titles) and is inscribed with the Biblical saying "Run to win," a phrase the devout Lombardi used that season to inspire the team.

Even though Lombardi is gone, the ring represents a cherished memory: Mercein helped the Packers run to win in 1967.

Making a Living Off the Land

Gale Gillingham
Offensive tackle, 1966-1974, 1976

Tommy Joe Crutcher
Linebacker, 1964-1967, 1971-1972

Gale Gillingham

He came out of Minnesota with enough fanfare and hype to match his lumberjack frame and billboard-sized publicity sheet, a 1960s version of Tony Mandarich. The world champion Green Bay Packers had made him their Number One pick in the 1966 draft. Although the Packers had a star-studded offensive line, heroes like Forrest Gregg, Fuzzy Thurston, and Jerry Kramer were aging and injury-prone. Everyone predicted that the 6' 5", 265-pound Gillingham would soon fill some big shoes at guard. To Gillingham's credit, he measured up to all the oversized expectations. By the end of the 1966 championship season, he was starting. By 1969, he was All-Pro.

Nearly 30 years after that thumbs-up debut and 20 years after retiring, the fanfare and hype are far from Gillingham's life. Today, he is the owner of Goedkar Realty in Little Falls, Minnesota, population 7,500. When asked if his status as resident celebrity helps him do business, he replied acerbically, "I really don't think people give a darn." (Little Falls also is famous for another resident, the late aviator Charles Lindbergh, who grew up there and whose home now is the city's main tourist attraction.)

Gillingham lives in the country outside of Little Falls, which is 100 miles north of Minneapolis-St. Paul and 30 miles from St. Cloud. He deals in farms, recreational land, and $50,000 homes. Hunting and snowmobiling are big in Morrison County. The largest employer is Camp Ripley, a National Guard training center. Another big employer makes boats. Gillingham, still an imposing, square-chested man, blends right into rural Minnesota with his beard, jeans, flannel shirts and his love for hunting.

The daily operation of a small business in a small town brings little adulation for Gillingham, but he no longer lives by the opinions of others. He's comfortable with his own opinions, of which he has many, and is as fulfilled with the work he does now as the work he did in the 1960s and 1970s. "I think I'm extremely good at it. I'm up front and people appreciate it." He approaches selling real estate in much the same way he approached blocking people like former Dallas Cowboys star Bob Lilly. He's committed and relentless. "As far as effort, yes. As far as enthusiasm, yes. But I have to be more of a negotiator. If you can't negotiate, you can't last [in real estate]."

Gillingham has been living in Little Falls ever since he was a teenager. He was born in Madison, Wisconsin, moved to nearby Stoughton at age five and moved north to Tomah, Wisconsin, at age 13. He moved to Little Falls three years later as his parents gave up farming and his father began selling real estate. He starred at the University of Minnesota as a tackle, and the Gophers also played him at running back, using his 5.9 speed in the 50-yard dash.

Upon retiring after the 1976 season, Gillingham went back to Little Falls, lost his Super Bowl I earnings in a failed cattle ranch, and eventually bought the real estate business. Although he was tempted to get into coaching, he has been content to stay in Little Falls and raise his family of three sons and one daughter. He is divorced. Although none of the boys played football, two of them, Brad and Karl, have surpassed Dad in the weight room as national-caliber power lifters. Dad still lifts four times a week at his private weight room, and at 280 pounds is just as big, if not bigger, than ever, but not as strong as his sons. "They're in their prime. I'm just an old guy now," he explained.

A less-than-joyous ending to his career might have contributed to Gillingham spurning the coaching world. The years 1966 through 1973 were mostly productive and enjoyable for Gillingham. He played occasionally early in 1966 and was starting by season's end. In 1967, he replaced Fuzzy Thurston in the starting lineup at left guard. Gillingham started ahead of Thurston in Super Bowl II, but Thurston swallowed his pride and tutored Gillingham for days prior to the game. "Everybody was helpful in those days. It was kind of like family," said Gillingham, a smashing drive blocker who now is ranked with the other great Packer guards, such as NFL Hall of Famers Jerry Kramer and Mike Michalske.

He missed virtually all of the 1972 season, when the Packers won their division, when he was hurt playing defense early in the year. Coach Dan Devine had decided that the best use for Gillingham would be as a defensive tackle. Did Gillingham agree with the decision? "Not when you're the best guard in the league."

His experience on defense was a prelude to his final two seasons. In 1974, front-office and sideline sparring led to Devine's resignation and the hiring of Bart Starr as coach shortly after the season ended. Gillingham was a team captain that year. "There was no such thing as not picking a side. We kept it together as best we could. It was the worst thing I've ever gone through in my life," he said.

Gillingham had four head coaches in less than a decade. When the Starr staff rolled in, Gillingham decided to sit out the 1975 season rather than play for Starr's offensive line coach, Leon McLaughlin. "I wanted to be traded. I didn't think I'd fit into that system, and I didn't. I had no faith in what they were doing. I had no faith in the line coach. I had enough of that crap. I had enough of losing. I didn't believe in anything we were doing as far as the offensive line goes. There was no football intelligence there at all. The assistants [Starr] started with couldn't beat Premontre [High School]."

Gillingham respected Starr as a person but not as a coach, saying Starr "didn't know his ass from page nine" when he took over. "He didn't know how to coach. I can't understand why they'd throw him in there when he wasn't ready. Then when he did learn how to coach they fired him."

When the Packers wouldn't trade Gillingham, he decided to come back in 1976. Although he started all year, he didn't return in 1977. He retired, citing philosophical differences with the coaching staff and knees that were weakened by surgeries in 1972 and 1973.

Gillingham was inducted into the Packer Hall of Fame in 1982 and returned to Green Bay with his sons in 1994 as the Packers' honorary captain for the home season opener. He attended the annual NFL alumni gathering of former Packers in September 1995, taking in the Packers-Giants game with his former linemate, Bill Lueck. "It was and still is a great organization. They had some bad years in between, but as far as I'm concerned Green Bay is the class of the league," Gillingham said.

Feelings like those help him forget the low pay—$17,500 as a rookie—he received for a decade of physical beatings. He has two bad knees today, along with bad shoulders, bad feet, and a bad back; he takes Motrin daily to relieve the pain. Yet he isn't complaining; he knew the consequences going in. "By the time you go through your freshman year at a major college if you don't know it's a damn tough business and a nasty business you're not smart enough to get through college. If you go through the [NFL] 10 years, the rest of your life will be changed."

The insidious effects of having played in the NFL go beyond the daily pain pills; they have sobered the futures of once-mighty men like Gillingham. Because the life expectancy of an NFL player is only about 50, Gillingham, who turned 50 in 1994, didn't take any chances of missing what the NFL owes him: His retirement pension. He's getting it now—just in case.

Tommy Joe Crutcher

When Green Bay beat Kansas City 35-10 on January 15, 1967, in Super Bowl I, Packer players were happy not just because they were world champions. Each player on the winning team also got $15,000, the biggest one-day payoff in team sports history. Tommy Joe Crutcher, a backup linebacker, was one of those happy players. That $15,000 helped set up his future. "I figured I'd better invest it or it would be gone," Crutcher said.

So not long after the victory, Crutcher went back home to southern Texas and looked at some land in the Rio Grande Valley. He liked what he saw—all 23,000 acres of it. He and several other NFL friends bought into a farm. Today he's general manager of a combination farm, grain elevator, and port elevator that is one of the industry leaders in Texas. "We've been fortunate. It's worked out well for me, the employees, and the stockholders too," Crutcher said.

Thanks to Super Bowl I.

The business is centered on farmland some 30 miles from McCook, Texas, about 300 miles south of Houston and near the Mexican border. A total of eight people along with Crutcher own the three divisions— Southwestern Farm and Ranch, Southwest Grain, and Port Elevator at Brownsville. During the harvest season in June and July Crutcher works long hours, but otherwise he works ten-hour days Monday through Friday overseeing up to 100 people. Southwest produces its own grain and cotton on its farmland, and it is also the central grain elevator for farmers from as far as 160 miles away. The grain processed at the elevator is sold and trucked across the Rio Grande River to Mexico.

With each shipment, Crutcher can give a little thanks not only to Super Bowl I but to the Vince Lombardi days in Green Bay, which he recalls in the wry, slow-talking Texas drawl that made him a favorite— along with his ability to win at poker—among Packer players.

Crutcher grew up on a farm in McKinney, Texas. A bachelor, Crutcher lives on his own 100-acre spread at Mission, about 15 miles from his office. He still tunes in the Packers on his satellite dish on Sundays.

The 6' 3", 230-pound All-American fullback from Texas Christian was the Packers' Number Three draft pick in 1964. The Packers switched him to defense immediately. While he never became a major force for the Packers, he still holds a unique place in team history. He is one of only a few players who played for the team twice, from 1964 through 1967 and again in 1971 and 1972. During his first tour of Green Bay, he found it nearly impossible to crack the star linebacking lineup of Ray Nitschke, Dave Robinson, and Lee Roy Caffey. The Packers carried just four linebackers in those days.

The highlights of his first stint with the Packers were Super Bowl I and the 21-17 win over Dallas in the Ice Bowl on December 31, 1967, details of which are frozen in his memory. On the key drive that led to Bart Starr's game-winning touchdown run, the Packers had third down and ten yards to go. If they hadn't converted, they likely would have tried a long field goal to try to tie the score at 17-17. Crutcher remembers Lombardi nervously talking to defensive coordinator Phil Bengston before the third-down play and saying, "If we don't make it we have to kick it, right?" Bengston, chain-smoking cigarettes, replied gruffly, "Yeah, yeah, we have to kick it." The Packers' hopes for a third straight title hung in the balance.

"It was going to be a long field goal, in the mid-40s at least, and with it as cold as it was I don't think Don [Chandler] had much chance of making it. But Starr threw a little flip pass to Donny [Anderson] and we got the first down. After that we were in decent field-goal range," Crutcher remembered.

As Bart Starr huddled the team on third down from the one before his now-famous quarterback sneak to win the game, Crutcher anxiously wondered if it would be the last play of the game. Only 13 seconds remained and the Packers had no timeouts left. "We weren't very well organized. If we didn't make it were we going to try a field goal or another sneak? I don't know if we would have had enough time left. Anyway, Bart made it."

After Starr's TD sneak gave the Packers a 20-17 lead, Crutcher remembers going onto the field as part of the extra-point team. He remembers because after standing around in minus-16 degree cold for much of the game, including the entire 68-yard, 12-play TD drive, the TV timeout before the kick seemed "like a hell of a long time."

Because of the cold weather, several players tried to prevent frostbitten toes by layering a sock, then a plastic bag and then another sock over their feet. It seemed to help some, but Crutcher remembers his toes still being "a little dark," a telltale sign of frostbite. He specifically remembers Ray Nitschke's toes being discolored after the game.

At one point during the game, a teammate told Crutcher that his nose was white, a sign that he had frostbite. He was told to stand next to one of the sideline heaters, but when he did other players told him that his nose would fall off if he did that. Eventually he was given a cup to place over his nose, and his body heat slowly warmed the appendage.

He recalls that the Packers were perceived to have an advantage because they were a cold-weather team, but he points out that the Packers had more players from Texas on their roster than the Cowboys. At halftime, the Cowboys switched from cleats to soccer shoes to gain better footing on the field, which had become frozen despite its coil-heated subsurface. The Packers stuck with their cleats, which Crutcher thinks was a mistake. "I think it was the first test for the [field] heating system. Vince was proud of his field. We were fortunate to get down there and score [at the end]."

Playing backup was a role Crutcher didn't enjoy. After the 1967 season, he explained his feelings to management and was traded, along with tackle Steve Wright, to the New York Giants. The deal brought the Packers defensive tackle Francis Peay, who still was on the Packer roster when Crutcher returned five years later. "I was happy with the trade. I made it known that I couldn't run down kickoffs all my life," Crutcher said.

With the Giants, Crutcher got his wish to become a starter. But in the last game of his second season there, in 1969, he suffered a severe knee injury and subsequently was traded to the Los Angeles Rams, where he spent the 1970 season on the taxi squad. After that season in LA, he was traded back to the Packers for the 1971 season. His role in Green Bay was again as a backup, although he started a few games his first season under Coach Dan Devine.

He still carries Lombardi's influences with him, even though now he "doesn't consciously think back" to his playing days. He particularly remembers Lombardi's maxim that players should put God first, family second, and the Packers third in their lives. "That's one of the things I think of more than anything. It's one thing I try to get instilled in the people in my company."

And what about Lombardi's most famous saying, that winning is the only thing? Did Lombardi really believe that? "In my rookie year, 1964, I went to camp with all the other rookies and free agents. The year before that the Packers had gone down to Miami to play in the [NFL] runner-up game. Vince asked us, 'Does anybody know where we finished last year? One of the guys raised his hand and said second place. Vince said, 'Wrong! We finished last! There are only two places. Either you're the champions or you're nothing.' "

After the 1972 season in Green Bay, Crutcher decided to retire because the knee injury limited his ability. Besides, he knew nothing would match his Packer memories from his first tour of duty.

CHAPTER

The Role Players

Marv Fleming
Tight end, 1963-1969

Carlos Brown
Quarterback, 1975-1976

Marv Fleming

You may not have heard about Marv Fleming in recent years, but chances are you've seen him. He's been a hungry quarter-pounder man for McDonald's, a loving father for Polaroid, and a thirsty big guy for Michelob and Pepsi, among other products. It seems as if the only thing Fleming hasn't done for 20 years is play football, which is how most people connect to the 6' 4", 225-pound former tight end for the Packers and Miami Dolphins. Aside from acting in more than 100 commercials and performing in films and television shows, the Los Angeles-area native and resident has been a successful businessman, sports agent, and executive agent since retiring from the NFL in 1975.

So many good things have happened to Fleming that he doesn't even want to be reminded that he hit 50 a few years ago. "Wait a minute. I don't even know how old I am. That's not important," he said. Fleming seems to be speeding up rather than slowing down. He plays tennis every day and tries to ski in the winter the 20 days a month he's at his Salt Lake City, Utah, home. The other ten days each month he spends at his Marina Del Ray, California, home near Los Angeles, where he swims regularly. He checks in at a svelte 225 pounds (15 lower than his NFL days), with "no gray hairs," he adds. He even planned to get married—for the first time—to a business executive from Toronto. "It's time for me to start to share my life with someone," he said, although he already has shared much of his financial success with his mother and a brother.

How can one person be so lucky? "I still live by the Packer rule: 'Get there early' and, 'The harder you work, the luckier you get,' " Fleming explained.

Fleming had been preparing for "retirement" for many years. He studied acting in London and graduated from the Los Angeles Institute of Theater and the Arts. He became a member of the Screen Actors Guild and began appearing in films. In addition to commercials, he made cameo appearances in the movie, "Heaven Can Wait," starring Warren Beatty, and in the 1970s hit TV series, "The Mod Squad." Eventually, Fleming's other work took so much time that he had to quit acting; he hasn't been on TV or in a film for more than two years.

Fleming represented ten pro athletes a year for several years. He now works exclusively as an agent for business executives. In his new specialty, he helped a female executive get a $1 million salary with Hitachi in Japan, including an up-front signing bonus of "over a half-million. That's never been heard of before." True to his motto (work begets luck), Fleming's willingness to take Japanese for seven months probably helped close the deal.

He started getting lucky when he was drafted by the Packers.

Actually, he was drafted twice in 1963 out of Utah, despite sustaining (and recovering from) a broken neck in college. The American Football League's Denver Broncos picked him in the second round, and the Packers took him in the 11th round.

Draft dodging is why he lasted so long in the NFL draft. According to Fleming, the Broncos put word out that he had signed with them, thereby scaring off other teams. It wasn't true, he said. "The Packers called me and asked me if I had signed. Green Bay offered me a $10,000 signing bonus if I signed by 9:00 a.m. I told them I'd wait until 1:00 p.m. until I talked with a friend. They offered me $10,000 more, and I said no. Money never meant anything to me because I never had any. I had to wait." Fleming's friend arrived before he signed, and he still got the $20,000 from the Packers.

Not only that, he got the rare opportunity to play for one of the great teams of all time, a team that had won titles in 1961 and 1962 and was on its way to winning three straight beginning in 1965. Fleming was one of three important rookies drafted in 1963, along with linebacker Dave Robinson and defensive end Lionel Aldridge.

Although just 20, Fleming was the starting tight end by the end of his rookie year, replacing someone he looked up to, Ron Kramer. Although Fleming didn't catch passes the way some tight ends do today, his job was to block, and he did that well on the famed Packer power sweeps. He did catch 119 passes for 1,300 yards and score 12 TDs for the Packers. He ranked among the team's top 25 receivers of all time for 25 years after he left.

Fleming, who could run the 100 in 10.1 seconds, caught three passes for 54 yards against Dallas in the 1966 NFL title game. He also caught two passes in Super Bowl I and four in Super Bowl II. He is one of only a few starting players from the Packers' championship teams who have not been chosen for the Packer Hall of Fame.

Fleming was often an object of Coach Vince Lombardi's wrath. He told former teammate Jerry Kramer in *Distant Replay* that "Lombardi pushed me and pushed me and pushed me. And then a lot of times he'd put his hand on my shoulders and say, 'Way to go there.' No one else saw him do it, but I saw it, felt it, and I said to myself, 'This man likes me, and it's OK for him to push me, it's OK.' I love it, that memory."

Fleming believes that under Lombardi in Green Bay he matured and learned lessons about what is important in life. Such as? "When you work hard you get lucky. I learned about life in Green Bay. It gave me that initial foundation. I learned what it takes to win. I say thanks to the guys who pushed me, like Willie Davis, Bart Starr, and Ray Nitschke. I was 20 when I got there, and lot of those guys had kids."

Despite all the joy he experienced in Green Bay, Fleming went to Miami in 1970 when the Packers didn't offer him enough money. "It was my best move, money-wise. I hated to leave my friends. The thing I did miss was football in Wisconsin. I loved it. Even though they had football in Miami, it was nothing like Green Bay."

At Miami, Fleming walked into another dynasty in the making. The Dolphins lost Super Bowl VI in 1972 but went undefeated in the 1972 season and won Super Bowl VII in 1973. They also won Super Bowl VIII. Fleming was in the lineup each time, in the process becoming the first player to take part in five Super Bowls and the first ever to get four Super Bowl rings. He also has his 1965 NFL championship ring from the Packers. Fleming made $13,000 his first year with Green Bay and over $100,000 with the Dolphins when he retired.

He still wears the rings as a reminder to himself of his ability to survive and succeed. "It's something I learned from Lombardi—the master—to be a survivor. That's the true mark of a champion."

Carlos Brown

When Carlos Brown was drafted by the Packers in the 12th round out of University of the Pacific in Stockton, California, in 1975 he was inexperienced and on no one's list as a quarterback with a future. He turned out to be one of the best role players in Packer history. Except he did it as Alan Autry on television and in the movies.

He's prime time now. In the 1995-1996 television season, he was on Wednesday nights in a CBS sitcom "Grace Under Fire" starring actress Brett Butler. He played Rick, Grace's boss. After the season, he quit the show and announced that he hoped to star in his own series.

He began his TV career in 1988 when he landed the role of "Bubba Skinner," a deputy in the long-running drama "In the Heat of the Night." The show, which starred one of TV's most famous actors, Carroll O'Connor, made the 6' 3", 220-pound Autry one of the most recognizable faces on television. In 1991, *TV Guide* called him one of "TV's handsomest hunks." It was the perfect role for the muscular Brown. With the show set in Sparta, Mississippi, he was right at home because he was born in

Shreveport, Louisiana. His southern drawl wasn't an affectation. He liked the fact that the show raised racial issues because he grew up poor, picking cotton alongside itinerant workers. He was the first member of his family to go to college, using an athletic scholarship to escape the cycle of poverty. When he got to college, he got his first taste of the good life—a phone. His family never had one.

In 1981, about the time he began his acting career, Brown met his father for the first time and took his father's surname, Autry. He was born Carlos Alan Autry, but when his parents divorced he grew up with his mother's name of Brown. Alan Autry appeared in several big-screen films with noted actors, including "Amazing Grace and Chuck" (with Gregory Peck), "Southern Comfort" (with Keith Carradine), North Dallas Forty (with Nick Nolte), and "Popeye" (with Robin Williams). He also landed guest appearances on popular TV series like "Cheers," "Newhart," and "St. Elsewhere." He was in the NBC mini-series "The Great Los Angeles Earthquake" and appeared in several TV movies.

As a Packer, neither his looks nor his talent got him far. In 1975, as Number Three QB behind John Hadl and Don Milan, Brown completed a respectable three of four passes and a TD. Brown's chance to be the Packer QB came late in the 1976 season. With veteran Lynn Dickey injured, Brown started games 11, 12, and 13. He completed just one-third of his passes and the Packers lost all three games, which were all played in foul late-season weather. In one of the games, against the Vikings, Brown led a 74-yard scoring drive that briefly tied the score on a frigid November day in old Metropolitan Stadium. "I think I played in the second coldest game on record there. The only thing colder was my statistics," Brown joked.

The next year, 1977, Dickey was healthy again and Brown was cut. Brown remembers going into Coach Bart Starr's office and being complimented by Starr as a hard-working player, but Brown also remembers being very upset. "I said something like I'd come back to haunt you. But I didn't know at the time that it would be on the television screen with one of my performances."

CHAPTER

The Enforcers

Steve Odom
Wide receiver, 1974-1979

Phillip Epps
Wide receiver, 1982-1988

Estus Hood
Cornerback 1978-84

Steve Odom

Steve Odom never really looked like a football player. At 5' 8", 174 pounds, and with a baby face, he was nicknamed "Leprechaun." Odom didn't scare defenders when he played wide receiver and returned kicks for the Packers, he simply outran them. That unassuming appearance, however, was advantageous for Sgt. Odom of the Berkeley, California, police department. Odom's looks may have saved his life.

Working a "deep undercover" in the narcotics division, Odom infiltrated the Berkeley drug culture to set up a bust on local dealers and buyers. For six months, he bought drugs for a fictitious heroin-addicted girlfriend and hung out with dealers and junkies. At one point, he even drove a getaway car on demand for two armed robbers, whom he later found out had served time on homicide charges. "I understood the relationship between narcotics and crime. The burglars, the robbers—they were the ones doing the buying," Odom said. "There were times when my life was in danger, and there were times when I didn't even know it was in danger."

One night during his undercover operation, his fame as a football player almost cost him his cover. He was in a dimly lit area approaching a dealer to make a drug purchase. While walking toward the dealer, Odom recognized the man as someone he went to grade school and high school with. Odom, who grew up in Berkeley, knew he was in trouble. Immediately the dealer thought he recognized Odom and began questioning him.

Odom reassured the man that he wasn't Odom and that they didn't know each other. "He told me my whole life story," Odom says, "About how I went to Utah and how I played for the Packers." The skeptical man pressed. "You sure look like him. Are you sure you're not Stevie Odom?" Odom finally said, "Come on. Do I look like a football player?" The man took another look at the tiny (for football) Odom and agreed. He dropped the argument. They made the deal. The man eventually was arrested— one of 40 caught in the operation—and realized his mistake when he again came in contact with Odom, this time at the police station.

After his undercover success, Odom, 43, was reassigned and promoted to director of the Community Services Bureau for the Berkeley police. In that position, he has a variety of duties, mainly developing a more community-oriented police force. "Officers are encouraged to go out of their cars and make contact with people, get to know the big as well as the little problems. It's a real partnership—the police with the community and other services in the community," said Odom, who works with businesses and neighborhood watch groups and gives crime prevention and safety talks.

Odom started his law enforcement career in Southern California, where he worked as a psychologist in Westminster after leaving the NFL. He has a master's degree in psychology and is only a few classes away from his doctorate degree. He saw a "neat integration of psychology and football into one occupation in law enforcement." He wanted to blend the ideas of using teamwork to overcome a problem along with psychology in assessing the problem.

In 1982 he was accepted into a police academy in Southern California. Four months later, he graduated first in his class and became a police officer in Westminster. "I was very proud of that. It was more difficult than training camp and graduate school—not that training camp wasn't tough. They really stress you to see how you perform. You're talking about life-threatening things that can happen to you."

After two years in Westminster, he moved to the nearby Huntington Beach police department before moving in 1985 to Berkeley, the city nicknamed "Berzerkeley" for its raucous 1960s anti-war protests and counter-culture, which still exists but to a lesser degree today. "I always say they should put a fence around Berkeley and charge admission," Odom joked.

He was living across the San Francisco Bay in Oakland when he lost his home in the Oakland Hills fire on October 21, 1991. The fire killed 25 people, destroyed 3,000 homes, and caused $1.5 billion in damages. Odom lost all his possessions, including his football memorabilia, such as autographed Packer footballs, scrapbooks, pictures, and trophies. "You can replace the TV, the car, but the photos, letters—you can't replace them," said Odom, who is divorced and has a son living in Eugene, Oregon.

The Packers' fifth-round draft pick in 1974, Odom held five National Collegiate Athletic Association kick return records. He could run the 100-yard dash in 9.4 seconds. While he didn't rack up impressive numbers as a wide receiver, he always came up with big plays either as receiver or kick returner. He has three of the longest plays in Packer history—all 95-yarders, including a 1974 punt return that is still a Packer record. He averaged close to 19 yards every time he touched the ball. He led the NFL in kickoff returns in 1978 with a 27.1 average, despite missing the final four games with a broken leg. In 1976, he was named to the Pro Bowl as a return specialist.

Odom wound up with 84 career receptions, which matched the number he wore. Yet he wasn't one to tabulate his statistics. He always saw his pro football career as a stage in his personal development. He took graduate courses in psychology while he was a Packer. His football career was a period that "provided a framework for a lot of growth and development. This wouldn't be the end. It would facilitate the rest of my life."

He remembers in his second season, 1975, the year after he had been Packer rookie of the year, a young boy approached him after practice to sign a Steve Odom football card. Odom, the longshoreman's son who collected football cards as a kid, then realized he was living a dream, a dream that he knew would have to end some day. As a Christian who tried to put God first in his life, he didn't let the ego-stroking atmosphere of the NFL undermine his sense of who he was. "Who I was not associated with what I did. That's the way of the world. People want to know what you do, not who you are. It's a huge drug. If you buy into that [in the NFL] it's hard because you'll almost never be able to reach that level again."

So he focused on what was attainable, what was real, and what made him truly happy when he played. He remembered getting a phone call in 1978 about an eastern Wisconsin boy named Greg Peters, a big Odom fan who had just lost both his legs in a farm accident. Odom showed up the next day at the hospital and promised the boy a game ball from his next touchdown. The next Sunday, October 15, the Packers played Seattle at Milwaukee. Odom mentioned the promise to the game's TV announcers. On the opening kickoff, Odom said a left-side return was called. "I took two steps left and there was nothing. I went to the center and it was like the parting of the Red Sea, and I remember thinking of Greg at that time." Odom went 95 yards for the touchdown and the Packers won, 45-28.

The TV announcers played up Odom's promise, and soon Peters and his family were flooded with donations, complimentary medical care, and other offers. "I knew at that time his family really needed it," Odom said. Peters eventually became a wrestler and went on to college, which pleases Odom. "I know he's doing well. Sometimes I think I only played football for one reason, Greg Peters. And if it was, that was just fine."

Phillip Epps

Scoring 16 touchdowns in seven years for the Packers doesn't compare with what Phillip Epps accomplished after only six months of working with juvenile delinquents. He helped steer a young man away from a life of crime and into school. "He had no father figure and his mom had drug problems. He had heard all his life that he'd be nothing but a thief or a thug," Epps recalled.

As assistant manager of a new program in Dallas, Epps noticed that the 17-year-old boy liked to lift weights. The affable Epps, who laughs easily and smiles often, worked on the friendship. The boy now is attending junior college and plans to play football. "I was always searching for something to get my adrenaline flowing like football, and this does. I like the rewards I get by seeing 17-year-olds turn their lives around," Epps stated.

After retiring from the NFL, Epps sold medical supplies for Damon Laboratory in Dallas for about five years, but he wanted to use the criminal justice degree he got at Texas Christian University. He was hired by the private Southwest Key Program, which sells its services to cities like Dallas. Epps worked out of the probation department up to six days a week with as many as five troubled 17- to 19-year-olds. In December 1995 he became a juvenile probation officer in Tarrant County, doing essentially the same work but now for the local government in the Dallas-Fort Worth area.

Epps always felt fortunate that he grew up with good parents in Atlanta, Texas, and that he got an education. He knows that many children come from splintered, troubled families and need someone to set them straight. The goal of his life's work now is to help rudderless youths steer away from crime and toward productive lives, help them become independent. In his work he helps them take care of family needs and find services that can aid their rehabilitation. More than that, he tries to become their friend, sometimes their only friend, sometimes their first friend. The salary, Epps says with a chuckle, isn't much, but "you can't be in it for the money. You've got to love what you do."

Unlike many of the youths he works with and many of the athletes he played with, Epps always has been focused. Even when he was a star athlete at TCU, he knew he would end up working for a living when his football days were over. He knew that the NFL probably wouldn't make him rich. He also knows of many of his NFL colleagues who didn't think that way and now have financial problems.

Although he never had a $1 million contract with the Packers, he invested well with his six-figure contracts and is "not really worried about" his family's financial situation. He and his wife, Janice, have two girls, 11 and 17, and a boy, one-year-old Phillip Jordan.

Epps knows about beating the odds. He was the Packers' 12th and final draft pick in 1982. He finished his career as the Packers' 10th best all-time receiver. From that draft, only first-round pick Ron Hallstrom and fourth-rounder Robert Brown were Packers longer than Epps.

At 5' 9½" and just 165 pounds, Epps had to rely on his speed and hands. He could run the 100 meters in 10.1 seconds, and while he was a Packer he ran the fifth fastest 60-yard dash (6.07 seconds) in American track history. He often competed in the World's Fastest Man contest. As fast as he was, Epps spent his first three years in pro football just sitting still, watching John Jefferson and James Lofton light up Lambeau Field. "I readily admit that I played *behind* those guys. I learned from the best. They were a big part of my development." Epps became a close friend of Jefferson's, mainly because Jefferson also was from the Dallas area.

When John Jefferson was traded to Cleveland in 1985, Epps found himself starting alongside Lofton. He started all 16 games, averaging 15.5 yards while making 44 catches. The next season he caught 49 balls. Injuries hampered him in 1987 and 1988. In 1989, after Sterling Sharpe's rookie season, Epps suddenly was expendable. Coach Lindy Infante cut Epps just before the regular season began. Epps spent the 1989 season with the New York Jets, then retired.

Epps may be best remembered by Packer fans for his catch that beat the Bears in 1984. Epps circled back to an under-thrown pass from QB Rich Campbell then eluded defender Terry Schmidt for a 43-yard TD to beat the Bears, 20-14, in the final minute at Soldier Field. But Epps' greatest memory isn't any one play. "The teammates are one of the things that stands out. I know it's a cliché, but [the friendships were] by far the most lasting experience."

He wants the members of his new team—those kids down at the probation department—to experience those same good feelings in their lives.

Estus Hood

When he replaced Willie Buchanon at left cornerback in 1979, Estus Hood had a high-pressure job to contain fast men. In a sense, life hasn't changed much for him. Since 1989 Hood has guarded federal convicts at the maximum security U.S. Penitentiary in Marion, Illinois, near the state's southern tip. As a senior officer specialist, he oversees inmates as they move from their cells to recreation and shower areas. At each site, Hood locks them into what are called "cages." Most of the convicts are confined to their cells 22 to 23 hours a day, Hood said. Among the fast men he covers now is infamous New York mobster John Gotti, who in 1992 began serving a life sentence at Marion for arranging the murder of his crime boss.

"This [prison] is for bad people," Hood said of Marion, adding that the only higher security facility in the country is the new supermax prison in Colorado. "There is a little danger to [the job]. Sometimes we respond to fights. But it's a relatively safe place" to work, Hood indicated. Hood is also part of a special SWAT team that gets called out to quell inmate uprisings at other federal prisons. Although he keeps his guard up, Hood has a "little interaction with inmates. You get a chance to steer a few on the right track, but very few. Some people you reach."

Hood, 41, lives in nearby Herrin, Illinois, with his wife and three school-age children. After retiring from football, Hood worked for two years in Golconda, Illinois, at a state agriculture department job corps center, where he was a recreation assistant. He also drove for United Parcel Service. Then one day at a job seminar he listened to the Bureau of Prisons recruiters. The security guard job "sounded pretty interesting. It was a good career goal for me," Hood said. He signed up, went through a three-week training program in Georgia, and began his new career.

Drafted in the third round in 1978 by the Packers, Hood had ten career interceptions. He started for the Packers in 1979 and 1980. His final four seasons, he was used as an extra defensive back in passing situations and played special teams. Born in Hattiesburg, Mississippi, he attended Illinois State, which retired Hood's number in 1995 (along with the ISU number of Mike Prior, a current Packer safety). "One of my goals in life was to play pro football. I attained that goal so I'm proud of it. Kids here still come to me for autographs. I look back with great memories," Hood said.

Between Lambeau and Lombardi: Men of the "Lost Years"

Bobby Dillon
Defensive back, 1952-1959

Dick Wildung
Tackle, 1946-1951, 1953

Earl Girard
Back, punter, quarterback, 1948-1951

Floyd Reid
Running back, 1950-1956
Assistant coach 1957-1958

From *1953 until 1963, one of America's Thanksgiving traditions was gathering around a black-and-white television, amidst the steamy smells of turkey and dressing, to watch the Packers battle the Lions in Detroit. The Lions had been playing Thanksgiving Day games as early as 1934 and began playing the Packers regularly in 1951. The game became part* *of holiday festivities nationwide in 1953 when it was beamed across the country and into living rooms for the first time. That first national broadcast turned out to be a memorable one.*

Bobby Dillon

Historic as it was from a broadcast standpoint, the Packers-Lions game November 26, 1953, was also one of the most unusual in Packer history. It wasn't expected to be much of a game. The powerful Lions, led by quarterback Bobby Layne, were on their way to a second straight NFL title. They were the team of the 1950s, much like the Packers of the 1960s. The Packers, at 2-7-1, were a disappointment, and Coach Gene Ronzani's job was in jeopardy. Rumors he would be fired had been so strong that some players were surprised he was even with them in Detroit.

Ronzani had become the second coach in Packer history in 1950 when he took over from Curly Lambeau, but Ronzani's teams had produced just 14 wins going into the Thanksgiving Day game. "We had read a lot of stuff in the papers that he was in trouble," recalled Bobby Dillon, the Packers' star defensive back, now a retired business executive who lives in Temple, Texas.

Dillon never will forget that Thanksgiving game, and not just because of television. It turned out to be the day the Packers almost upset the powerful Lions, the last game Ronzani coached the Packers, and the day Dillon experienced the high and low points in his great career.

Kickoff was at 11 a.m., but the lights had to be turned on because a light snow was falling. A crowd of more than 52,000 was on hand, and for the first time thousands more watched on 97 television stations across the country. (The game is considered the first televised nationally on Thanksgiving Day, according to Joe Horrigan, historian at the Pro Football Hall of Fame. The Lions may have televised previous Thanksgiving Day games but only to local or regional audiences, he explained.) That season was the Packers' first on TV. The team received $15,000 for the Thanksgiving game TV rights. The Packers also had a three-game, $15,000 contract in 1953 with the Dumont network; two of those games were on Saturday nights, a sort of forerunner to Monday Night Football.

For their holiday game on November 26 at Briggs Stadium (now known as Tiger Stadium), the Packers wore dark blue jerseys with white pants rather than the all-gold uniforms they sometimes chose. To everyone's surprise, the Packers took a 15-7 halftime lead behind quarterback Vito "Babe" Parilli. He had been the Packers' Number One draft pick out of Kentucky the year before, when the Packers went 6-6 and seemed to be making progress under Ronzani. In fact, Ronzani was awarded a three-year extension of his contract after that season.

Early in the third quarter, the Packers drove to the Lions' three-yard line and had a chance to take a big lead. But the Packers fumbled away, and the Lions seized the opportunity. Layne dropped back and heaved the ball 57 yards down the sideline to Cloyce Box, who was being covered by Ace Loomis. The ball dropped perfectly into Box's hands as Loomis made a diving lunge, but Box was on his way to a 97-yard TD pass, third longest in NFL history at the time. The Packers fell apart and lost 34-15. "We couldn't hold them, and our offense couldn't move in the second half," Dillon recalled.

Almost swallowed up in the Thanksgiving Day fiasco was Dillon's great and sad day. Dillon, a second-year speedster out of the University of Texas, set a Packer record and tied an NFL record with four interceptions. He recalls picking off at least two passes by Layne, the future Hall of Famer, but believes that Layne didn't play the whole game because of an injury. The Lions won despite having 6 of their 18 passes picked off by the Packers—two others by Loomis—and losing two fumbles. "I'm not sure it was the best game I played, but I was in the right place at the right time and made some good moves," Dillon remembered.

Dillon that day became the sixth person in NFL history to intercept four passes in a game; since then ten more players have reached that mark. Dillon was the only Packer with four interceptions until Willie Buchanon stole four San Diego Charger passes on September 24, 1978, in San Diego.

Dillon's great day, however, had a painful ending. With less than two minutes to play, he moved up to tackle a Lion running back. Packer defenders swarmed the runner, and Dillon was caught underneath on the hard baseball infield. "They snowed me under and my legs split." Dillon was carried away on a stretcher with torn ligaments in both knees. "They operated on the worst one. They didn't want to operate on both. By the time I got off crutches on the first one, the second one was good again."

After the game or early the next morning, Ronzani was fired and the Packer board appointed assistants Hugh Devore, Ray "Scooter" McLean, and Chuck Drulis to handle the team for the remaining two games, although Drulis also was fired several days later. Ronzani, a native of Iron Mountain, Michigan, had played college football at Marquette University in Milwaukee and played quarterback for the Chicago Bears, along with such greats as Bronko Nagurski and Beattie Feathers. He was a controversial coach who was disliked by many of his players.

For some unknown reason, Ronzani didn't disappear when he was fired. He actually traveled with the team for the final two games of the season. The Packers at that time traditionally played their final games out west against the Los Angeles Rams and San Francisco 49ers. Ronzani apparently bought his own train ticket and accompanied the team on the 2½-day trip west. "That was bizarre, really bizarre. I'm sure he got a lot of publicity out of it. I'm not sure what his motive would have been otherwise," said former Packer Clayton Tonnemaker, who was not one of Ronzani's supporters. Ronzani's presence didn't help any; the Packers lost 48-14 to the 49ers and 33-17 to the Rams to close the unusual season at 2-9-1.

The day after the Thanksgiving game, Dillon went to see Ronzani at his office. It was a fond farewell. "He told me that I had been invited to the Pro Bowl. He knew before the game on Thursday and was going to tell me afterward. He told me he believed I was the finest defensive back he had ever seen. He was a very friendly guy. I never had any problem with him," Dillon said.

Fortunately, the injury didn't hurt Dillon's career. He recovered to become All-Pro in 1954, 1956, 1957, and 1958 and played in the Pro Bowl from 1956 through 1959, when he retired. He was inducted into the Packer Hall of Fame in 1974 and was voted to the club's all-time team in 1969 and modern era team in 1976. In just eight seasons, he had 52 interceptions—a Packer record—and still ranks among the all-time NFL leaders. Of his 52 career thefts, Dillon said, "I felt pretty good about it, and I still do. We were able to do some things defenders can't do now, but they threw the ball only 20 times a game and now they throw it 30 or 40 times a game." Dillon led the Packers in interceptions every year but one, his last. In three seasons, he had nine interceptions per season.

It appears only two things have kept Dillon out of the Pro Football Hall of Fame: He didn't play long enough and didn't play for a winner. In his eight seasons, the Packers had a winning record just once, 7-5 in 1959. Dillon averaged more interceptions a season—6.5—than many defensive backs in the Hall, including:

- Dick "Night Train" Lane (Rams, Lions, Chicago Cardinals), who had 68 in 14 seasons for a 4.3 average. Lane set an NFL record with 14 thefts in 1952.

- Jack Christiansen (Lions), 46 in eight seasons, 5.7 average. In the Lions' 1953 title season, Christiansen led the league with 12 interceptions.

- Emlen Tunnell (New York Giants, Packers), 79 in 14 seasons, 5.6 average.

- Mel Blount (Pittsburgh Steelers), 57 in 14 seasons, 5.1 average.

- Herb Adderly (Packers), 39 in nine seasons, 4.3.

- Willie Wood (Packers), 48 in 12 seasons, 4.0.

Paul Krause holds the NFL record with 81 interceptions, but he got them in 16 seasons, a 5.0 average.

"I had 52 interceptions in eight years and Wood had 48 in 12. It helps if you played for a winner. Ray Nitschke said one time, 'Of all the people I know who are not in the Hall, he deserves to be in.' I don't think I'll ever make it now. At one time I did. It would be nice, but I've resigned myself that it's just not going to happen." Dillon noted that he also averaged 20 yards per interception return.

Dillon might be in the Hall today if he had played just a few more years for some of Lombardi's winning teams and raised his interception total into the 60s. But by 1959 Dillon was more concerned with his second career. While playing for the Packers, he began working for Ralph Wilson Plastics Co. in his hometown of Temple, Texas. "I got to know people while I still was playing. They [Wilsons] gave me a leave of absence to play," Dillon said. After 1959 he decided to give up football, even though while playing under Vince Lombardi in 1959 Dillon could see changes on the horizon. "I played eight years and that was plenty. My daughter was starting school and my wife wanted me to quit. I would have liked to play some more, but I had to make a choice. The company couldn't hold the job for me, and I probably would have played only another two or three years. There wasn't any money [in football]. I was making $16,000 to $17,000."

For nearly 30 years, Dillon worked his way to the top. In 1986 he became president of the company, which then employed 2,300 people at two plants and had 15 national distribution centers. Wilson Plastics is the maker of Wilson Art, a laminate used to make kitchen countertops. The company is the largest manufacturer of the product in North America. Dillon retired in 1995 at age 65. He, his wife, and their two children own the 800-member Racquet Club of Temple.

When asked to name the toughest players of his era, Dillon picked a group of Hall of Famers:

- At quarterback: "Johnny Unitas [of the Baltimore Colts]. Bobby Layne [of the Detroit Lions] probably was the best competitor if you had to get into the end zone, but overall I'd take Unitas."

- At wide receiver: "Ray Berry [of the Baltimore Colts]. I don't ever recall him dropping a ball that was catchable. He and Unitas were the first pair to work on timing. Berry was the first guy to work on out-of-bounds moves, the first to come back to the passer."

- At running back: "Jim Brown [of the Cleveland Browns] was just starting when I was ending, but he was tough. And Hugh McElhenny of the [San Francisco] 49ers."

- At defensive back: "Jack Christiansen" [of the Detroit Lions].

Regarding Dick "Night Train" Lane of the Lions, Dillon said "He made the Hall of Fame by being a gambler. He played the ball. He got a lot of publicity out of the interceptions. He wasn't too highly regarded. You could beat him anytime you wanted, at least our receivers thought so."

Dillon played with Nitschke for just two years but could see greatness on the horizon for the young linebacker. "He was a highly touted fullback. He had all kinds of talent. He wanted to make all the tackles no matter where the play was. You could see he was going to be outstanding if he learned the system, and he was a very smart player."

Like Nitschke, Dillon was smart and talented, so much so that he beat receivers, made tackles, and made all his interceptions with one eye closed. At age 10, Dillon was hit in the face when someone carrying a board in front of him swung around and smashed his glasses. The glass shattered into his left eye and blinded it. Because of the injury, Dillon's parents didn't let him play football until he was 15, when he already was a senior in high school. He eventually wound up at the University of Texas and was drafted by the Packers in 1952 in the third round.

Prior to arriving in Green Bay, Dillon was at the College All-Star game. After giving him a pre-game physical, a doctor informed Dillon that with one eye it wouldn't be safe for him to play. The doctor feared that Dillon could lose his other eye. At that time, the only players wearing the optional face masks were linemen, said Dillon, who did not wear one. "I said to the doctor, 'That's OK. I'll just get to Green Bay three weeks earlier,'" Dillon recalled. The doctor replied, "You're playing pro football? Get back in the damn line!"

Dick Wildung

When Dick Wildung thinks about the years he played for the Green Bay Packers, he summarizes it with a joke that he and a former teammate used to tell. "We got rid of the only two coaches the Packers [had] ever had," he said with a chuckle. As a standout two-way lineman from 1946 through 1953, Wildung played for the Packers' first-ever coach, Curly Lambeau, before Lambeau left the Packers after the 1949 season. Then Wildung played under the Packers' second coach, Gene Ronzani, who was fired after the 1953 season.

"Bob Forte and I were the only ones left from Lambeau's teams. We were the only guys who played for the only two coaches the Packers ever had," he said. Both Wildung and Forte left the Packers after 1953, preserving their niche in Packer history. Forte died in 1996.

Wildung, now living in Bloomington, Minnesota, was the Packers' first-round draft pick out of the University of Minnesota in 1942, but he didn't put on a Packer uniform until the 1946 season. Like many other college athletes at that time, he had joined a Naval officer training program in college that enabled him to finish school. He was on PT boats during the war. The lightly armed, fast boats were used to disrupt enemy supply routes. He saw action in the Philippines for one year.

After a standout pro football career, he was inducted into the Packer Hall of Fame in 1973 along with many stars of the 1940s. In 1993, he was also inducted into the University of Minnesota Athletic Hall of Fame. He grew up in Luverne, Minnesota, in the sparsely populated southwest corner of the state, was an All-American at the University of Minnesota, and played on the Gophers' undefeated 1940 and 1941 national champions under Coach Bernie Bierman. Wildung also is a member of the College Football Hall of Fame, inducted in 1957.

At 6 feet, 225 pounds, Wildung was the prototype quick tackle of the run-oriented college and pro game of the 1940s. He played offensive guard and tackle and defensive tackle for the Packers. He was one of the blockers in 1949 when Tony Canadeo became the first Packer ever and one of the first in the NFL to crack 1,000 yards rushing (he gained 1,052).

The Packers were not successful in the late 1940s. They won their sixth NFL title in 1944, but after Don Hutson retired in 1945, the team went into a slide on and off the field that led to Lambeau's departure. The Packers were 6-5 in 1946 and 1947 but fell to 3-9 in 1948 and to 2-10 in 1949, their worst record ever. Wildung thought highly of Lambeau but said the coach didn't keep pace with the changes in the pro game. "The game kind of passed Curly by. We still were playing the Notre Dame Box and everybody else was in the T-formation. The T took over after World War II. The Notre Dame Box had a balanced line with guard, tackle, and end on either side of the ball but it didn't spread the ends out. They played outside the tackle just about a yard. It was a direct snap to the tailback, like the single wing. The quarterback wasn't up under the center. It was inevitable where pro football was going," Wildung explained.

Some of the criticism of Lambeau was fiscal, related to his purchase of Rockwood Lodge, a training camp and practice facility near Green Bay. It turned out to be a fiasco when the Packers couldn't practice there because of the hard ground. "It seemed like a hell of an idea. But there was not one foot of black dirt over rock. It was tough on the players. Many of them got shin splits. I got shin splits and I never had them in my life," Wildung recalled. His rookie year with the Packers, 1946, was the first year they practiced at Rockwood. "In 1947 we finally went to town to practice."

Wildung didn't play in the 1952 season. He had opened a hardware store in Redwood Falls, Minnesota, with his brother-in-law. But his brother-in-law died and Wildung was forced to take care of the business. He returned to play the 1953 season, mostly for financial reasons, before retiring for good and returning to Redwood Falls to operate the store until 1959. At 32, he was the oldest Packer on the team when he retired, when football still was a part-time job. "Then, you played five or six months, went home, and worked."

After football, Wildung worked 25 years in sales for Borchert-Ingersoll Inc., of Eagan, Minnesota, a seller of heavy equipment, retiring as vice-president of sales. He then spent eight years selling automobiles in the Twin Cities.

Wildung was pleased when in the early 1990s the NFL Players Association granted a monthly pension to old-time NFL players. The pension is about $60 per month for each season played, or in his case about $420 a month. "It was kind of a gift. I never expected it."

Earl Girard

When he was drafted in the first round by the Packers' Curly Lambeau in 1948, Earl "Jug" Girard couldn't have been happier to be heading back home. He grew up just north of Green Bay in Marinette, Wisconsin. Four years later, when he was traded to the Detroit Lions, Girard couldn't have been happier to be leaving. "It was not too good to be playing too close to home. There were too many outside activities. People [from Marinette] came down. Your life was not your own. I was happy to get away from all the hustle and bustle."

He also was happy to leave the Packers because the organization was suffering through one of the darkest periods in its history. During Girard's four years in Green Bay, the Packers never won more than three games in a season, going 11-37 during that time.

"Lambeau was kind of tough and he was getting ready to pack it in. He had his day and we appreciated it. We didn't have too much [talent] besides [running back Tony] Canadeo, and he was getting past his prime. The team was pretty much done and gone with. Nobody said anything about it, but that was the general feeling."

After playing for the Packers through 1951, Girard was sent to Detroit, where he played through 1956. He finished his career with

Pittsburgh in 1957. After he went to Detroit, the Lions won NFL championships in 1952 and 1953. "Green Bay just didn't have enough money to get the ballplayers they needed, and consequently they did go down, and I was part of it," Girard said.

Girard still lives near Detroit in Royal Oak, Michigan. After retiring from football, Girard and a Lions teammate owned a cocktail lounge in the Detroit area for about 10 years. He also worked as an industrial buyer at Great Lakes Steam and Supply for 15 years before retiring.

Girard was a versatile performer. At 5' 10", 170 pounds, he led the Packers in interceptions with five in the 1951 season, one reason why he drew the interest of the Lions. In addition to playing defensive back, Girard was also a quarterback and a punter. He led the Packers in passing in the 1949 season—Lambeau's last—even though he completed just 35.4 percent of his passes. Girard thinks he was an adequate quarterback in college but not a pro-level quarterback. He is the only All-American quarterback ever at the University of Wisconsin, earning the honor in 1944.

He'll never forget returning to Green Bay for the first time with the Lions in 1952. He had a good day punting, caught two TD passes, and rushed for 61 yards. The Lions won that game 52-17. "I just had a hell of a day. I felt sorry for Green Bay. They weren't in the same class we were. You hate to rub it in on guys you played with for four years."

Floyd Reid

When Floyd "Breezy" Reid left the Green Bay Packers after the 1958 season, he was leaving on the edge—on the edge of history. Reid could tell that the Packers were on their way to something big. And that was before Vince Lombardi was hired in 1959 as the coach. "The 1958 team won only one game, but as a team you could see they were coming," Reid said in an interview before he died in 1994.

"[In 1958], Starr was in his third year. You could see he was going to come. There were Boyd Dowler, Jerry Kramer, Jim Ringo, Forrest Gregg—you could see that nucleus coming together," Reid remembered. For Reid it was a bittersweet memory. After all, he played for seven Packer teams that never did better than .500, and a few years after he left the Packers became a dynasty.

Reid referred to that period from the middle 1940s through the late 1950s as the Packers' "lost years." They suffered through financial trouble, many losing seasons, and coaching problems, especially when founder and 29-year coach Curly Lambeau left in 1950 to coach the rival Chicago Cardinals. "People just don't talk about the '40s and '50s. It's like they don't exist. People don't write about it or talk about it. It's the '30s or the '60s."

The Packers won four of their 11 world titles in the 1930s and five in the 1960s (in addition to 1929 and 1944 titles). Reid felt that the Packers made some "bad draft choices after the war" after winning their 1944 title and "they didn't have the money to spend."

The Lambeau resignation followed by the signing of Gene Ronzani as coach brought Reid to the Packers in 1950. As a former Bear, Ronzani knew the Bears' talent and grabbed Reid off the Bears' waiver list. Reed, a speedster out of the University of Georgia, became one of the top backs in Ronzani's two-set backfield.

Reid remembered one particularly frustrating game during Ronzani's tenure. On October 12, 1952, the Packers were playing a home game at Marquette Stadium in Milwaukee against the powerful Los Angeles Rams, who were led by Elroy "Crazy Legs" Hirsch, Norm Van Brocklin, and Bob Waterfield. The underdog Packers led 28-6 with four minutes to play. Unbelievably, the Rams went wild and caught up. "They scored on the last play of the game and we got beat [30-28]," Reid said. "Everybody was stunned."

Reid led the Packers in rushing in 1953 with 492 yards and again in 1954 with 507 yards, ranking in the top ten in the NFL both years. After his strong 1953 season, Reid held out in 1954 to get a $600 raise, boosting his contract from $6,600 a year to $7,200. "That's how tough it was," he recalled.

That was coach Lisle Blackbourn's first year, and Reid thinks the holdout might have been a factor in Blackbourn cutting him with two games to go in the 1956 season. Reid was only 29 then, but he figured his career was about over anyway so he went into coaching. "Then you didn't train as hard as they do now. You worked in the off-season then. When you hit the 29- or 30-year-old mark, hey, you figured you were done. You never heard of a quarterback 39 years old. They were just getting into conditioning then. In those days you'd run a 50-yard dash once or twice a year."

After coaching the backfield with the Packers in 1957 and 1958, Reid went to coach the backfield at Virginia Tech in 1959. He coached under Buster Ramsey with the Buffalo Bills in 1960 and 1961, the first years of the American Football League. He then went to work full time for General Motors, putting in 24 years in a supervisory position in materials handling in his hometown of Hamilton, Ohio, before retiring. He died of a heart attack in March, 1994.

The Early Line

Lon Evans
Guard, 1933-1937

George Svendsen
Center, 1935-1941

Lon Evans

Lon Evans never forgot the night in Chicago when a man walked over to him on Soldier Field and asked if he would like to play professional football for the Green Bay Packers. Evans, a strapping 6' 3", 225-pound college lineman from Texas Christian University, didn't quite know what to say at first. "I didn't know anything about Green Bay. I didn't even know where it was," Evans remembered. Nor did Evans know who the man was. Evans had only vague knowledge of pro football, a game played in the North and East but not common to the South during those early Depression years. But the man was offering $90 a game. Evans loved football and the money sounded awfully good. He agreed to play for the Packers. The man was Curly Lambeau.

Evans made a wise decision. He played for some of the great teams and with some of the great players in early NFL history. Although he played just five years for the Packers, retiring after the 1937 season, Evans was All-Pro three times, was part of the club's first true world championship team (1936) and played with the first seven Packers who were inducted into the Pro Football Hall of Fame.

Evans was in Chicago because he had been invited by *Chicago Tribune* sports editor Arch Ward to play in the 1933 World's Fair All-Star game. After he agreed to play for Lambeau, Evans found himself being courted by owner George Preston Marshall of the Redskins. After the Redskins heard that Lambeau offered $90 a game, they counter-offered. But Lambeau matched the counter-offer and told Evans, "I'll raise it to $110 after three games if you're doing all right."

Evans made $125 per game the next year and wound up his career making $150 a game. For the 1936 title game, seen by 6,000 fans, each Packer received $750, according to Evans. "It was a very hard life. We would play a league game on the weekend and play a semi-pro team on Wednesday to get an extra $50. We played a lot of games, and you had to be able to fill in at two or three positions," Evans explained in *The Purple Lawman: From Horned Frog to High Sheriff,* a story of his life. "The Packers roamed the country playing exhibitions, mostly with pick-up teams, teams we had never heard of before or since. Sometimes we went three, four weeks without a payday because the cities we visited didn't make enough off the game. We'd have to wait until we played in Chicago or New York." Ticket prices in the 1930s were 55 cents for a "regular" seat and $1.65 for a "first class" seat, Evans recalled.

When Evans played for the Packers, they had a heated rivalry with the Bears even though the teams had played fewer than 20 times. "One time we played them when [the Bears] had a particularly tough tackle named Ted Rosequist, from Ohio State. A Packer fan came down out of the stands in the fourth quarter and decked Rosequist. Rosequist sued the fan—but in a Green Bay court. The judge naturally was a Packer fan and he threw the case out, saying, 'Somebody should have done it earlier in the game.'"

When the Packers played late-season away games on the East Coast in the mid-1930s, they often practiced at Fordham University in the

Bronx, New York. There Evans first encountered a small (180-pound) but determined right guard named Vince who wore Number 40. The young man "would come to me to ask questions about how to play guard," Evans recalled. The young man's last name was Lombardi, a standout at the school from 1934-1936. Lombardi would watch the Packers prepare for games against the New York Giants and then ask the team members for tips. "Years later, he still remembered those days after he was winning Super Bowls," Evans said.

Interviewed several months before he died in December 1992 at the age of 81, Evans still had fond memories of playing in Green Bay, although he said it was the coldest place on earth. He left the Packers after the 1937 season to go into officiating, which he thought offered a more stable future. "I could still play real well, but I thought I should get along to something that I could do a little longer," he said.

As an official, Evans encountered the ebullient George "Papa Bear" Halas, then coach of the Bears. "Halas was a great showman and a master of crowd appeal. I was officiating, and during the game my penalty flag fell from my pocket. Halas came running and screaming on the field like a wild man. I explained to him what had happened. He said, 'You mean there is no penalty?' I replied, 'Yes, that is correct.' With that he began walking backwards, bowing like a Japanese houseboy. The crowd loved it!"

Evans spent 30 years officiating high school, college, and pro football. He also sold women's lingerie and helped build World War II bombers. After his officiating career ended, he spent 25 years as the popular sheriff of Tarrant County, which includes the Dallas-Fort Worth area.

Evans was inducted into the Packer Hall of Fame in 1978. He and Pro Football Hall of Famer Mike Michalske were the guards who led the way for two other hall of famers, halfback Johnny "Blood" McNally and fullback Clark Hinkle, on the powerful 1936 team. The quarterback was Arnie Herber, another future hall of famer. Receiver Don Hutson was Herber's favorite target in what was one of the game's first great passing attacks. That team finished the regular season 10-1-1. In the NFL championship game, the Packers beat the Boston Redskins 21-6 at the Polo Grounds in New York. It was the Packers' first title under the league playoff system, which was established in 1933. Prior to that, they won the 1929-1931 world titles based on league standings.

Evans called his fellow guard Michalske "the fastest, most movable man I ever saw in football. He was probably the greatest football player I was ever around. He was a fullback at Penn State. Man, he could move. In those days, the guards pulled out and blocked the linebackers and ends. In those days, we used to move. We had to move. We made a pretty good pair. We'd lead the play. We used to take 'em on," Evans said. Michalske was the first guard elected to the Pro Football Hall of Fame.

Evans remembered Johnny "Blood" McNally as a "true character. You never knew where he'd be or what he'd do." Evans wrote this about the unpredictable McNally, a Wisconsin native from the west-central city of New Richmond: "Once in the early '30s we were practicing in New York and Johnny showed up late. Coach fired him. He then ran two laps around Central Park and went back to the hotel. We were playing on Sunday. When we got up and read the Sunday paper, there was this headline that said, 'Johnny Blood Scores Five Touchdowns for Staten Island.' He'd gone over and hooked up with a semi-pro team. He would spend time every day in the Green Bay library doing research for the book he later wrote on the Malthusian theory of economics. He also wrote beautiful poetry."

Then there was the time McNally needed some spending money. Lambeau wouldn't give him any and locked his hotel door to keep McNally out. "Johnny, never one to give up, leaped across an airshaft eight stories above street level, in a driving rainstorm, in order to climb through the window of Lambeau's hotel room. The ashen-faced Curly was shocked into giving it to him," Evans remembered.

Evans recalled the great Bears runner Red Grange and how frustrating it was trying to tackle him. One time, big Packer tackle Cal Hubbard (280 pounds) "caught Red and carried him for about 10 yards while the referee kept blowing his whistle. Cal turned to the ref and said, 'I've intercepted the sonuvagun, let me run with him.'" Hubbard went on to be an American League baseball umpire and is the only person in both the pro football and pro baseball halls of fame.

As for Hutson: "No doubt he was one of the best players [of all time]. He was not a real big guy but he was real, real fast. He could catch the football in any way you could imagine. Hutson used to stuff *Saturday Evening Posts* and *Colliers* magazines under his long underwear before Packer home games. He never did get used to Green Bay weather."

George Svendsen

George Svendsen still gets worked up about pro football on Sunday afternoons. He thinks there's been malaise in the NFL the last 50 years, and he doesn't like it. Svendsen, now 83 and living in the Minneapolis area, can't accept the practice of substitution, and he thinks today's offensive linemen are too big. If Svendsen's tough attitude is any indication of the type of men who played pro football before World War II, the period was appropriately dubbed the Iron Man era. "We used to pride ourselves in playing 60 minutes. If you didn't, you were mad," Svendsen remembered.

Svendsen believes that because of the physical nature of football, players should go both ways. "I think you lose continuity when you have to go watch from the sidelines. We didn't want to leave the field. If some guy had just beaten your brains out, you could turn right around and do it to him," Svendsen explained. He didn't know any other way. During his seven seasons with the Packers, when he wasn't centering the ball to quarterbacks Arnie Herber or Cecil Isbell, Svendsen was playing linebacker. It might seem preposterous nowadays to tell Brett Favre he must play linebacker or tell Reggie White to play guard. But when Svendsen played, everyone, including star receiver Don Hutson, went the distance.

Svendsen believes that NFL players are more talented now than in the 1930s, but he despises the size and immobility of the offensive linemen. "I don't like these 300-pound linemen. You might as well put 300-pound stumps out there. They can't move. They're not athletes," he insisted.

In Svendsen's days, the linemen not only were decent sized—like 6' 3", 265-pound Packer Cal Hubbard—but they were known for their quickness and agility. "To me the correlation between lifting weights and playing football is for the birds. Cal Hubbard was 265 and he could run like a deer." Svendsen admitted that the "physical condition of some guys [today] is fantastic. Their speed and agility is amazing," he said, especially referring to the linebackers.

Svendsen was one of the mainstays of the talented Lambeau Packer teams of the late 1930s. In seven seasons, he played in three title games. The Packers beat the Boston Redskins 21-6 to win the 1936 title at the Polo Grounds in New York during Svendsen's second season. In 1938, the New York Giants beat the Packers 23-17 at the Polo Grounds before a record crowd of 48,120. In 1939, the Packers got revenge, winning the title by shutting out the Giants 27-0 behind Herber and Isbell at State Fair Park in Milwaukee before 32,279 fans.

After the 1941 season, Svendsen joined the military and didn't get out of the service until 1945. Instead of attempting to play again, he returned to the University of Minnesota as an assistant coach. He had played for the Gophers from 1932-1935.

Right behind George at Minnesota was his brother, Earl, another standout center. Earl followed George to the Packers, playing in 1937, 1939, and 1940, taking off the 1938 season to try coaching. But after 1940, Earl was traded to Brooklyn and the brothers wound up playing against each other in a 1941 game. They had also faced each other in 1937 when Earl played on the College All-Star Team, which embarrassed the champion Packers with a 6-0 win. George was inducted into the Packer Hall of Fame in 1972, and Earl followed in 1985. Earl also lives in the Minneapolis area. They retired from the family's Twin Cities electric business, Boustead Electric. George now has two sons helping in the business.

George Svendsen still has vivid memories of his playing days. In his first game as a Packer in 1935, "I recovered a fumble, intercepted a pass and had 10 tackles," he recalled. The Packers lost at home 7-6 to the Chicago Cardinals. "[Green Bay] was some town. If we beat the Bears, they would shut down the town. One year we beat the Bears in Chicago [to take the division lead]. There was a parade down main street when we got back, and we celebrated all night long."

On fall Sunday afternoons these days, Packer fans statewide drop what they're doing and turn on their TVs. In the Packers' 1930s heydays, the fans did the same thing—only they turned on their radios. "When we played, people turned on their radios and that was the only thing going on until the game was over," Svendsen remembered.

Although he was a solid performer, Svendsen was one of the lesser-known players on Lambeau's power-packed teams, which won five titles from 1929 to 1939. The Packers of the 1930s were much like the Packers of the 1960s—they had Hall of Fame talent and a Hall of Fame coach. Svendsen hasn't forgotten them.

Curly Lambeau (player, coach 1919-1949), "was a prime egoist in a way, but a positive guy who never thought he would lose. He always thought he could win, and when you look back at his record, he could. He knew how to handle all the players. He put a lot of faith in the ballplayers. In 1941 we had a brain trust—myself, Hinkle and Hutson—a players' council, that met with him before games. We were like assistant coaches. The credit for the Packers' innovative passing attacks should go to Lambeau. His pass patterns were ingenious. He could attack a defense like nobody ever saw. He was the first to use the pass the way it is today. Even today I can recognize some things on TV that we used to do."

Don Hutson, who is retired in Palm Springs, California, "had kind of a funny gait, a gallop. He had two speeds, one was fast and the other was faster. I still can see him running down the sidelines, cutting over the middle and Arnie [Herber] heaving it to him. He could go deep like nobody. He used to drive [Chicago Bears Coach George] Halas nuts. Halas hated to see him come to town." Hutson supposedly had a loping run because he had flat feet.

Hutson and Svendsen were rookies the same year. In fact, they arrived in Green Bay the same day, Svendsen said. "I don't think anybody knew who he was, but it didn't take long. He had a fantastic pair of hands." Some Packers and fans weren't happy that Lambeau had signed Hutson, thinking Hutson was too skinny. But Svendsen said Lambeau was sold on Hutson when he saw him practice for the 1935 Rose Bowl game, in which he scored three touchdowns. Hutson ran the 100-yard dash in 9.7 seconds.

In his second game as a Packer, September 22, 1935, Hutson beat Chicago defenders Gene Ronzani (the future Packer coach) and Beattie Feathers (the NFL's first 1,000-yard rusher) on a deep route for a long touchdown pass from Arnie Herber. Herber faked a hand-off to halfback "Blood" McNally, drawing in the defensive back Feathers, and Herber heaved the ball 66 yards in the air to his wide-open rookie. The Hutson era was under way.

Clark Hinkle (fullback, kicker, linebacker 1932-1941) "could do it all. He was very versatile. He had a heart as big as a football. He wasn't a very big fellow, about 205 [pounds]," Svendsen remembered. Hinkle, considered one of the NFL's fiercest competitors ever, was the NFL's all-time leading rusher when he retired.

The unpredictable Johnny "Blood" McNally (halfback 1928-1936) "made the easy catches hard and the hard ones easy. He was one of the most gifted guys you've ever seen. He was about 6' 2½" and he could run like hell. Hutson challenged him to a 100-yard dash when he got to Green Bay. Hutson could run the dash in 9.8. Johnny [at age 33] just barely got beat. The question always was when he would show up for camp. He was one original. Lambeau knew he had a talent there; he learned now to live with him."

"Iron Mike" Michalske (guard 1932-1937) "was the best guard who ever played. He had tremendous strength and speed. They called him the guard of the century. He was only about 6-feet, 220 pounds but he had good speed and was strong as a bull."

Arnie Herber (QB 1930-1941) "probably had the strongest arm I've ever seen. He really could throw the ball and was accurate. One time he threw a football through a window at 50 yards—three times in a row."

CHAPTER

Healing Hands

Malcolm Snider
Guard, 1972-1974

Like any pro football player, Malcolm Snider experienced the emotional extremes of pro football, the scalp-tingling rushes of joy when the team played well or moved toward the playoffs and the depths of disappointment when a 100 percent effort wasn't good enough, when an injury destroyed months or years of work and hope. Malcolm Snider's NFL experiences have served him well in his new career as an orthopedic surgeon. He knew from his NFL days that life and work weren't always comfortable. He also knew, as a former offensive lineman, that taking on the most arduous and seemingly thankless tasks with maximum effort could bring worthwhile results.

When a migrant worker was brought into the emergency room in Salem, Oregon, with a crushed pelvis, Snider calmly worked through the situation. The man would have been in the hospital for three months without an operation to restructure the mangled bone. It was a procedure Snider never had done, but he pushed ahead. After consulting with other physicians to prepare his plan, he operated successfully. The next week, Snider proudly watched the man walk again.

While Snider doesn't command much attention among the legions of well-known former Packer stars, he commands much respect in his new career. In 1978, four years after he retired, Malcolm Snider became Dr. Snider, a graduate of the University of Wisconsin Medical School. He now is an established surgeon with his own practice in his hometown, Salem, Oregon, a city of 100,000 people about 50 miles south of Portland and about an hour's drive from Mt. Hood and the Cascade Mountains.

Unlike many 1970s Packers who struggled in their second careers, he's one of the ex-pro football players who has taken success well beyond the football field. He has the satisfaction of reaching the pinnacle of two professions.

Despite his choice to shorten his NFL career (1969-1971 with Atlanta, 1972-1974 with Packers), Snider cherishes his playing days for a couple of reasons: He never truly expected to make it to the NFL, and while being a doctor was his childhood dream, being a football player was, too. Of course, there are the valuable football lessons he learned that have given him the life experience any surgeon would covet. "A day doesn't go by that I don't remember [football] in one way or another. It was a major influence in my life. There never has been or ever will be anything like that in my life again."

Despite the sometimes taxing aspects of his job—his short weeks are 60 hours long—Snider "dearly loves" being a surgeon. He spends three days a week performing surgery at Salem Memorial Hospital. He does joint replacement surgeries, such as hips and knees. He is associated with a group of orthopedists but has an independent practice. He also helps outpatients with a multitude of muscle, bone, and joint problems.

A large part of his practice is sports medicine. Donating his medical assistance to local high schools and a college, Snider frequently finds himself on the football sidelines on Friday nights at North Salem High, where he played in the early 1960s. He performs many operations to repair football-injured knees, shoulders, and other joints. "I'm giving something back. One [prep football player] tore up each knee in successive years and was able to come back successfully," Snider said with pride.

Snider lived in Madison, Wisconsin, until 1983 when he completed a required five-year residency, the culmination of a long schooling and training period that began while he still was with the Packers. He applied to medical school when he was an undergraduate at Stanford, where he was named the school's best offensive lineman of the decade. But when he was drafted in the third round by the Falcons in 1969, he couldn't pass up a chance to play in the NFL.

But by 1973, Snider was with the Packers and was taking medical school classes at the UW. On days off during the football season, he would drive from Green Bay to Madison, about 130 miles. "I would spend 18 hours dissecting a cadaver then drive back the next day. During the off-season I would go to school full time." The UW was "perfect," Snider said, because he could do independent study his first two years of medical school. "It was the only thing I could have done. I was fortunate to be traded to Green Bay."

Snider is one of those Packers most often remembered as the answer to a trivia question. Offensive linemen who play just three years simply don't have long-standing name recognition, not in the land where Hall of Famers once trod. Who is Malcolm Snider? In 1972, the Packers traded speedy running back and kick return specialist Dave Hampton to Atlanta to get him. Snider still doesn't understand the trade. He was threatening to play out his option in Atlanta. He wanted to go to Canada and play in the Canadian Football League while attending medical school. Coach Norm Van Brocklin of the Falcons didn't want Snider to get away for nothing. "I was trying to get something going with medical school and he didn't like it," Snider recalled.

So Van Brocklin put Snider on the trading block, telling Packer Coach Dan Devine that Snider wanted too much money. Devine took the hook and traded Hampton for Snider. "I showed up on [Devine's] doorstep, and he said, 'Here's the money you want.' I said, 'Money has nothing to do with it.' His teeth about fell out. Van Brocklin sold him a bill of goods," said Snider. The trade came during the last week of preseason in 1972, and while it definitely helped the Packers that season, in the long run it wasn't a good deal. While Snider had retired by 1974, Hampton remained productive with the Falcons, rushing for 1,002 yards in 1975. "[Devine] traded a 1,000-yard rusher for a journeyman lineman," Snider admitted.

Devine tried to help Snider get accepted into medical school in Madison, but Snider figures Devine was only trying to save face. "I never knew what his motives were. If I left for Canada, he'd have egg all over his face." Snider appreciated the effort, but he said Devine's good words didn't help because medical schools were overrun with applications, and the administrators didn't "know or care who the coach of the Packers was." He got into medical school on his own merit.

After the dismal 1974 Packer season, Snider retired and went to school full time. The stress of pursuing dual careers became too much, along with "nagging injuries" and the difficult Packer seasons in 1973 and 1974. "It was not that much fun playing ball. It wasn't a positive experience in 1973 and 1974." Snider had his own problems. While he played guard all during the 1972 season, he was occasionally shuffled to tackle in 1973 and 1974, which he didn't like. "In '73 I had some notorious *faux pas* playing tackle."

Snider, divorced and remarried with a grown son and stepson, calls pro football "an amazing experience, both good and bad. I would like to have had the body of a 22-year-old and the maturity and experience of a 40-year-old when I played. But all in all I wouldn't trade it for any experience in my life. I feel incredibly grateful."

CHAPTER

Legacies:
Once They Were Packers

David Beverly, *Punter, 1975-1980:* David Beverly had a decision to make. He was 30 years old, and he felt he wasn't improving as a punter in the NFL. Heading into the 1981 season he knew his job would be on the line because the Packers had spent a third-round draft pick on another punter, Ray Stachowicz. So Beverly did what few NFL players would: He cut himself from the team, rationalizing that he needed to get started on his second career. "I didn't even show up for camp." He gave the job to Stachowicz, who lasted just two years.

Coping with defeat and a bit of boredom contributed to Beverly's no-looking-back exit from the NFL. "In Green Bay, with the constant losing and turnover of players, it wasn't much fun. It gets old in a hurry. I was still enjoying the Sundays, but Monday through Saturday got very old. I didn't like practicing. Most of the guys got tired of it."

Although he had studied textile management at Auburn University, Beverly took an interest in the stock market while playing for the Packers. About 18 months after retiring, he became a stockbroker near

Houston. He went to work for Paine-Webber in 1993 in a three-man partnership that specializes in retirement investment programs. More significantly, that same year he began taking courses from Landmark Education, "a corporation that is committed to people fulfilling the real possibilities of their lives." The courses changed his life. "You can have a committed life or a justified existence. Before I took the seminar I had reached the point where I was not who I could be . . . I was more concerned with how much more money I could make, how much vacation time I had, and what new car I was going to get. I'm somewhat of a new creation. It's given me a new vitality. The future looks a lot different," Beverly said. As a result, Beverly, 44, developed more committed relationships with family members. And he has kicked football far into his past. "Are you kidding? I can't get my leg waist high."

Beverly grew up in southern Alabama in the tiny town of Sweetwater, where he was one of 39 kids in his senior class. He knew heat and humidity, not the snow, sleet, and icy winds that often swirled about Lambeau Field and County Stadium. His best season was 1979, when he averaged 40.4 per punt and ranked fourth in the NFC. "That first year, in 1975, I was very homesick and lonely. I roomed with [place-kicker] Joe Danelo in a hotel next to the stadium, and neither one of us had a car. We each put in $250 and bought some old blue car. We weren't living the glamorous life. I was so lonely. My wife called once and I remember holding the receiver up to the window, and she said, "What's that? I told her it was the wind. I said, 'You think we're having fun up here?' "

Willie Buchanon, *Cornerback, 1972-1978:* Willie Buchanon, the son of a minister, grew up in the San Diego area, played ball at San Diego State, and finished his career with the San Diego Chargers after the Packers traded him following the 1978 season. Predictably, he now lives near San Diego. He owns a real estate business.

In fact, the best day of Buchanon's career came September 24, 1978, in San Diego when he intercepted four passes in a 24-3 Packer victory. Although Buchanon wanted to stay in Green Bay, the next year the Chargers offered him a $70,000 raise—more than the total salary he was asking of the Packers—and the Packers wouldn't budge so he took his 9.4 hundred-yard dash speed home. He had been drafted Number One by the

Packers in 1972 and was NFC defensive rookie of the year, admired by his Packer teammates as a total package of speed, power, and intellect. Buchanon turned his talents to helping the Chargers to three straight division titles before retiring. The rising star of the Charger offense at that time was young wide receiver John Jefferson.

After he retired, Buchanon taught for several years at the elementary, high school, and junior college levels. In the mid-1980s, he started Buchanon and Associates real estate agency, which deals mostly in commercial properties and appraisals. He has a variety of outside interests. He's on the California State Athletic Commission, which regulates boxing, the martial arts, and pro wrestling. Since 1979, he has been a singer and dancer with a San Diego production company. He also started the Athletes for Healthier Youth program, which has reached 100,000 San Diego kids since 1985. Buchanon moderates discussion of a four-part message regarding goals, abuses, decisions, and persistence. He gets San Diego Padres, Chargers, and ex-athletes like John Brockington and Steve Scott to give talks. "I do it because my family upbringing taught me the value of giving something back to the community," he explained.

And the worst day of Buchanon's career? That's easy. On October 21, 1973, he broke his left leg in two places while covering Los Angeles Rams receiver Jack Snow. The Packers lost 24-7 in LA.

Mike Butler, *Defensive end, 1977-1982, 1985:* The loss of Mike Butler in 1983 may have cost Bart Starr his job, but don't blame Butler. He was drafted in the first round in 1977 along with another first-round pick at defensive end, Ezra Johnson. In 1983, Butler hoped the Packers would meet his salary demands and re-sign him. Coach Bart Starr hoped as much and was assured by his superiors that it would happen. It didn't.

Butler believes that the Packers would have improved on their 8-8 record in 1983 and made the playoffs—thereby saving Starr's job—if their Butler-less defense hadn't been so porous. "They missed the playoffs by one game. I know I could have helped that," he said. Who can argue that Butler was missed? Starr's job came down to the Packers holding off the Bears on the final drive of the final game of the season. The Bears marched down the field and kicked a field goal to win 23-21 and knock the 8-8 Packers from the playoffs.

Butler played in the USFL with Tampa Bay in 1983-1984 but returned to the Packers in 1985 and retired after that season. Butler still lives in Tampa Bay, but he works in many cities assessing public housing projects for the federal government, a line of work he got into soon after retiring from football. Much of the money he made in football was lost when his investments soured, leaving him to scramble for a second career. "It didn't totally wipe me out, but it put a pretty good hurting on me," he said.

Ron Cassidy, *Wide receiver, 1979-1984:* Ron Cassidy could consider his six years with the Packers as a black period in his life. He caught just 14 career passes while playing behind James Lofton and John Jefferson. Worst of all, he lost his 3 ½-year-old son, Connor, in Green Bay in a tragic home accident and subsequently went through a divorce.

Cassidy was at a team meeting during the second week of the regular season when he got a phone call. Connor had been killed when an electric garage door came down on him at the family's home. "I never would have played a down in the NFL if I could have him back," Cassidy said. "We were really close too. I used to take him to the weight room. Everybody knew him. It had quite an effect on the team when it happened." The accident had "a big effect" on Cassidy's marriage, although it didn't cause the divorce that followed, he said. His ex-wife and their two young daughters live in Provo, Utah. Cassidy works in auto sales in the Los Angeles area.

Cassidy, an eighth-round draft pick from Utah State in 1979, a year after Lofton was drafted, especially remembers the 1983 season after sitting out all of 1982 with a rotator cuff shoulder injury. In 1983 the Packers chose wide receiver Mike Miller, a track speedster out of Tennessee, in the fourth round. "He was the NCAA 200 champ. He came into camp driving a new Datsun 280-Z. He thought he was hot stuff. The first day of camp I saw him run a route, and I said, 'No way.' I had him. He could run, but he wasn't a receiver." Miller was gone before the season began. "It was a very satisfying thing," Cassidy recalled.

Although he grew up in Southern California, Cassidy found Wisconsin to his liking. "I played on softball teams in the summer and met some really great people. I played on the Packer basketball team. We went to places like Marshfield. I would say, 'Where in the world is that?' I'd dread going, but we'd wind up just having a great time.

"I played longer than I thought I would and a lot longer than every-one else thought I would. It's really something to be proud of when the average career is only three, three and a half years. Nobody can take that away from me."

Despite his undistinguished career, Cassidy already has a prominent spot at the Packer Hall of Fame—not in it but outside of it. In front of the building stands the statue of receiver Number 88 catching a pass. When the sculpture was dedicated on June 8, 1985, Cassidy still was on the Packer roster. He wore Number 88.

Dan Currie, *Linebacker, 1958-1964:* In the 1958 draft, the Packers helped lay the groundwork for the fabulous 1960s (and thereby financial security) by drafting Nitschke, Kramer, Taylor, and Currie on their first five picks—four guys who today don't even need first names in Packer fan discussions.

What fans might not remember, however, is the order those four were taken by outgoing coach Lisle Blackbourn. Jerry Kramer? He was the last. Ray Nitschke? He was taken fourth. Jim Taylor? He was the Pack's second choice. Dan Currie, the least known of the fab four, was the first-round pick. The Packers had two third-round picks that year, with run-ning back Dick Christy actually being chosen before Nitschke. Christy subsequently was traded to Pittsburgh and never played for the Packers.

Currie, a 6' 3", 235-pound All-American center from Michigan State, was the only one of the fab four who wasn't around to taste all of the Packers' success. He was with the Packers at left linebacker for the 1961 and 1962 titles, but was traded after the 1964 season. In a roundabout way, Currie helped the Packers win the three later titles. He was worth enough to enable Vince Lombardi to acquire wide receiver Carroll Dale from the Los Angeles Rams. Dale gave Bart Starr one more target at wide receiver to complement Boyd Dowler and Max McGee.

The trade to LA made sense to Currie. The Packers had too much talent at linebacker and not enough at wide receiver. Along with Currie, there were Nitschke, Dave Robinson, and Lee Roy Caffey. "It wasn't any great shock. I knew [Lombardi] had to get Robinson in the lineup. You'd only be a fool not to think that. Robinson was an All-Pro, and he's got to play. Lombardi and I had a couple of fights over a couple of dollars. He said he had to get somebody with some speed because at that time he didn't know how much Max had left. He had enough talent at linebacker. He didn't want to get stuck holding the ball without any receivers," Currie remembered.

After two years with the Rams, Currie suffered a knee injury and retired. Yet he still smiles when he looks back. He made All-Pro in 1961 and 1962, was on two Packer championship teams, and played for a decade. "How much more do you want? The Lord doesn't always dish things out like that." Being inducted into the Packer Hall of Fame in 1984 "was a very pleasant surprise. I didn't think I'd make it." Currie credited his teammates. "You've got to be surrounded by good people to be good."

Currie, who grew up in Detroit, has good memories of Green Bay. "We lived over on the east side by St. Mary's Catholic grade school. I'd go to early Mass, have a pregame meal and take a cab to the game. After the game, Kimberly Clark [a paper manufacturer] would have tailgate parties. We would walk over there and have a couple of drinks, and we got to know them very well. We had a very nice social life, and we had a lot of fun."

While most people remember the gruff side of Lombardi, Currie remembers the human side. "Lombardi was a pretty funny guy. A lot of people didn't know that. He knew his team had to laugh, even if he was the brunt of the joke. He'd make a *faux pas* occasionally. He'd let us laugh at him. One time, he was as mad as a hornet because he didn't think we were putting out. He said, 'I wish I could play. I'd show you.' The next Sunday we had a home game. There was a big pileup in front of the bench and Vince couldn't get out of the way. He got hit by Nitschke and went over backwards about three times and lost his hat and glasses. Ray picked him up and he got mad at Ray. When we saw the play in the [team] movies, we were all laughing and we said, 'Run it back, run it back.' Vince ran it back a couple of times. He let us laugh at him. Then he got mad and yelled, 'Let's get serious now.' "

Currie also remembers being pitted against Lombardi in one of Kramer's $2-a-man cribbage tournaments. "I played Vince in the second or third round. He was a good player. The whole team was behind me telling me how to play. Vince got mad and yelled, 'Leave him the hell alone and let him play his own hand.' I eventually beat him, and he went storming out."

Although many of his ex-Packer teammates went on to successful business careers, Currie has found life after football far from euphoric. He hasn't found the lucrative career that capitalizes on his name or football contacts. "You run into a lot of 'You haven't done this' or 'You haven't done that.' I've run into a lot of difficulty. . . . You sure as hell don't get any help. You do it by yourself." Currie is divorced and has six grown children (four girls and two boys). He recently lost his ex-wife to cancer and a brother to Lou Gehrig's disease. "I have to make a considerable effort to stay in touch with the kids because they don't have their mother anymore."

Since 1982, he has worked as a security guard at the Stardust in Las Vegas, where he still follows the Packers enthusiastically. He also is starting a business selling rare coins as investments. His customers build a portfolio by monthly investments in rare coins. "Only 1 in 100 people are financially secure at retirement. I'm working like hell to get this business off the ground so I won't have to do this the rest of my life," Currie said from the Stardust.

Hank Gremminger, *Defensive back, 1956-1965:* Hank Gremminger still practices one form of discipline that Vince Lombardi taught. He believes there is no team like the Packers, even though he faces heavy pressure almost daily to switch allegiances. He lives near Dallas. Although the Packers haven't won an NFL championship since tie-dye shirts were in, Gremminger refuses to give in or give up on the Packers. He's one Texan who still loves Wisconsin. "This ol' boy will never be a Cowboy fan. Never," Gremminger said emphatically.

After playing his last down for the Packers, Gremminger moved back home to Texas, where he was born, raised and still makes his living. For more than 20 years, he has owned and operated Hank Gremminger Inc., a home construction business just west of the Dallas-Forth Worth metropolitan area. He lives six miles from the suburb of Weatherford on a ranch, where he and his wife raise beef cattle on the side.

Gremminger has 1961 and 1962 title rings to show his Cowboy detractors, points out that the Cowboys never beat the Packers while he played, and puts in one final plug: The people in Wisconsin "are the finest you'll ever meet. They are second to none. They made us feel like one of them."

Jim Hill, *Safety, 1972-1974:* He once did play-by-play for regional telecasts of NFL games on CBS, but Jim Hill loves where he is now as sports anchor at KCBS in Los Angeles, one of the country's largest media markets. "I've got the best job in the world here. Absolutely the best job in the world. Just about every major sports figure at one time or another comes through LA. This morning I played golf with Julius Erving and Bill Russell. Michael Jordan comes through, and we play golf. It can't get any better than this," Hill enthused. "I know how lucky I am. The best thing for people to realize is what they do best. I have a pretty good idea what I do well in life, and this is it."

Hill got his start in broadcasting at WBAY in Green Bay while playing for the Packers. He has been in Los Angeles, including 12 years at KABC, since retiring from football after the 1975 season. "The best days of my career and worst days of my career were right there in Green Bay," Hill said. "They were the best days because of the [1972] playoffs and because it looked like we had the makings of a team that could win and win big for several years. The worst days were at the end when we all scattered. I left for Cleveland, Ellis went to the Oilers, MacArthur Lane went to the Chiefs. It's a big mystery. How could a team that was so good one year come apart?"

Hill recalls coaches and players bickering and back-stabbing one another over "petty jealousies. It was like, 'What's the latest rumor today?' " He remembers safety Al Matthews getting into a fight with assistant coach Don Doll at the Left Guard in Green Bay. A tennis racquet was used in the fight, and the next Sunday at Lambeau Field a banner read, "Hey, Al, what a racquet."

Bob Jeter, *Defensive back, 1963-1970:* In 1960, Bob Jeter was graduating from the University of Iowa and had no plans to play pro football, even when the Packers drafted him in the second round. He served in the

Marine Corps, then played briefly in the Canadian Football League. He was sitting in Canada watching the Packers win the 1961 NFL title 37-0 over the New York Giants when he realized his mistake. "I told my roommate that I could be playing in that game." Coach Vince Lombardi still wanted Jeter and by 1963 he was in a Packer uniform. "It was the best move of my life. I never dreamed that I'd be in the '65 title game and the first two Super Bowls."

Jeter was a backup wide receiver to Boyd Dowler and Max McGee in 1963 and 1964 but was switched to defensive back in 1965. That's when he got his big chance. Early in the 1965 title game against Cleveland, Packer right cornerback Doug Hart went down with an ankle injury. Jeter was sent in. His job was to cover the legendary Paul Warfield. "He was one of the few guys I couldn't intimidate. I'd give him a nice pop, and he'd pat me on the butt and say, 'Nice hit Jeter.' I knew I was in for a long day."

It was a long day—but only for Warfield and the Browns. After Jeter was assigned to him, Warfield didn't catch another pass that day and the Packers won 23-12 at Lambeau Field. "That's the game that stands out most in my mind," Jeter recalled. He was especially proud because he had started the 1965 season on the injury list; during an exhibition game against the Browns, he suffered four broken ribs from a hit by fullback Jim Brown.

After his stellar performance in the title game, Jeter went on to star for the Packers. He started every game at right corner in 1966 and 1967, making All-Pro and the Pro Bowl in 1967 and the Pro Bowl again in 1970. After making 22 interceptions for the Packers in eight seasons, Jeter was traded to the Bears in 1971. He was a player-coach in 1972-1973 before retiring. Jeter was inducted into the Packer Hall of Fame in 1985.

For the past two decades Jeter has remained in Chicago and worked in a variety of jobs, including selling health and beauty products, boxes, radio advertising, and aluminum siding. In September 1994 he started a new job as a security guard at the Everett M. Dirksen Federal Building in downtown Chicago. After putting in so many years as a traveling salesman, he liked the 4:00 p.m. to midnight shift and the short drive from his Chicago home. In April 1995 he worked 12-hour shifts after the federal building in Oklahoma City was bombed. Security was tightened again that fall when a bomb was mailed to a federal judge in Chicago, but the bomb was spotted by one of Jeter's colleagues. "We have to monitor everyone who comes in the building. I get a chance to meet a lot of different people," Jeter said. "A lot of them remember me from when I played for the Packers."

When he's off duty, Jeter loves to golf. On a good day, he's a low-handicapper, capable of breaking 75. He spent much of his free time in recent years traveling to Wisconsin to watch his sons Robby and Carlton play at the University of Wisconsin-Platteville. Both were all-conference players in the early 1990s. Basketball actually was Bob Jeter's favorite sport while growing up in Union, South Carolina, and he only went out for football to prove to his friends that he wasn't too scared to play. Jeter doesn't spend much time reminiscing or looking over his memorabilia, he said. Besides, any game balls he ever saved disappeared while Robby and Carlton were growing up. "I don't ever hardly think about football. It's all behind me."

Larry Krause, *Running back, 1970-1974:* Growing up in the 1960s in Greenwood in central Wisconsin, Larry Krause was as big a Packer fan as any kid could be. Today he's a middle-aged businessman, still a Wisconsinite and still a big Packer fan. On autumn Sundays at his Waunakee home he still tunes into Packer broadcasts.

There's one difference between Krause and the average Packer fan. He played for them for five seasons. He was just a 17th-round draft pick from St. Norbert of De Pere, Wisconsin—the Packers' summer training camp site. He never started a game and seldom carried the ball from formation, but he starred on special teams and was dependable in emergencies.

It seems apropos that Krause's tenure as a Packer ended with Devine's. Unlike many of his teammates, Krause liked Devine. He blames management, not Devine, for the rough ride from 1971-1974. "The players in general were pretty much behind Devine, but it was an unfortunate situation for him to be in. The consensus [among fans and media] was that he wasn't the right guy for the job. In his last year, there were a lot of rumors that he would be fired. That caused dissension. I thought he was an excellent coach and he brought in some excellent people—Bill

Tobin and Bob Harlan, who's now the president of the club. Dan Devine was a smart guy, and he knew how to surround himself with good people. I felt there wasn't a real commitment to him on management's side.

"He had a difficult task at hand with the situation we were going through at that time being the first non-Lombardi person. That caused him a lot of problems. They required him to keep Dave Hanner as defensive coordinator. Hanner was the guy who thought he was going to get the job. It's hard when you keep part of the old and part of the new. There's a natural friction there. If Dan could have had entire control and started with everybody from his side it would have helped. There was a division of loyalty there, too much tension from upper management level and it filtered down."

One thing football taught Krause was humility. Now a manager of the Madison, Wisconsin, branch of Milwaukee's Security Bank, he speaks to high school students about pro football. He impresses upon them that 90 to 95 percent of pro athletes, even with today's huge salaries, "are normal guys who have to work when they're done" playing.

Mark Lee, *Cornerback, 1980-1990:* Mark Lee is hoping to be remembered for something other than his ability to bump-and-run against star receivers. He wants to make a difference in the lives of some troubled young girls. As part owner of the Berkeley, California, Academy for Delinquent Girls, he speaks several times a month to teens who need help. As a former NFL star and someone who also had to overcome childhood obstacles, he knows that his abilities now lie in his life experiences, not his foot work. Lee was one of 13 children in a one-parent family in Hanford, California, near Fresno, where he lived in a poor and troubled section of town. "By my senior year in high school, I knew the scouts were looking at me and realized that was my ticket out."

Since being cut by the Packers in 1990 and playing that season with San Francisco and New Orleans, Lee has lived in Redmond, Washington, near Seattle, with his wife Lorrie and their three children. He flies regularly to Berkeley, where his brother, psychologist Charles Blakeney and his brother's wife, Ronnie, run the two small group homes funded by the state. The two homes have 20 to 25 girls between the ages of 12 and 18, most of whom have criminal records.

"I try to get across to them to be good citizens," Lee said. "Most of them are abused or have drug-related problems. Most don't believe it if you tell them you love them because that's never been told to them. You have to get their trust, get them to believe in themselves."

Much of Lee's free time now also goes into operating a home shopping business with his wife. He also hopes to return to college and get the 20 credits he needs to finish a bachelor's degree in psychology.

Packer fans remember him for his 31 career interceptions (fifth best in team history), including 10 in 1986. His brightest moment came during the playoffs in the strike-shortened 1982 season. In the second round against Dallas, Lee intercepted a Danny White pass and returned it 22 yards for a touchdown in the fourth quarter to bring the Packers within 30-26. They wound up losing 37-26.

Dale Livingston, *Kicker, 1970:* In the mid-1980s Dale Livingston was diagnosed with Hodgkin's disease, which is cancer of the lymph nodes. Doctors operated to remove cancerous lumps in his neck and groin and also removed his spleen. After chemotherapy from August 1988 to May 1989, no traces of cancer have been found in his annual blood tests. "It's a 90 to 95 percent cure rate after four or five years," Livingston said. "Every year now is one on my side." However, every day when he showers he checks for lumps under his arms and in the groin area.

After his treatment, Livingston gave up 16 years in the life insurance business to teach eighth-graders with learning disabilities in the Freedom school district near Green Bay. He had to return to school to get certified in his specialty. He also hoped to teach children with emotional disabilities. "I just feel this is what I'm supposed to do." he explained. One of Livingston's two sons, ages 24 and 21, is learning-disabled but is able to work as an auto mechanic. His wife, Liz, is an elementary school teacher.

With the Packers, he made 15 of 28 field-goal attempts and was the team's leading scorer for the season with 64 points. However, he had five kicks blocked and was just six of 11 from the 20- to 29-yard line. Livingston appeared to be the kicker for 1971 until he was cut late in the preseason by new coach Dan Devine. According to Livingston, the cut came after he had a run-in with Devine's 15-year-old son. The boy was holding the ball in practice for Livingston, and when he began telling

Livingston how the ball should be held, Livingston told the boy to get "the hell" off the practice field because he didn't belong there. Devine heard about the exchange and criticized Livingston for using foul language in front of his son. Livingston stood his ground. "I knew then that was it." Livingston got cut, and he's sure the argument was the reason. The Packers went through three kickers that season—Lou Michaels, Tim Webster, and Dave Conway. Combined, they made 14 of 25 field-goal attempts.

Livingston, meanwhile, kicked for a semi-pro team in Manitowoc in 1971. He played briefly for the LA Raiders and in the World Football League the next three years before hanging up his shoes for good in 1974.

Mike P. McCoy, *Defensive tackle, 1970-1976:* At 6' 5", 280 pounds, Mike McCoy never had trouble getting people to listen to him. But when the former defensive tackle towers over a podium and talks to youths about drugs, alcohol, and other social ills, magnetism takes over. There's something about a big, ex-pro football player talking about life that kids can't seem to resist.

That's what McCoy has found since working for Bill Glass Ministries, a program started by the former Cleveland Browns star. Wherever McCoy speaks throughout the country, he's certain to command an attentive audience. "We tackle life head-on—the pressures that young people face with sex, drugs, relationships," McCoy said.

McCoy worked until 1993 with SportsWorld Ministries, a similar organization featuring former athletes speaking from a Christian perspective. He became a dedicated Christian after he developed a close friendship with wide receiver Carroll Dale. The Dales are godparents for the oldest of Mike and Kia McCoy's four children.

McCoy tells kids about some of the pro athletes he has known who have ruined their careers, and sometimes their lives, by abusing drugs and alcohol. "Young people have the image that if you make it in pro sports you've got it made, but that's not always true," McCoy explained.

McCoy was the Packers' top draft pick in 1970—the second player taken overall behind Pittsburgh's Terry Bradshaw. The Packers got the second pick by trading three veterans—Elijah Pitts, Lee Roy Caffey, and Bob Hyland—to Chicago. After six years with the Packers, McCoy was traded during the 1976 training camp to the Super Bowl champion

Oakland Raiders. He spent three seasons with the Raiders and two with the Giants before retiring in 1980. When he was traded by Packer Coach Bart Starr, McCoy says he was bitter, but only for a day. "I wanted to be like Ray Nitschke and be a Wisconsinite all my life."

McCoy had been back to Green Bay just once since the 1976 trade— to speak to a youth group—but returned in September 1995 for the Packer alumni gathering. Still wide from crew cut to hips and walking with his trademark waddle, it was easy to envision him once pushing offensive lineman for a living. When he came through a door, another ex-Packer commented, "I thought it was two men."

Terdell Middleton, *Running back, 1977-1981:* Terdell Middleton rushed for 1,116 yards in his second year with the Packers. He was one of the team's heroes during that roller-coaster 1978 season, when the team shot out to a 6-1 start. No Packer running back topped 1,000 yards for another 17 years, until Edgar Bennett succeeded in 1995. That's one reason Middleton, hardly a household name, still gets his football cards in the mail to autograph.

From his home in Memphis, Tennessee, Middleton quickly placed himself among the Packer backfield elite. "Fourth Packer ever to rush for 1,000 yards and fifth most yards in a season," he rattled off statistics. But he did it half in jest because these days his ego takes more of a pounding than a massaging at the Memphis Fire Department, where he is a lieutenant. "They always say, 'Hey, butterfingers,' " he said with a laugh. "I've got to work on my basketball game. No one picks me on their team and I can't understand it. I tell them, 'Hey, you've got an All-Pro athlete here.' "

After Bart Starr released Middleton just before the 1982 regular season, he caught on with Tampa Bay for 1982 and 1983. He then returned to his hometown, Memphis, signing as a free agent with the Memphis Showboats of the USFL for the 1984 season. When financial problems began plaguing the USFL, he figured he'd "better start pursuing other interests."

He took a job with the fire department in 1984. He likes the three 24-hour shifts a week that allow him time to work on a degree in business management at Memphis State, where he was a star when the Packers drafted him in the third round in 1977. Middleton, 41, married with no children, returned to school in 1995.

"I went from one men's club [NFL] to another men's club. The gang has changed, but the characters have remained the same. You meet the same guys in the fire department. The same kind of mentality."

Middleton led the National Football Conference of the NFL with 11 rushing TDs—one of them a 76-yard run—and tied Walter Payton for most overall TDs in the NFC in 1978. His new nickname was "TD." To cap off his season, Terdell made the NFC's Pro Bowl squad, but the good times didn't last. He dropped off to 495 yards in 1979, 155 in 1980, and 181 in 1981. His 2,044 career rushing yards still rank him among the Packer elite.

Mark Murphy, *Safety, 1980-1991:* In early 1995, Mark Murphy took another step in his second football career: He became defensive backs coach for the University of Akron, an NCAA Division I program. Previously he coached two years at tiny Malone College in his hometown of Canton, Ohio, where he still lives with his wife and four children, and commutes 25 miles to Akron.

Football still has a lock hold on Murphy, although growing up he had no strong desire to be a pro athlete. The Pro Football Hall of Fame was just across town, but he never visited the Hall as a kid and had no pipe dreams of someday seeing himself there. When he lost all his hair in third grade because of a disorder caused alopecia, Murphy dove into sports because they were a hideout for him. His struggles over his appearance motivated him to succeed in athletics. "The early years were tough because other kids can be cruel. It made me be a tough kid. I had my share of fights. I played football and baseball. One had a helmet and the other a hat. It was a way to kind of get lost in something and take my mind off my hair," Murphy recalled.

Hairless but smooth on the football field, he starred at a small college, West Liberty State in West Virginia. He made the Packers as a free agent in 1980, ironically missing that season when he broke his wrist in his first pro game, an exhibition game in front of family and friends at the Hall of Fame in Canton. Committed to proving himself, he improved each season, leading the Packers in tackles 1988-1990.

Jim Ringo, *Center, 1953-1963:* For 35 years, Jim Ringo was a football nomad, playing in two cities and coaching in five others from coast to coast. The travel, for games, camps, meetings, and scouting, ran into hundreds of thousands of miles. Ringo put down roots a few years ago in the remote town of Findley Lake, New York, population 600, located southwest of Buffalo in western New York, about 12 miles from Lake Erie. The emphasis now is strictly R&R. Ringo watches football from his secluded house and angles for bass, pike, or musky on Findley Lake.

He has gotten far away from the high-profile life he lived as an NFL coach and NFL Hall of Fame player. When Ringo, 63, isn't fishing, he's often in his woodworking shop. "I'm doing things I would like to have done for many years. I live in a very, very remote place. It gives you a different perspective that football isn't everything," he said.

Ringo coached with the Chicago Bears 1969-1971, went to Buffalo 1972-1977, to New England until 1981, to the Los Angeles Rams for 1982, to the New York Jets for 1983-1985, and back to Buffalo. Ringo become head coach of the Bills midseason in 1976, when O.J. Simpson starred with the team. He left the Bills after the 1977 season. "You would like to be a head coach, but not by default," he said, referring to the fact that he was chosen to replace Lou Saban when Saban resigned. "Management thought I'd be able to replace Lou, but it didn't work out that way. On both parts, it was best for me to get out of there."

Ringo was offensive line coach or offensive coordinator in his other coaching jobs. As offensive coordinator in Buffalo, his "Electric Company" Bills line blocked for Simpson during his record-breaking 2,000-yard season in 1973, and Ringo was named NFL assistant coach of the year by the National 1,000-Yard Foundation. The sight of a sad Simpson sitting in a Los Angeles courtroom in 1995 being tried for double murder bothered Ringo because his image of Simpson was far different. "He always had a smile. He had a hell of a nice side to him." Ringo was disturbed by stories that painted Simpson as a dark, occasionally brooding figure and sometimes as a petulant, uncoachable athlete. "Several articles mentioned that people had a hard time coaching him. I wonder who the hell they talked to. He was one of the most enjoyable people around, one of the easiest players I coached. He was a class person. He held parties for the players and every other thing. I never saw that dark side of him. I never knew he had a dark side. I felt so sorry, some of the stuff that has been said about him."

Little bad has been written about Ringo. He was a seventh-round draft choice from Syracuse, won All-Pro honors six times, and played in ten Pro Bowls. He was chosen for the Pro Football Hall of Fame in 1981. Part of Ringo's success was his durability, although he was just 6' 1", 235 pounds. He once held the NFL record for consecutive games played—at 182. Ringo retired in 1967 at age 35. Amazingly, he was chosen for the Pro Bowl that year, 15 years after being drafted by the Packers.

Although Vince Lombardi traded Ringo in 1964, Ringo developed a respect for Lombardi that went far beyond coaching. "A lot of people claim Vince Lombardi could walk on water. We knew he could. Things were very bad up through the '58 season. In '58, it was a hell hole because we won only one game. In two short years, he had us playing for the championship in Philadelphia. It was him. You knew it was him because we had all the same people."

Ringo had one opportunity to return to Green Bay as an assistant coach but turned down the offer. He knew he never could go back and duplicate what had been done under Lombardi. "I love Green Bay and I love all the people there, but when you return as a coach it's different. Forrest [Gregg] found that out. It was the same with Bart. People form a different opinion of you based on how you coach."

Del Rodgers, *Running back, 1982-1984:* Getting a Super bowl ring with the San Francisco 49ers in 1990 was a dream come true for Del Rodgers and the culmination of a successful NFL career. When he woke from the dream, he found himself on TV. Rodgers now is the weekend sports anchor for NBC affiliate WXIA in Atlanta, the nation's 10th largest TV market. He moved up quickly after starting his broadcasting career at a small station in Salinas, California, for which he did his first broadcast story, a first-person account of going to the Super Bowl with the 49ers. His new career was off and running. After three years in Salinas and one year at KIRO in Seattle, he found himself in Atlanta, the sports center of the South.

"I say my prayers every night and always make sure to take advantage of things that come my way," Rodgers said. "Football is something to prepare yourself for life. There's no question that if I had gone from college to life, I wouldn't have been as successful as I am today. I learned from playing in the NFL."

Rodgers was the Packers' third-round draft pick in 1982 out of Utah. He led the team in kickoff returns in 1982 and 1984 and was a reserve running back. He missed the 1983 season with a broken neck.

Dave Roller, *Defensive tackle, 1975-1978:* Mark Gastineau pranced, Lawrence Taylor prowled, and Tim Harris pointed his imaginary six-shooters. During the 1980s, sacking the quarterback became a big-time, big-money part of the NFL. Dave Roller would like to take a little credit for that.

During the late 1970s, the pudgy, 6' 2", 260-pound Roller jumped from the World Football League to the NFL and the Green Bay Packers. In no time at all, he danced his way into the hearts of Packer fans. Roller put some spark into the difficult first years of Bart Starr's teams. Whenever he sacked the quarterback, the Packer doughboy would juke and jiggle over his fallen victim, to the delight of Packer fans.

"I was doing it before Gastineau—since I had been in high school," said Roller, a Dayton, Tennessee, native who now lives in Alpharetta, Georgia, a suburb of Atlanta. "I'm sure it turned some people off, but we had some lean years there and if the fans didn't yell for that they wouldn't have yelled for anything. It wasn't to highlight Dave Roller so much as it was to spread enthusiasm and get people excited."

Among the Packer people Roller enthused week after week was a group of fans from Port Washington, Wisconsin. They started a Roller fan club and always hung out a "Dance, Roller, Dance," banner at Packer home games. Roller was even given a key to the city. "I've got it hanging on my wall. It says, 'From Mayor George O. Lampert, Dec. 9, 1973. Honorary citizen.'" Right next to Roller's key to the city of Port Washington is a picture of himself doing his dance over fallen Bears QB Bob Avellini.

Not far away are other Packer mementos, including a game ball from September 18, 1977, when the Packers beat the New Orleans Saints 24-20. Roller sacked Saints QB Archie Manning four times on the Superdome turf that day. Roller, who had eight sacks to lead the team that season, his best with the Packers, was used mostly in pass-rushing situations.

While Roller takes credit for causing some excitement, he would like to be remembered for his professional contributions as well. Roller believes players like him helped make quarterback-sacking important in today's game. It wasn't until the mid-1970s when the Packers even began keeping statistics on defensive players. Sack statistics weren't kept for many years, and originally quarterback sacks were referred to as quarterback dumps. "We helped bring it to the forefront. Now they even have stats on quarterback hurries. All those things weren't notarized then."

He played 1979 and 1980 with the Minnesota Vikings before retiring during training camp in 1981. It was a good place to finish because Roller figures he had a favor coming from Vikings Coach Bud Grant. Once as a Packer Roller sacked Viking QB Fran Tarkenton, and their momentum carried them off the field to the feet of Grant at old Metropolitan Stadium. Roller was penalized for a late hit, and a "stone-faced Grant" told the official that Roller was a "detriment to the game" and should be thrown out. Roller was ejected. After showering, Roller was headed to the Packers' press box but got off the elevator and found two machine guns pointed at him. "I said that all I did was sack Tarkenton." Roller had gotten off on the wrong floor, the floor where Vice President Hubert H. Humphrey was watching the game.

Roller, 46, seldom dances now, but he plays survival war games with paint-pellet guns on the weekends. As during his football days, he isn't concerned about staying in shape. He weighs about 300 pounds, 30 to 40 more than when he played. "I don't really work at it. I was down to 230 but I didn't feel too comfortable. People said I looked half dead. I said, 'I can go back up.'"

Part of his weight problem is related to work, said Roller, who works out of an office in his home. He has worked in real estate since the mid-1980s and today is employed by DBSI, a syndicated real estate developer from Boise, Idaho. It's Roller's job to convince financial planners that their clients should invest in DBSI. Roller travels around the country meeting with brokers and making his sales pitch. "You eat all the time. It's just like football."

"Barty" Smith, *Fullback, 1974-1980:* Fullback Barton "Barty" Smith retired from pro football in 1980 because he couldn't run effectively anymore with his battered, surgically repaired knees. So what's Smith's favorite form of recreation these days? Running. Despite five knee operations that hampered the Packers' 1974 first-round draft pick throughout his seven-year career, Smith puts on his running shoes daily now. "I rarely miss a day. I run 30 to 40 miles a week. My shortest run any day is five miles. I often do a long run on the weekends," he said.

Smith, now vice-president of Loveland Distributing, a Miller beer wholesaler in his hometown of Richmond, Virginia, has run three Richmond Marathons. His best time is 3 hours, 45 minutes. "Not bad for a guy 225 pounds with five knee operations," Smith, 43, said with a laugh. "I don't have any trouble running straight ahead. Only when I try to make lateral movements do my knees give me trouble."

Great physical condition was why the Packers drafted the 6' 4", 235-pound Smith out of Richmond University in 1974. He was expected to take the place of star fullback John Brockington, whose production had begun to slip. Smith never got the chance to show his real abilities. In the Coaches' All-America game prior to the Packer training camp that summer, Smith severely injured a knee in the second half. "I even remember the name of the guy who hit me—Ozell Collier of the University of Colorado. It was a clean hit. He caught me when I was crossing one leg over the other going down the field. He cut my legs out. It's the old saying. I should have zigged instead of zagged." Smith remembered that shortly after he was taken from the field, Packer director of scouting Bill Tobin was at his side. Within an hour, they were on a plane to Green Bay, where Smith was operated on the next day.

Although Smith did return to action late in his rookie season and was fully recovered heading into 1975, he doesn't think he ever returned to his collegiate form. "I was foolish to believe—you read it in all the medical journals—that you come back stronger than ever after the surgery. I was a little naive. I never had my confidence after that."

He had a second knee surgery halfway through the 1976 season. Despite his limitations, Smith was the standout offensive player on the Packers' 4-10 team in 1977. He led them in rushing and receiving. He ran for 554 yards (3.3 average) and caught 37 passes for 340 yards (9.2

average). Smith's strong play enabled the Packers to release Brockington in 1977.

Smith's best year may have been in 1978. That year, rookie James Lofton led the Packers in receiving with 46 catches, but Smith wasn't far behind with another 37 catches. In addition, Smith rushed for a career-high 567 yards and did much of the lead blocking as Terdell Middleton rushed for more than 1,000 yards.

Smith was off to a good start in 1979 when he suffered another knee injury and missed the final 10 games. In 1980, he suffered his fifth knee injury and underwent his fifth surgery. His only carry of the season came in the final game, for three yards against Detroit. It turned out to be the last carry of his career.

Ray Stachowicz, *Punter, 1981-82:* People around the NFL were second-guessing when the Packers used a third-round draft pick in 1981 to take a punter, Ray Stachowicz. Logic was that high draft rounds were reserved for impact players. Punters had always been late-round picks or free-agent grabs because of their unpredictability—unless they were someone special. In 1981, the Packers thought they had that someone in Stachowicz. "It was a compliment to me," said Stachowicz, who now lives in Brecksville, Ohio, near Cleveland, where he grew up and where he works at Oakes Equipment Co., a family-run machining business.

It wasn't a compliment to the Packers two years later when Stachowicz was cut and replaced by an 11th-round draft pick, Bucky Scribner. What went wrong? To this day, Stachowicz isn't sure why the Packers gave up on him so quickly. In 1981, Stachowicz averaged 40.6 yards per kick, ranking 11th in the National Football Conference and 18th in the NFL, hardly what the Packers envisioned with such a high pick. Yet, that 40.6 average was better than any Packer had done in the tough Wisconsin weather since Ron Widby in 1973. "You can't compare someone in Green Bay with LA—no way," Stachowicz said.

The next year Stachowicz did not improve—averaging 40.4 and ranking 17th in the NFL, but it was the strike-shortened year and virtually all of his kicking came in the cold, late-season weather. After many losing seasons and with the team on the upswing, Coach Bart Starr wasn't taking any chances going into the 1983 season. He drafted Scribner on the 11th round to push Stachowicz—or to push him out. Three games into the pre-season, Stachowicz was out cold. After tryouts with Chicago and Detroit failed, Stachowicz took the first train to Brecksville.

Eric Torkelson, *Running back, 1974-1981:* He wasn't fast and was always a backup, but somehow Eric Torkelson survived eight seasons with the Packers. He still hasn't left Green Bay either, living there with his wife and three daughters. And he still specializes in making the cut—he sells orthopedic surgical equipment to surgeons and hospitals in central and southeastern Wisconsin for Stryker Corp. of Kalamazoo, Michigan. He's on the road daily. "My job starts very early in the morning. Surgeries often start at 7:00 or 7:30 in the morning, and if the customer's hospital is two hours away, I've got to get up and get there. That's how they try out the equipment," Torkelson explained. He sells power saws and drills and other accessories for total joint (knee and hip) procedures.

Torkelson, who works in a daily jog of four to six miles and who skied two American Birkebeiner cross-country marathons in the late 1980s, likes the independence of selling. He likens it to the do-or-die situations he faced each year in training camp. "You're on your own completely. I like that part of it. It's been perfect for me."

Torkelson starred on special teams in 1974 and 1975. Then from 1976 through 1979 he started 22 of 60 games, rushed for slightly more than 1,000 yards, and caught 51 passes. But statistics don't tell the Torkelson tale. Torkelson survived because he always played to his ability and was dependable on special teams, meaning his value went beyond his role as a running back. Many Packer fans remember that Torkelson played well when others didn't, such as in the rain, snow or mud, especially at Milwaukee County Stadium. "I was just as fast on snow as I was on a dry track." His sure-footed, high stepping style got him yards when there didn't appear to be any and even though he said he had no speed. "I performed when I was expected to, and that had something to do with my longevity."

In 1979, the Packers made running backs their first two draft picks, choosing Eddie Lee Ivery and Steve Atkins. Strangely enough, 1979 was Torkelson's best year. He started the last eight games at fullback and rushed for 401 yards after Ivery and Smith suffered injuries. After missing 1980 with an injury himself, Torkelson was cut early in the 1981 training camp, then re-signed by the Packers. He was cut again at the end of the 1982 camp and retired.

Gary Weaver, *Linebacker, 1975-1979*: On Saturday mornings, Gary Weaver can still be found at training camp—at a local San Francisco-Oakland area field drilling about 30 teenaged football players. The camp has no name and no official status. For Weaver, a successful business-man with some time on his hands, it's simply a chance to plant some seeds and see if they grow. "I do it because I enjoy seeing the kids blossom," said Weaver, 40. "I have a lot to give to kids."

To get into Weaver's camp, a player simply has to ask—and show up. Weaver lets you miss camp only twice or you're out. "If a kid wants to learn with me, all he has to do is get up and get out of bed. I just want kids to learn the fundamentals." And when a Saturday morning camp session is over, Weaver takes his troupe out for lunch. "We also talk about life, family, drugs, eating habits," Weaver said, adding that the kids come from all races and economic levels.

Weaver, who is divorced with one son, spends 20 to 25 hours a week with his protégés. He can afford that because his specialty advertising business, GLW Associates, is going strong after 15 years. Weaver's company helps other businesses advertise by putting logos and names on thousands of items, such as key chains, pencils, and refrigerator magnets. "It's a good business. I'm happier now than when I was playing football. I'm in control of my life."

His life wasn't always so good. Growing up in Muscle Shoals, in the northwest corner of Alabama, he saw little of his alcoholic father after his parents divorced. After starring at Fresno (California) State, he played for Oakland two years, was cut and picked up by the Packers. Weaver learned from Coach Bart Starr "how to be a good person. From watching Bart, he gave me a direction."

Weaver was team comeback player of the year with a record 124 solo tackles in 1978 after a knee injury. However, in 1978 the Packers drafted linebackers John Anderson (first round), Mike Hunt (second round) and Mike Douglass (fifth round). In 1979, the Packers drafted linebacker Rich Wingo, who became an instant starter. By 1980, Weaver, although only

31, was gone from the NFL. Life has been getting better ever since, he said. "Last week things were going so good that I walked down the street and something was telling me that life is not supposed to be this easy."

Jesse Whittenton, *Defensive back, 1958-1964:* Jesse Whittenton's greatest football moment came in 1961 when the Packers beat the New York Giants to clinch the Western Conference title. With the Giants leading 17-13, Alex Webster ran 22 yards to the Packers' 30-yard line, where Whittenton stripped the ball. The Packers then scored in five plays and won 20-17. Four weeks later, they thrashed the Giants 37-0 in the first NFL championship game ever played in Green Bay. It turned out to be the first of the Packers' five titles in a seven-year span.

By 1964, Whittenton had played in three straight Pro Bowls and was just 30 years old, but he retired to run a golf course and real estate development with his cousin near his hometown of El Paso, at the southwest tip of Texas. "Vince [Lombardi] told me I'd be crazy to turn down this development. It worked," Whittenton recalled. Asked if he regretted retiring early from the NFL and missing the three straight Packer championships beginning in 1965, Whittenton replied, "If I hadn't done that, I wouldn't have gotten into golf."

Who could argue? While running the private Horizon Hills Country Club, Whittenton took in a young pro who needed a place to work. His name was Lee Trevino, a Dallas-born Hispanic whom nobody had heard of at the time. They became best friends. In fact, the day Trevino arrived in El Paso in 1966, he and Whittenton teamed up and won a best ball match. It was at that little course in El Paso where a previously unknown Trevino, the head pro, used to hustle players in the mid-1960s. "He didn't hustle people. People hustled themselves. They didn't think a Mexican could play," said Whittenton.

When Trevino went on tour in 1967, Whittenton sold him his car and along with his cousin backed Trevino financially. When he started winning prize money, Trevino bought a share of Horizon Hills. As a measure of thanks for giving him his start, Trevino in 1967 made the two cousins partners in his winnings "indefinitely. Years later I really regretted that," Trevino wrote in his autobiography, *They Call Me SuperMex.*

In 1968, Trevino won the U.S. Open and went on to become one of the richest golfers of all time.

Whittenton, inducted into the Packer Hall of Fame in 1976, became an outstanding golfer himself and played on the PGA Senior Tour in the late 1980s.

CHAPTER

He Wasn't a Packer

Robert Bosco
Quarterback 1986-1988

Robbie Bosco, 33, is already seven years into a coaching career, but he has few doubts that he could have been in the middle of a great NFL career. In Bosco's mind, he still is the second-team All-America quarterback who came from Brigham Young University in 1986, when he was the third most accurate passer in the history of college football.

If there was a silver lining to the rotator cuff shoulder injury that killed Bosco's promising NFL career, it occurred before his career did. Now Bosco at least can dream about how good he could have been. No one can take that away from him. No, he never split the defense with a game-winning touchdown pass, but he also never threw an ill-timed pass into a crowd of defenders. He never played in an NFL game.

Bosco's pro football career forever will be young and unfulfilled, a sort of John F. Kennedy legacy. People always will wonder how much he could have accomplished, how much history he could have rewritten. To ease the pain, that's how Bosco chooses to remember it. With confidence, he said, "If I was healthy, I still would be playing."

Coming out of BYU, Bosco was a laser. He finished behind only Jim McMahon and Steve Young (also both BYU players) and ahead of John Elway in NCAA career passing efficiency. Among Bosco's numerous NCAA records were 12 straight 200-yard passing games, 338 completions in one season and 511 attempts in one season. Bosco was 24-2 as a starter at BYU. In one 1985 game against New Mexico, he passed for 585 yards.

Now the laser arm is powerless and he coaches quarterbacks and receivers at BYU in Provo, Utah. He works for LaVell Edwards, the same man he played under. But Bosco can't lead by example; the arm still hurts when he "tests it" so he doesn't bother trying. He has slipped quietly back into the shadows. He likes to play golf (shooting in the upper 70s) and play around the house with his three girls and one boy. Provo is only 45 minutes from Salt Lake City so he occasionally goes to Utah Jazz games for entertainment. Having converted to the Mormon religion when he was in college (his mother was Mormon), Bosco couldn't be happier at the BYU, a Mormon school. "I'm lucky to be able to raise a family in this kind of environment," he said.

His shoulder problems actually began at BYU during his senior season, but the injury didn't stop the Packers from drafting him in the third round in 1986. The shoulder bothered him throughout training camp and he went on injured reserve. By October 1986 he was visiting renown sports specialist Dr. Frank Jobe in Los Angeles. "I went down there, and they operated the next day."

Jobe gave Bosco a 50-50 chance of playing again. For two years Bosco and the Packers believed he still could play. The following year, 1987, was a washout. "I wasn't even close" to being able to play, Bosco said. But heading into the 1988 season, he thought his hard rehabilitation work had paid off and that he had totally recovered. Packers Coach Forrest Gregg had predicted that Bosco would challenge for the starting QB job. Bosco was under the close supervision of Packer trainer Dominic Gentile. "Every day Robbie gets a little stronger," Gentile said early in 1988.

The big test came during training camp. Two-a-day practices revealed just how weak Bosco's shoulder still was. "I felt I was throwing pretty good. Then we went to two-a-day practices and [the shoulder] just couldn't hack that. I couldn't throw it the way I used to." The Packers finally gave up on Bosco, and first-year coach Lindy Infante released him. In the 1988 training camp, the coaches never told Bosco that his arm was weak. They didn't have to. He knew. "I wasn't even close. I had a hard time throwing spirals."

Why did it take two years for Bosco to realize his shoulder would never be as strong as it was in college? He wasn't trying to fool himself or the Packers. Many days during the two years he thought the shoulder was dead. Other days he felt life. For example, scar tissue from the surgery often fooled him. Tearing the scar tissue was something "you had to go through. Every once in a while I would throw the ball and tear scar tissue, and it felt like I was tearing my arm part. I felt it was over, but it healed up. After a while it kept getting worse and worse."

So all the athletic promise of a young man from Roseville, California, all the Zeus-like potential of someone who could lead the football warriors, amounted only to one training scuffle. Robbie Bosco played in one preseason game in 1988 for the Packers. He never played in an NFL game that counted. Because of that, his name cannot be found on the Packers' list of more than 1,300 former players. Only players who have appeared in a regular-season game join that honor roll.

In the minds of Bosco and the many who recognized his talent, the belief always will be: He could have been. Yet in Green Bay Packer and NFL history, Robbie Bosco knows this: He officially never was.

Bibliography

Abitante, Pete, and Chuck Garrity Jr., eds. *NFL Record and Fact Book*. New York: NFL Properties, 1987.

Ashe, Arthur Jr. *A Hard Road to Glory*. New York: Amistad Press, 1993.

"Blacks in Sports." *Ebony*. August (1992).

Chalk, Ocania. *Pioneers of Black Sport*. New York: Dodd, Mead, 1975.

Evans, Lon. *The Purple Lawman*. Fort Worth, Texas: Summit Group, 1990.

Gentile, Domenic. *The Packer Tapes*. Madison, Wis.: Prairie Oak Press, 1995.

Goska, Eric. *The Packer Legend in Facts*. Milwaukee: Tech/Data, 1993.

Halas, George S. *Halas on Halas*. Chicago: Bonus Books, 1986.

Huizenga, Robert. *You're OK, It's Just a Bruise*. New York,: St. Martin's Press, 1994

Johnson, Chuck. *The Green Bay Packers: Pro Football's Pioneer Team*. New York: T. Nelson, 1961.

Kramer, Jerry. *Distant Replay*. New York: Putnam, 1985.

Kramer, Jerry. *Instant Replay*. New York: World, 1968.

Kramer, Jerry. *Lombardi: Winning is the Only Thing*. New York: World, 1970.

NFL's Official Encyclopedia and History of Professional Football. New York: Macmillan, 1973.

Nitschke, Ray. *Mean on Sunday*. Garden City, N.Y.: Doubleday, 1973.

Starr, Bart. *Starr: My Life in Football*. New York: Morrow, 1987.

Torinus, John. *The Packer Legend*. Neshkoro, Wis.: Laranmark Press, 1982.

Trevino, Lee. *They call me SuperMex*. New York: Random House, 1982.